W9-AFN-233

WITHDRAWN
L. R. COLLEGE LIBRARY

372.5
M18a

47885

DATE DUE			

Frontispiece
"MY PICTURE" *drawn by Nancy—Grade two*

Art for Primary Grades

BY *Dorothy S. McIlvain*

DIRECTOR OF ART, SPOKANE PUBLIC SCHOOLS

CARL A. RUDISILL LIBRARY
LENOIR RHYNE COLLEGE

G. P. Putnam's Sons · *New York*

372.5
M 18.a

47,885
Sept. 1964

Copyright © 1961 by G. P. Putnam's Sons.
All rights reserved.
No part of this book may be reproduced in any
form, by mimeograph or any other means, without
permission in writing from the publisher, except
by a reviewer, who may quote brief passages in a
review to be published in a magazine or newspaper.
Published simultaneously in Canada by Longmans,
Green & Company.

Library of Congress Catalog Card Number: 61-13155
Manufactured in the United States of America

To my sister
MARGARET

Acknowledgments

This book evolved from years of experience with primary classroom teachers and their children.

My appreciation can never be adequately expressed for the inspiration I have received from working with primary teachers and children of the Spokane Public Schools and with children in Delaware and North Carolina.

It has been my privilege to be associated with Marjorie Pratt, Director of the Elementary Curriculum in Spokane. Her interest in my program in child art has given me the confidence I needed to complete this book.

I am indebted to Leila Lavin, formerly Assistant Superintendent, in charge of Elementary Education in Spokane, for her sympathetic attitude toward the importance of the art program in filling the needs of the child.

A special expression of gratitude goes to Shirley Cross, Curriculum Assistant in Art, and to each one of the art teachers in the Spokane Public Schools for their cooperation and inspiration.

A particular acknowledgment is due the primary grade teachers who created an atmosphere conducive to child art expression, and to the children whose work illustrates this manuscript.

I am further indebted to: Sherman Blake for his fine photography; Mrs. Glennavon Loosmore for her patience and accuracy in typing my manuscript; Beverly Combs for her explanatory line drawings.

Preface

No one thinks as a child does. No one lives in the same imaginative world. Every morning begins a new day, full of delightful things to see and to do. A child's art is honest, direct, and simply stated. Expression comes from what the child knows and imagines.

I have written this book because I believe all children have within themselves ideas waiting to be expressed. The years are so few in which children are without traditional patterns and conventions. This book is my answer to the need voiced by mothers, by classroom teachers, and by students for a comprehensive and practical book which applies directly to the teaching of art in the primary grades. My aim is to supply concrete assistance to the untrained teacher in art so that the reader concludes, "This is not hard to do; I can do this."

One of the primary teacher's greatest needs is for worthwhile but quiet projects requiring initiative on the part of the child, to be used during the period when part of the class is reading. Suitable lessons, which children can do independently, are included. The text is simply written to help teachers who will not have supervisory assistance in art. Guidance is given for planning art experiences in terms of the growth and developmental learning of the young child.

The art experiences in this book relate to play, to the home, to happenings in the community and to the child's visual and imaginative world. Many of these activities are related to the social studies, the science, the stories and the special days children have in these grades. The text includes steps in developing each new art experience to include the preparation of the classroom and materials; the motivation of boys and girls; discussion periods to stimulate thinking by arousing their curiosity, imagination and inventiveness; ways to develop observation and appreciation; the value of the art experience to the child. Adults with imagination and with an understanding and love for children can develop creative expression in children.

Important to the creative expression of children is the way the teacher stimulates thinking. Of equal importance, however, are the things said to children that restrict or inhibit their natural artistic expression. I have included, therefore, a section suggesting ways to counter the blocks resulting from such inhibitions, and suggestions for treating individual differences, for recognizing these differences and dealing with them is essential for creating conditions favorable to self-expression.

The personality traits commonly found in the five-, six-, seven- and eight-year-old child are described, because awareness of these traits helps adults understand what the child sees and what he thinks and feels about things he sees, touches, and hears.

Physical development of the child is also considered, for it affects the choice of art processes and is a factor in determining a child's interest span. The degree of maturation of vision and of ability to coordinate the hand with the eye and mind determines the kind of experiences which are understood by the child and therefore the selection of art materials.

Every teacher in the primary grades needs to remember that art is not subject matter to be learned, but a creative way of doing things. Doing things stimulates the imagination; children learn new ways of using materials and a best way. The feel of forms and textures, the beauty in things around them, the joy experienced in using color and shaping new forms are all necessary parts of each child's understanding of the world.

Children's desires to make things with their hands is satisfied by experiences given in the use of different materials for modeling, constructing, weaving, and printing. The child's need for dramatic play is answered in the sections on puppets and mask-making. Opportunities are suggested for children to share ideas and materials in the organization and execution of murals, dioramas, sand-box projects, box movies, and peep shows.

I believe children learn best what they discover for themselves. In art they learn by discovering for themselves what they can do with art materials. Qualities are revealed to them by touching, seeing, and manipulating the materials. Thus does the child discover how to make new forms, alter forms, select, and arrange forms. Painting, modeling, and constructing help him to answer the questions, "What?" and "Why?" They help him describe and live an experience more fully. The child gains confidence in his own ability to express his ideas.

Contents

Acknowledgments   viii

Preface   ix

I   The Child   1
The Five- and Six-Year Old   1
The Seven-Year Old   4
The Eight-Year Old   5

II   The Teacher   8
Creating an Atmosphere Conducive
    to the Growth of Self-Expression   8
Blocks to Creative Expression, and
    Possible Remedies   10
Treating Individual Differences   14

III   The Primary Classroom   17
Activity Areas in the Classroom   17
The Playhouse   21
Display and Bulletin Boards   23
Arranging Plant Material   29
Constructing Rooms for a Doll House   34
Building Blocks   36

IV   Wood Construction   38
Equipment   38

The Child Constructs a
    Form with Wood   39

V   Materials for Children to Explore   45
Stabiles   48
Mobile Space Design   49
Collage   52
Texture Design   54

VI   Beauty in the Child's World   57

VII   Art Materials and Their Use   61
Fingerpaint   62
Wax Crayon   66
Chalk   71
Tempera and Powder Paint   74
Watercolors   76
Easels   78

VIII   The Child Encounters the Brush   83

IX   The Beginning of Representation   89
The Child's Perception   89
Gradual Development of Children's
    Art Expression   90
Class Discussion About Children's
    Paintings and Drawings   94

X   *Observing Color in Things
    Children Know*   96
    A Color Portfolio of Children's
    Paintings   *(follows page)* 98

XI   *Stimulating Ideas in Children*   100
     Subjects for Children's Pictures   101
     Things Children See and Do Which
       Provide a Succession of Ideas   104

XII   *Growth in Representation*   107
      Drawing People   107

XIII   *The Community*   118
       Suggestions for Trips of Interest 118
       Bulletin Board   122
       People in the Community   125
       Play Experience   127
       Different Ways to Use Art Materials 133
       A Trip to the Zoo   135

XIV   *Related Subjects for Group
      Projects*   143
      Booklets Children Can Make   143
      Moving Picture Box   144
      Making a Mural   145

XV   *Seasonal Experiences*   149
     Fall   149
     Winter   153
     Spring   156
     The Farm   166

XVI   *Prints*   178
      Stampings   178
      Monoprints   185
      Stencils   187

Screen Prints   194
Blueprints   199

XVII   *Cut Paper*   201
       Guidance for Learning to
         Use Scissors   201

XVIII   *Box Animals*   216

XIX   *Papier-Mâché*   224
      Papier-Mâché Animals   225
      Laminated Paper   227

XX   *Masks*   230

XXI   *Puppets Children Can Make*   235

XXII   *Weaving*   242
       The Process of Weaving   244
       Weaving With Rags   246
       Weaving or Darning in an
         Onion-Skin Bag   248
       Spool Knitting   249

XXIII   *Stitches*   251

XXIV   *Clay*   255
       Modeling Materials   255
       Preparing the Classroom   257
       Things to Make with Clay   259
       Growth in Clay Modeling   264
       Pottery: The Coil Method   268
       Finishing Clay Pieces   270
       Skills Acquired   271

XXV   *Art Fulfills A Basic Need*   273

Appendix   275

Bibliography   287

Index   289

Illustrations

"My Picture" — *frontispiece*   *Drawn by Nancy*   GRADE 2   ii

Floor Plan for Primary Classroom   18

Tool Cabinet   19

Paint Cart   19

Proper Storage for Brushes   20

Play House (A Group Project)   22

Examples of Bulletin Board Arrangements   24

Bent Coat Hanger   25

Peep Show   25

Organization of Bulletin Boards   26

Second-Grade Bulletin Board. Cut-Outs
    Illustrate a Story: The Little Red Hen   28

Bulletin Board to Direct the Study of Animals   GRADE 3   29

Suggestions for Arranging Flowers, 5 Drawings   31

Suitable Backgrounds for Flower
    Arrangements, 4 Drawings   32

Constructing Rooms for a Doll House,
    4 Drawings   GRADE 3   34

Boxes Used for Doll House Furniture   35

Block City   37

Boat Shapes Made From a Few Basic Pieces
    of Wood   41

"An Airplane"   42

Making Stabiles   47

Framework for Mobiles   50

A Pleasing Texture Design in Grouping of Materials and Colors   53

Different Textures			55
Shells of Varying Shapes, Patterns and Textures			56
Looking into the Heart of a Flower	*7-year-old child*		58
Watching His Pet Hen Eat from His Hand	*5-year-old child*		59
Going Round and Round *(Fingerpainting)*			63
Making Upward Flame-like Movements *(Fingerpainting)*			65
Making a Tree			65
Crayon Strokes Defining a Bird, House and Fence	*by Ann*	GRADE 2	67
Crayon Strokes Defining a Train and Its Background	*by Rhona*	GRADE 2	67
Crayon Drawing of Bear	*by Carolyn*	GRADE 3	68
Forest Animals	*by Linda*	GRADE 2	68
Clown Scratched From Paint and Crayon			69
Design of Crayon Rubbing	*by Alan*	GRADE 1	69
Crayon on Cloth	*by Third-Grader*		70
Chalk Rubbing	*by Carol*	GRADE 2	72
A Tree in Chalk	*by Larry*	GRADE 1	72
A Mare and Her Colt	*by Karen*	GRADE 3	73
Double Easel			79
A Bench Easel			81
Double-Table Easel			81
Evidence of Growth in Two Paintings (a) (b)			86
Making Stripes With a Paintbrush (a) (b)			87
Simple Shapes	*by Jim*	GRADE 1	91
A House with Smoke	*by Barrett*	KINDERGARTEN	91
A Figure Done in Crayon and Paint	*by Teresa*	GRADE 1	91
Important Parts of the Face	*by Cathy*	KINDERGARTEN	92
"A Fine Pattern of a Man"	*by Judy*	KINDERGARTEN	92
Simple Shapes That Tell a Story	*by Yvonne*	KINDERGARTEN	92
"Boys and Tree"	*by Ullrick*	GRADE 2	93
The Bottom of the Ocean	*by Roberta*	GRADE 3	93
A Jewel-Like Pattern	*by a First-Grader*		95
The Inside of His House	*by a Second-Grader*		95
Her Own Picture With Her Bird	*by Sandra*	GRADE 2	95
"Mother Working in the Kitchen"	*by Wayne*	GRADE 3	101
"My Family"	*by Sandra*	GRADE 2	101
"A Clown Doing Stunts"	*by Jimmy*	GRADE 2	102
"In the Auditorium"	*by Mary*	GRADE 2	102
"Games We Like Outdoors"	*by Paul*	GRADE 1	103
"Jumping Rope"	*by a Third-Grader*		104
A Clown	*by Kathie*	GRADE 1	105
"Birds"	*by Barbara*	GRADE 2	105
A Picnic	*by a Third-Grader*		106

"Dolores When She Was a Baby"	by Dolores	GRADE 1	109
"The Family"	by a Third-Grader		112
"Going for a Walk"	by Deborah	GRADE 1	113
"Skating"	by Jennifer	GRADE 3	114
"Pushing-Out People," with Chalk		GRADES 2, 3	115
Cut-Out Painting on Cut-Paper Mural	by Joyce	GRADE 1	116
Cut-Out Figures Arranged for a Bulletin Board	by the First Grade		117
"What I Saw at the Bakery"	by Chris	GRADE 2	119
"At the Post Office" — a Sand-Table Project	by the Second Grade		120
"Men Working at the Post Office"	by Bonnie	GRADE 2	120
"Children Going to School"	by Holly	GRADE 1	121
"Steam Shovel"	by Mark	GRADE 2	122
"Tractor"	by Carl	GRADE 2	122
"The Bricklayer"	by a First-Grader		123
"Houses"	by a Second-Grader		125
"Our Neighborhood" (A Mural Painted in Powder Paint)	by Second-Graders		125
People in the Community — a Group Project	by Third-Graders		126
"The Fireman"	by Jerry	GRADE 3	127
"At the Gas Station"	by Ila	GRADE 2	127
"The Policeman"	by Patty	GRADE 2	127
"The Postman Comes to Our House"	by Jane	GRADE 2	127
Kinds of Trucks — a Group Project	by Second-Graders		128-9
Mural — a Group Project	by Second-Graders		130
Mural — a Group Project	by Second-Graders		131
"The Roundhouse"	by Steven	GRADE 2	132
"Freight Trains"	by Grant	GRADE 3	132
"A Community Map"	by Second-Graders		133
Construction in Third Dimension			134
"Two Giraffes"	by Jimmy	GRADE 1	136
"Lion"	by Bill	GRADE 3	136
"The King"	by Bobby	GRADE 1	136
"Other Animals Seen in the Zoo" — Class Project	by the Second Grade		138
"Zoo Animals" — Painted Mural	by the First Grade		139
"Circus Parade" — Cut-Paper Mural — Class Project	by the Second Grade		138-9
"A Small Bear Climbing a Tree"	by Harry	GRADE 2	140
"Tiger"	by Dennie	GRADE 2	140
Some Animals Done in Clay	by Second-Graders		141
Accordion Book — Project	by Second-Graders		144
Making a Moving Picture Box			145
A Box is Used for a Moving Picture			146
"Shepherds with Their Sheep" — in Powder Paint	by Second-Graders		147

A Circus Mural	by Second-Graders		147
"A Tree"	by Yvonne	GRADE 1	150
"A Tree"	by Sharon	KINDERGARTEN	151
Thanksgiving Day Bulletin Board			153
"Hibernating"	by Karen	GRADE 3	154
"Bare Branches with Snow"	by Freddie	KINDERGARTEN	155
"Mural"	by a Second-Grader		156-7
"Snowmen" — A Wrapping Paper Design	by a Third-Grader		157
"Flowers"	by Barbara	GRADE 1	159
"Flowers"	by Second-Graders		159
Crayon on Cloth Wall-Hanging	by the Third Grade		160
"Kites" — A Springtime Mural	by the First Grade		161
"Rabbit"	by Linda	GRADE 2	162
"Bird"	by Karen	GRADE 2	162
"Squirrel"	by Clark	GRADE 2	163
"Squirrel"	by Marcia	GRADE 1	163
"A Fuzzy Animal"	by Carol	GRADE 2	165
Diorama of Bears and Their Environment			165
"A Jumping Frog"	by Richard	GRADE 1	167
"Our Cow, Molly"	by Joy	GRADE 1	168
"Cat"	by Margaret	GRADE 1	168
"My Cat"	by Linda	GRADE 2	169
"My Cat Likes to Lie on Her Rug by the Fire"	by Susan	GRADE 3	169
"Spotted Horse"	by a Second-Grader		171
"White Colt"	by Margaret	GRADE 1	171
"Horses with Their Colts"	by Jerry	GRADE 1	171
"A Big Fat Pig"	by Jack	GRADE 2	171
"Rabbits in Their Burrow"	by Jefferson	GRADE 2	172
"Tractor"	by a First-Grader		175
"The Bulldozer"	by John	GRADE 1	175
"In the Country"	by Gail	GRADE 3	175
"Working on a Combine"	by Bobby	GRADE 3	175
"A Turkey with Bright Feathers"	by Mary	GRADE 1	176
"The Farmer"	by a First-Grader		176
"The Farm"	by a Second-Grader		176-7
"A Hen Family"	by a First-Grader		176
Printing With Stamps — Example of Repeat Designs			180-1
Repeating Shapes for All-Over Design			183
Monoprint	by Ann	GRADE 2	185
Brayer Prints			186
Stencil Design			188
Paper Cut-Outs for Chalk Stencil			190
Rubbing Design			192

"Stenciling"	*by Esther*	GRADE 2	193
Screen Stencil Print			195
Two Screen Prints Over Colored Papers	*by Bob*		196
Screen Stencil Print — Positive and Negative Shape			197
Screen Printing Using Wax Crayon — A Positive and Negative Print			198
Two Examples of Prints from Adhesive Paper Stencils			200
Cut Paper Picture Frame			202
A Paper Chain in a Wooden Frame			203
Melodie and John Weaving Paper Strips		GRADE 3	204
A Row of Figures Cut on a Fold to Hold Hands		GRADES 2, 3	205
Variations of Basic Cut-Paper Forms — For Grades One, Two, Three			207
Standing Cut-Paper Forms			208
Imaginary Animals Cut on a Vertical Fold	*by a Second-Grader*		209
Paper Cut-Out Buildings			210
Place Cards		GRADES 1, 2, 3	211
The Same Bird Shape Used With Varying Wings			212
Animal Forms		GRADES 2, 3	213
Kings and Queens		GRADES 1, 2, 3	214
Composite View of Materials Needed for Making Box Animals			215
Diagrams Illustrating Ways to Join Boxes for Parts of the Body Together			217
Making Necks			218
An Animal from Cut Paper			219
Making Ears and Horns			220
Making Noses and Eyes			220
Box Animals Made by First-Graders			221
A Fantastic Paper-Cup Dragon's Head		GRADE 3	221
Two Dragon-Type Animals in Paper		GRADE 2	222
A Guinea Hen Made From Discarded Materials		GRADE 3	223
Animals Made From Rolled Newspapers		GRADES 2, 3	226
Preparing Newspaper for Lamination			228
Laminated Paper Land Formations			229
Head-Shaped Mask			231
Strip-Paper Mask			231
Detail for Nose and Mouth of Mask			232
Paper-Bag Base for Mask		GRADES 1, 2	233
A Box-Mask Made From Cardboard		GRADE 3	233
Examples of Divisions of Space Suggested by Primitive Masks			234

Back of Cardboard Puppet Showing Position of Child's Hand		236
Animal Puppet		237
Components of Hand Puppet		238
Diagram to Show Stringing of Puppets		240
A Stocking or Cloth String Puppet		241
Simple Looms		243
Cardboard Loom		244
Navajo Loom		245
Third-Graders Weaving on Simple Looms		247
Materials Used in Spool Knitting	GRADES 2, 3	249
Second-Graders Spool Knitting		250
Simple Ways to Vary a Running Stitch		252
Variations of Basic Stitches and Their Combinations		253
A Simple Stitch Design on Burlap		254
Timothy Engrossed in Rolling Out the Clay		256
Gregor Puts His All into Shaping a Clay Bowl		257
Karla Is Stimulated and Intrigued by Her Discoveries with Clay	KINDERGARTEN	258
Examples of Useful Gifts Made from Clay		261
Sgraffito Tile Design		262
Sgraffito Design on Low Clay Bowl		263
Preparing Clay to Make Legs		265
Animals Modeled in Clay with Texture Added	GRADE 3	267
Demonstration of the Coil Method		269
Four Clay Bowls		271
Wall Plaque With Relief Design	*by a First-Grader*	272

Color Plates

COLOR PLATES
(*following page* 98)

Arrangement of Colored Paper Shapes

Imaginative Shapes in Dream World
Crayon and Water Color, Grade 3.

"Taking a String for a Walk"
Crayon and Water Color by Donald,
Grade 3.

A Little Girl Surrounded by Jewel Like
Colors
Painted by Joyce, Kindergarten.

Day and Night
Painted by Ginney, Kindergarten.

A Little Girl with Her Pet
Painted by Debra, Grade 1.

Mother Hen with Baby Chickens
Painted by Elizabeth, Grade 1

My Friends
Painted by Judith, Grade 3. Judith likes
to paint designs.

Birds Singing
Drawn in Crayon by Karin, Grade 3.
Karin has spread the wings of her birds
to show how they fly, making a delightful design.

Going for a Walk in the Park
Drawn in Chalk by Doreen, Grade 3.

A Boat with Shooting Guns
Painted by Paul, Grade 3, with exploding
movement in the sky, water and boat.

Buildings, Land, and Boat
Painted in rich strong colors by Eddie,
Grade 2.

A Bird in a Bed of Flowers
Painted by Janice, Kindergarten.

Mother Bird with Baby Birds in a Nest
Painted by Linda, Grade 2.

A Clown Doing Tricks
Painted by Dean, Grade 2.

A Lion Where It Likes to Be
Drawn in Crayon by Marlene, Grade 3.

"Springtime"
Painted by Marie, Grade 1.

Playing Indian
Painted by Lynda, Grade 2.

ART FOR PRIMARY GRADES

CHAPTER I

The Child

THE FIVE- AND SIX-YEAR-OLD CHILD

THE FOLLOWING CHARACTERISTICS serve as a guide for the kindergarten and first-grade teacher in understanding the art expression of five- and six-year-olds; procedures developed through actual classroom experience follow. One must remember that in every group of children some are developed more and some less than the majority, and each child's previous home experiences influence his or her readiness for school, such as places he has visited and things he has done.

PHYSICAL CHARACTERISTICS

EACH CHILD NEEDS to become acquainted with the use, need, and importance of body parts, that his hands are small, his arms and legs short; and that he has legs for walking, running, and jumping; feet for walking and supporting his legs; arms for reaching; hands for holding, lifting, and carrying things; eyes for seeing; mouth for eating, talking, and singing.

Muscular control is not developed to a high degree. The child does not have fine coordination between his hands and eyes. For this reason big tools which help him work need to be used. Small tools are not recommended. Free arm movements in rhythm, in painting with a large brush, and hammering large-headed nails into boards, are a few ways to develop muscular coordination.

The larger muscles of the limbs and trunk are developed to a higher degree. It is important for the young child to run, jump, swing, tumble, pull, push, and to move his body rhythmically to music. These acts coordinate and develop the larger muscles as well as give a feeling of freedom and rhythmic movement.

The child lacks strength in his hands. Manipulation of materials chosen to strengthen the hands of a small child includes building with wooden blocks; using both hands at once to paint or finger paint; modeling with clay and other plastic materials; sorting materials such as nuts and bolts; fitting parts together such as parts in an erector set.

A five- and six-year-old child uses his whole body in active play, in rhythm, and in constructing things. He enjoys manipulating materials of different kinds with his hands. He does not enjoy sitting still for long periods of time.

MENTAL CHARACTERISTICS

THE CHILD OF FIVE AND SIX *is seeking ideas* and *to understand about things he sees and feels.* The child finds out about things by continually questioning, by asking "What?" and "Why?" and by experimenting with materials. Most of the child's day is filled with undertakings of uncertain outcome and discovery.

Perception. Children of five and six see big areas and major differences in the contours of things, instead of seeing fine details. The child sees only one viewpoint, height and width. Each object is complete in itself, such as a house, a tree, an animal or a person. In the beginning things are not seen as part of their environment.

Being small, the child's line of vision is low, and he must look up to see many things. Objects for him to observe and enjoy must be placed on his eye level.

The child lives partly in an imaginary world. He does not have a tendency to view or represent things as they are seen by adults. The child combines what he knows with what he sees and imagines. His imaginary concepts are real to him. He exaggerates things he knows and hears. He states as true things he wants to happen. He will imitate a person or animal and identify himself with a character he wishes to be.

He does not reason the way an adult does. He thinks differently and draws what he knows and thinks is important about a subject during the time he is drawing — not what an adult sees.

The child's interest is focused on one thing at a time. The relative size of things is unimportant to the child. Proportion is not his purpose. The child may exaggerate size, color, and pattern to make parts important; likewise, he may minimize size or color or leave out things unimportant to him.

The five- and six-year-old child does not understand space. The child understands and is interested in his immediate surroundings. He knows the meaning of up and down and of in front and in back. He does not understand about distant places or about things in space.

The five- and six-year-old child has not developed a sense of time. He lives in the present and easily forgets what he did the day before; he does not distinguish one week from the next or a period of time.

He does not know how to wait a few days or a week to do something. The child thinks of time in terms of events such as "the day after my mother took me to the circus" or "the time my puppy was born."

The creative abilities of children lie in the use of materials to satisfy curiosity about how they feel and what will happen. The child creates by first manipulating and experimenting with art materials as a form of play. He draws, paints, builds and models for his own pleasure. It is important to the creative expression of a child for him to be free from fear of any kind.

The five- and six-year-old child is interested in the nature of things. He is interested in active things that concern himself. He likes to explore and experiment to find out how things move, what he can do with them and to discover new things. He enjoys touching the surface of things to find out how they feel as well as their color, sound, and movement.

The five- and six-year-old child likes to solve his own problems. A child can assemble his own toys and use them for a purpose. He starts with a raw material such as a lump of clay, and with his own resources, he shapes a form. He joins different sizes and shapes of wood together with nails to make a train, truck, boat or an imaginary object.

The young child has his own kind of humor. Things funny to a child need to be seen or heard by him, such as noises, funny faces, or someone doing tricks. His own symbolic drawings are serious and honest expressions. Often these are humorous to an adult but not to a child.

The five- and six-year-old child has a short interest span. He desires quick results and is able to concentrate on one thing only for a short period of time. The child works with enthusiasm as long as his interest and inspiration lasts. He needs time to complete his plan and work. He calls his work finished when he has completed his first impression, when he is fatigued, when he has lost interest or when his attention has been distracted. His concern is not whether he finishes or not but in the manipulating of materials. As the child develops physically and mentally he will be interested in producing a completed work.

Outside factors which influence the creative responses of a young child are weather, his home life, and events at school and in the community.

EMOTIONAL CHARACTERISTICS

THE CHILD OFTEN manipulates art materials for pure joy. He chooses colors which have emotional appeal to him. In the beginning he does not relate the color to the object. He may not be able to tell in words what or why he painted, modeled in clay, or pounded nails into wood.

The five- or six-year-old is easily excited or overstimulated. He forms concepts and images from things he imagines. His imagination may exaggerate events within his experience or may intensify feelings which he has toward an event.

Imaginary fears begin in a child as a result of things people say, from incidents described by adults as fearful, or the way events are described by adults. A child yields readily to adult suggestion. A few examples follow:

Lightning and thunder, for instance, can be approached as fascinating phenomena to watch rather than as potentially harmful ones to be avoided. Fear of the dark can be replaced by the enjoyment of discovering bright, colored lights in the dark and the stars in the sky. Fear of a policeman can be overcome by knowing some of the ways he can help boys and girls.

A child's likes and dislikes are often formed by a parent or teacher. A child thinks of clay only as a plastic medium to be formed by the hands; clay as "dirty" is an adult idea. A child thinks of the beautiful colors in paint and the joy in their use; paint as "messy" is an adult idea. The child likes attention and asks questions for information from adults. This is one way the child gains in understanding his environment.

Social Characteristics

THE FIVE- AND SIX-YEAR-OLD child needs to learn how to be a member of a social group. He has not relinquished his home ties and feels insecure in a group. He does not always understand the difference between "yours" and "mine." He may be selfish about sharing his property or be angered by interference with his possessions, plans, and purposes. He wants to take home the things he makes. The child needs help in learning to share with the group and meeting new situations. The child is predominately interested in himself and is not interested at first in what other people think about his work. He desires recognition, affection, praise and approval. He is eager to assume responsibility, and with help progresses in the care of his person, of his possessions and some responsibility toward others.

THE SEVEN-YEAR-OLD

EACH GROUP OF CHILDREN varies in physical, mental, emotional, and social development. Characteristics of seven-year-old boys and girls which may be used as a guide for understanding their art follow. Previous experiences have become part of the child's life.

Physical Characteristics

THE SEVEN-YEAR-OLD seems to possess continuous energy. He enjoys play acting — like being a cowboy, dressing up, riding in a wagon. He likes to run pulling a kite behind him. He likes to do things requiring motion in using his hands and legs. Art activities which require making new forms, joining forms or altering forms appeal to the second-grader. He shows growth in the coordination of his hands and eyes. His small muscles have developed sufficiently to make it possible for him to form legible letters in writing, but his coordination is not sufficiently developed for fine details which require close control, such as fine paper cutting or sawing irregular shapes.

Mental Characteristics

THE SEVEN-YEAR-OLD is interested in how things work and how they are made. This interest helps give purpose to his observation. He is able to retain information or visual images he has formed. Thus he profits from taking well-organized trips. His interest is in what he is making, and he works very hard to accomplish it. He has developed likes and dislikes. These influence his choice of activities and art mediums for self-expression.

The seven-year-old relates things to each other in forming sentences, just as he relates shapes in his art work. He thinks of certain things as belonging together — a house, child, and tree beside a street with cars — and he combines them in a picture. Many boys and girls of this age are interested in details of machinery — the wheels in a clock, the moving belts in a bottling machine, or the swinging arm of a bulldozer. Those who observe keenly enjoy drawing every part and telling about its use. In his drawing the second grader adds what he knows to what he sees. For this reason he often shows the inside and outside of a building in one picture, thus telling the observer both. Often the child turns his paper around as he draws each side of a street or playfield, depicting one side of the street on the top of the paper and the other side on the bottom. The second-grader does not examine critically essential elements.

His imagination often adds charm to his work. He likes to pretend, and to make imaginative animals and people. He does not think abstractly or understand esthetic values.

The interest span of the second grader is still short. He concentrates on one thing at a time and should be given but one step at a time for a process that requires several steps to complete.

EMOTIONAL CHARACTERISTICS

THE SEVEN-YEAR-OLD creates from an inner feeling of impelling desire to express an idea. He does not create from formulas outlined by a teacher. If the child fears he will not do something right or that he will make a mess, he may draw very small or refuse to use art materials at all. The child reacts to experiences that arouse curiosity.

SOCIAL CHARACTERISTICS

THE SECOND-GRADER IS oriented to the classroom environment and needs to associate with other children both in play and in group projects.

THE EIGHT-YEAR-OLD

CHILDREN GROW AND DEVELOP in their ability to observe, to create, and to use tools at different rates. Previous experiences at home and in school affect their readiness for art activities in the third grade, as observation, self-expression and love.

PHYSICAL CHARACTERISTICS

THE EIGHT-YEAR-OLD is energetic and alert. His growth in motor ability has increased his control over materials and tools. The third grader still does not have highly developed small muscles. Tools need to be large, such as large-eyed needles to use with heavy thread, big nails to use with soft wood and medium-size scissors to use with large sheets of construction paper. A third-grader enjoys putting materials together to make a new form. He likes to use what he has made — to beat a drum which he has made by stretching skin over a barrel or to manipulate a puppet he has made.

The third-grader enjoys constructing objects with moving parts, such as wheels on a wagon.

The eight-year-old's perception has developed, and he sees sharper distinctions between one object and another. He observes finer differences and details of pattern. He desires his own expression to represent what he observes. He notices nearness and distance. He places distant objects higher up on the paper. He overlaps objects to show one is in front of another. He sees the top, side, front and back of objects. He represents these different points of view in one picture, like a square table top with the profile of a chair.

Mental Characteristics

The eight-year-old is inquisitive. He desires to know how or why things happen; how things are made and what comes next. He has keen interests and does not hesitate to try new things. He likes to work with the unfamiliar.

An eight-year-old is capable of comparing one color, shape or size with another, and of reasoning and deciding which one is better for a given purpose. The third-grade child is interested in facts about things he has seen and read about. He can find and use source materials. Some third-graders use the same symbols to represent a person, a tree, a house or an animal that they used in the second grade. Stimulation produced by rich experiences which include the child's sense of touch leads to a symbol showing more active thinking.

The eight-year-old begins to notice the proportions and actions of the human figure or animal form and represents more clearly his visual image of them. He desires his own expression to represent what he observes. He adjusts the size of objects to the length and width of the paper, and relates objects to each other in order to convey his idea. The child thinks in terms of what he is trying to impart.

The longer interest span of the third grader is noticeable in the details he adds to his work. He desires to produce work that is acceptable to his classmates, for third graders are capable of evaluating each other's work.

The third grader is imaginative and enjoys action plays in which he can pretend. He is resourceful in combining materials to make his own costumes, as well as the stage sets. He works with energy and enthusiasm until he achieves the result he desires.

The eight-year-old understands simple directions and can follow several successive steps in a process. He is able to plan and to make suggestions about ways of carrying out a project in art.

The third-grade child has developed individual ways. He is beginning to be interested in the result as much as in the "doing," thus running paint or a wrinkled piece of paper is disturbing to him because he feels his work is spoiled. He needs sufficient guidance in developing his skills, to help him to produce an art work that satisfies him.

Emotional Characteristics

Third-grade boys and girls do not know how to express esthetic feeling or to portray a mood in color. They are becoming more individual, and are sensitive and aware of what is involved in accomplishing chosen goals. They need security and confidence in their own ability to succeed. A child often needs guidance in the best way to use material to achieve the desired result. Fear causes him to draw in a tight small way, in one corner of the paper, to copy, or to hide his work from view.

For true creative work the child needs experiences enabling him to identify himself with the idea he is trying to express. The more intense his feeling or reactions to the experience, the greater will be his concentration and creative power of expression.

SOCIAL CHARACTERISTICS

THE THIRD-GRADER IDENTIFIES himself with his environment. He realizes the need to cooperate with others. He contributes to group discussion and group planning as well as to work with others in shared activities. Children of this age like subjects that are related to a group, such as "Things we do together," "Places we go," or "My family."

CHAPTER II

The Teacher

CREATING AN ATMOSPHERE CONDUCIVE TO THE GROWTH OF SELF-EXPRESSION

THE TEACHER NEEDS many qualities. Among them these are essential: 1) an understanding of children, to make possible an agreement in feeling between the teacher and the child; 2) the ability to value the creation of new images made by the child, in order to develop the imagination of that child; 3) a knowledge of how children grow and what their interests are at different ages in order to select art activities and materials; 4) an appreciation of children's spontaneous and creative efforts in order to increase their worth to the child, as well as to develop creative self-expression.

Furthermore, to open the eyes of children to the beauty in their surroundings, the teacher must recognize beauty in nature and in man-made objects. The teacher needs a creative point of view and a willingness to try new things. A classroom arrangement conducive to exploring untried materials.

ENCOURAGING GROWTH IN SELF-EXPRESSION

By LISTENING WITH enthusiasm to what a child has to tell, a teacher encourages the expression of ideas.

By having an inquiring, open-minded attitude toward things a child says and does, a teacher gives children confidence in themselves.

By being impartial and fair, a teacher can help a child gain faith in adults.

By speaking to a child in a manner that considers his affairs as important, a teacher strengthens the child's feeling of worth.

By being interested in the activities a child likes, a teacher becomes closer to a child because of the interest common to the teacher and the child.

By recognizing that each attempted action is a step toward a child's further growth and understanding, the teacher encourages the child to experiment, to find out what he can do with each different material.

By being able to laugh and sing with children, the teacher gives them the feeling that he is human and enjoys the things they enjoy.

By adjusting quickly to the sudden changes in a child's temperament — from a burst of energy to drowsy inactivity — the teacher gives the child a feeling of mutual understanding.

By regarding busy, happy activity as the best discipline for young children, the teacher values what is purposeful.

By giving a child an opportunity to discuss his ideas, the teacher can help him clarify his thinking.

By arousing a desire in the child for self-achievement, the teacher helps him appreciate the results of his own efforts; thus his own ideas become significant to him.

Promoting the Development of Self-Expression

By basing comments upon the child's experience rather than on the quality of work alone, the teacher draws the child's attention to his own expression of his idea.

By emphasizing the good parts of a child's work, the teacher instills in the child a feeling that he has succeeded.

By praising the child's own way of doing things, the teacher gives the child a feeling that he has a contribution to make.

By saying, "I know you can do it," the teacher encourages the child to try.

By asking questions which help the child form a mental image of what he desires to do, the teacher helps him think out his own problems.

By asking the child for information, the teacher gives the impression that he wishes to learn from the child.

By wording questions so as to give the child the impression that he is capable of answering, the teacher gives the child a feeling of worth. The teacher values the individuality of the child in his art.

Stimulating Thinking

By guiding the observations of a child, the teacher encourages exploration and discoveries.

By making the beauty and character of simple things a child sees a part of daily class observation and discussion, the teacher develops esthetic taste in children.

By enlarging upon the prevailing interest of the child, the teacher helps the child develop ability to express ideas.

By focusing the child's attention on the good qualities of his art work, the teacher gives the incentive for further development in self-expression.

By giving direct help to a child in answer to "How can I do it?", "What makes it go?", or "Why is it like that?" the teacher satisfies the child's desire to know.

By selecting from a confusing group a simple subject which interests the child, the teacher makes it possible for the child to give his full attention to one thing at a time. The teacher helps the child describe one thing about his subject that is important.

BY SELECTING materials suitable to the child's physical and mental capabilities, the teacher avoids frustrating the child.

By helping the child find the art medium best suited to the expression of his emotional experiences, the teacher frees him from restraint.

By considering the muscular control and mental abilities of a child in the choice of tools, the teacher offers the child the opportunity to do his best.

By choosing art mediums in which each child attains satisfactory expression, the teacher increases the child's desire and potential capacity for self-expression.

By offering and teaching a technique when the child needs help in expressing himself to his own satisfaction, the teacher makes clear why and how tools should be used in certain ways.

BLOCKS TO CREATIVE EXPRESSION, AND POSSIBLE REMEDIES

Adverse criticism confuses a child. The child rebels and says, "I can't," or changes his own way of expression to please the teacher. For example:

    a. Expressions which imply that a picture is incorrect such as, "No one has ever seen a tree like that," or "Grass is never red."

    b. Directing attention to inaccuracies, such as in rendering the proportions of the human body, before the child sees or understands them.

Instead of seeing "mistakes," try to understand the mental and physical growth of the child. What does the child see? How does he feel about what he sees? What does he imagine while he is thinking and working? Recognize the natural way children express their ideas by making parts they feel important appear large or by using colors they like. Enjoy the simplicity and directness of children's art. Praise the child for his own best work. Look for free rhythmic movement, balance of color, and clear, bold rendering, not for accurate likenesses. There are no mistakes in a child's art.

Do not direct the attention of small children to details, for this makes them confused and tearful, and they will say, "I can't do it."

Their vision is not developed sufficiently to see small details. Recognize this stage of growth and help them see by observing and commenting on large similarities and pronounced differences in shapes, such as roundness and squareness. Point out shadows of buildings and trees as examples of simple shapes.

Do not assume or suggest, that every stroke a young child makes with a brush or crayon should transmit a thought or feeling, and do not require children to explain their marks and unrecognizable forms, or you will confuse the child.

Every child needs to go through a natural period of growth in the use of art materials. Before making marks and forms that have meaning, the child handles art materials as a form of play — without any definite aim making lines, shapes and forms merely for the fun of it, and in handling the art materials discovers what they are like and what he can do with them. Plan days or weeks for introducing different materials.

Assigning a project beyond the child's understanding or physical ability frustrates the child.

If you discover that the child knows nothing about a subject you have chosen from his own experience, or if you cannot possibly explore its possibilities with him, change to a subject the child knows about.

Stress placed on the "correct" word, color, or shape rather than on the idea, creates anxieties in the young beginner about *how* he expresses himself, and puts a damper on his eagerness to express himself.

Remember that there are many different colors, shapes and sizes, and that each child thinks and sees differently. Stress the way he expresses his own ideas of what he himself has seen, felt, or imagined.

Stress on precision, exactness, and neatness makes the child fear the teacher's disapproval — whether expressed or only intimated.

The small child does not have sufficient coordination, interest span, or understanding to produce exactness or precision. Encourage a clear, honest rendering fitted to the child's own ability. Guide children to form good work habits with each material.

Imposing adult standards of realism on a child's work when the teacher is helping him, discourages a child.

Find out what a child knows, sees and imagines. Children in the symbolic stage do not see fine differences in forms which differentiate a species such as a cat from a dog. The child may differentiate an animal from a man by making a long horizontal body with four lines for legs to represent an animal and vertical shapes or lines with perhaps a rounded head to represent a man.

As the child's observation of real things develops and he feels the living quality of animals with their movements and use of body parts he will draw the milk bag or horns of a cow, the whiskers of a cat or the long jumping legs of a rabbit.

Comparing a child's work with that of adults discourages a child because he does not have an adult's ability.

Value each child's honest expression. Children's art has characteristics of its own. Although adult illustrators often try to make child-like drawings, children can never do adult work. Encourage children to be themselves.

Comparing one child's work with another's discourages individual self-expression.

Each child has a unique contribution to make. Rather than noting the similarities or pointing out that one child's work is better than another's, draw attention to what is good in each, by such comments as: "John has repeated his blue," "Mary has told many things about the bakery she visited," or "See the beautiful bright colors."

Materials such as "clay too wet" or "too hard," or "paper too rough," which do not fit the child's fingers or coordination discourage him. The child develops a dislike for using these materials.

Art materials that are "just right" help ideas to grow. Their use becomes natural, not a hazard to overcome. Paints need to be thin enough to flow easily from the brush. Clay for modeling must be plastic and not sticky. Paper for finger painting should be smooth and slippery.

Dictating every step of a project to a child by showing him *how* to do something makes the child lose confidence in his own expression and ideas, makes him timid, imitative and dependent upon help. This child will say, "I can't," when left to express himself without help.

Give children an opportunity to participate in the planning of each project. By experimentation encourage the children to discover what they can do with each new material, and in progressive steps guide them to success in terms of their own satisfaction.

Asking the child to explain what he has done in a way that makes him feel the teacher does not understand his work tends to make the child lose confidence in the teacher.

Children often express in easel paint, clay, or fingerpaint something they cannot say in words. Art expression does not need to be explained. The joy children have in "doing" is sufficient.

Not recognizing the seemingly incomplete, meager attempt of a child as an honest expression or as the fulfillment of his dream, perhaps a wonderful one to the child, creates a barrier between adult and child. The child feels grown-ups do not understand.

The adult must sense and be close to the inner being of a child, and outwardly must show enthusiasm for each experience of the child. The child needs to feel that grown-ups care, and respect his ideas.

Laughing at something the child has not intended to be funny gives him the feeling that the teacher does not understand or that he is making fun of the child's work.

Children's work needs to be taken seriously. If the child's purpose is to make a funny person or animal, the child wants his picture to amuse those who see it. Many of his pictures are symbols for his ideas — he reduces people to very simple shapes, he finds names for his symbols in his imagination. Adults do not see or think like children, and cannot fully understand a child's reactions. Instead of laughing at childlike expression, enjoy its honesty and symbolic qualities.

Standing over a child while he is working when the child has not asked for help disturbs the child.

Creative thinking evolves through concentration. An adult needs to stay in the background, ready with encouragement and suggestions.

Pushing children when they are tired and they say they are finished results in labored work.

Children are finished when their interest span has ended; when they do not know the next step; or when they have completed their work to their own satisfaction. Very young children often cover up work that is completed because they love to manipulate the brush. Nothing is gained by insisting upon children continuing when they are fatigued or think they are finished. Then, a complete change of activity is needed. When the child is refreshed, if he wants to add to his work, he should have the opportunity to do so.

Allowing insufficient time for a child to finish a picture or complete a form which the child has in mind often makes the child revert back to a previously-learned form of expression.

The normal child works with all his faculties for a short period of concentration. Once he has started using a material he needs to complete his work while his idea is clear in his mind. He does not remember his original idea a few hours or a day later, nor is the beginner ready to do step-by-step processes. He thinks and acts in the immediate present.

Teaching a technique as an isolated activity or as an end in itself has no meaning to a child.

A child is ready to learn the next technique when he asks for the knowledge that technique provides. When the child reaches the stage of dissatisfaction with his results and asks how to use a certain tool, or how to make some specific thing such as "wool on a lamb" or "a man riding a horse," or how to make parts stay together in clay or wood, then give the child the technique he needs, or guide his observation of the object to see the details he needs.

Designating certain children as *the* artists in the room and making apologies for the work of other children hampers growth in individual expression.

The use of art materials enlists the imagination. They offer an opportunity for making choices and finding different ways of doing things. Each child is able to grow in self-expression with the use of art materials. No single accomplishment should be considered superior to another, for one boy or girl may model well in clay, another construct well with wood, another make fine plant arrangements.

Saying to a child, "When you are older, you will do this a certain way," inhibits the child.

Being a child, thinking with a child's mind, playing with all the imagination, joy, and energy of a child, is special. The child has no tradition to confuse his thinking. A simple example is the profile of the animal form which the child draws as having four legs. An adult sees two legs in a profile view. The child draws four legs because he knows an animal has four legs. In his honesty he draws what he knows, not what he sees.

If adults whom the child likes and desires to please, such as mothers, fathers, and teachers do everything for their children, by making all the initial steps for children to follow, they shake the child's confidence by not accepting the child's honest attempt. These children refuse to work independently and ask continually for help. They lack confidence in their own ability.

You can build self-confidence in the child at school by selecting materials that encourage the child to explore — such as, a lump of clay he can squeeze, pat, roll, or punch holes in; wire he can bend to different forms; colors of opaque paint he can intermix to find out how many colors he can make; scraps of wood he can move about and nail together into new forms.

Allowing a child to copy and praising him for work he has copied destroys creative growth, stifles imagination, stops spontaneity. The child's perception becomes confused and complex. He does not have the opportunity to form his own idea or conception of a subject. He reproduces without understanding meaning, he does not have the pleasure of making his own selection, nor of choosing his own treatment; consequently, he cannot grow with the progression of his work. He is robbed of the joy in achievement that comes with the completion of a creation of his own. Copying is based on the assumption that the child has no ideas of his own, and the child senses that his own work is not acceptable.

Find out why the child has copied. Instead of asking children to duplicate something set before them, substitute an experience with interest and meaning for them. Guide children in their observation of things in their environment so that ideas are stimulated and mental images formed, by asking them for the specific characteristics that distinguish one thing from another — such as, the antlers of a deer from the horns of a cow or the large blade in front of a bulldozer?

Instead of criticizing the child for the way he does his art work, praise the child's own work. Only exhibit the child's own work.

For a child lacking ideas of his own, try

to find his interest — in school and out of school — and use this interest, something he knows about from experience, to stimulate his thinking and visual images. (Example: The child likes airplanes. The teacher says, "Have you watched the airplanes land at the airport? Before a plane is ready to leave, what do workers do to prepare for the flight? Where do airplanes go? How does the inside of an airplane look? Where do people sit? Where is the pilot?")

For the child who repeats one thing which satisfies him because it gives him a feeling of security, change the medium entirely. Suggest experimentation with the following materials, to enable the child to make new discoveries:

1. Fingerpainting.
2. Intermixing colors to make new colors.
3. Using discarded materials such as bent wire, buttons, shavings, bits of cloth, or colored paper to make a collage.
4. Using wooden sticks of different shapes to stamp a design.
5. Modeling with clay.

All of these may be shared with the group.

TREATING INDIVIDUAL DIFFERENCES

For the child who is uncertain of his own abilities, feels inferior, or whose work is hesitant and cramped.

Treatment: Give finger paint, which allows for large movements with no hazards to overcome in the way of tools.

Encourage using a brush, full of paint, to make a bold, firm stroke, using a free arm movement swung from the shoulder, to carry the paint as far as it will reach on the paper.

Large movements on the blackboard made with a wet brush as far as the child can reach will also help to release the child who has been using cramped, uncertain or disconnected strokes.

Encourage the child to try different mediums on different days, to broaden his interests and to acquaint him with the possibilities of various materials.

For the child using methodical, rigid, and unimaginative forms.

Treatment: Suggest bodily movements, like rhythm bands, singing, and dancing.

For the child hesitant to try something new.

Treatment: Suggest that he express in color some personal experience, and tell us how the experience made him feel. Find what the child is interested in at home.

For the immature child who is slow to retain or understand the subject.

Treatment: Provide more information about materials. This child is probably in the manipulative stage, and helping to mix paint, or simply passing materials may be his contribution.

For the child who evades work, withdraws from the group, who lacks interest and understanding, or feels he has nothing worthwhile to say or contribute.

Treatment: Assign a responsible task, such as sorting the crayons into groups with like colors together; assign an individual something he is able to do, such as caring for a pet or arranging objects attractively for everyone to enjoy; guide the child to decorate paper with a design to be used as a mat under a plant, book, or clay object. Each one of these helps the child feel he is a necessary member of the group.

For the child who begins several projects and does not complete any, who is emotionally unstable, has a very short interest span, or the second grader who does not relate ideas.

Treatment: Find the child's interest. Help him clarify his own idea by asking questions which make him think and recall things he has experienced.

Encourage him to tell all he knows about one thing, such as his wagon. What makes his wagon go? [Wheels] How many wheels does his wagon have? How does he use his wagon? Does he ride in his wagon? How does he ride in his wagon? Does he carry things in his wagon? How does he pull his wagon?

Help the older child relate ideas through a personal experience, such as observing things he sees in looking out the window or going for a walk.

Give the emotionally unstable child color so that he can paint how he feels.

For the child doing stereotyped, imitative work.

Treatment: Praise the child for every attempt which is his own. Give the child a definite, tangible experience such as a visit to a bakery plant, a milk factory, or a pet store. Help the child to discover for himself what things are like and how they work. Encourage the child to use art materials to express what he saw when he visited the pet store. Do not use color books and patterns which cause children to lose their creativeness and to become stiff and conventional.

Help the child to find his way to his own discoveries and expression by stressing the many different ways materials can be used.

For the child with little imagination.

Treatment: Guide the child to see the beauty of pattern in animals and plants, such as that of the turtle's shell, the butterfly's wings, or the caterpillar's back. Direct his attention to the rhythmic movement of the swimming goldfish or the bending of trees in the wind. Inspire the child to show the movement of things he has observed with chalk or paint, or to make an all-over repeated pattern for decorative paper.

For the child who becomes very skillful with one expression and thus produces automatically.

Treatment: Change the medium to one which requires the child to think and to make new discoveries.

For the spoiled child who is seemingly pleased with nothing.

Treatment: Try to know this child. Is he an only child? Is he given everything he wants? Does he think he is superior to the other members of his group? Has he been given too much attention at home, for things he does well and things he does poorly? Has too much adult influence made him dependent on adult standards? Are his emotional problems centered on himself?

Give this child art experiences which offer opportunities to rid himself of tensions — such as modeling clay, finger painting, or using color to express how he feels.

Watch this child as he works to determine what absorbs his attention and interest. Help him develop his interest by offering new experiences and materials; give him materials to manipulate and arrange, such as wire to bend or discarded materials to arrange in a collage or stabile (see Collage, page 53; Stabile, pages 48, 49).

Give this child a part in some group project — painting a mural or constructing a building for a community — and be sure he realizes that the part he contributes is needed for the whole.

This child needs to be aware of values, to appreciate things, to feel real materials such as smooth plastic clay, soft fur, smooth hard pebbles; to see the beauty of color and pattern on animals' backs, the many colors in flowers; to feel the freedom of body movement in running and playing and the joy of having fun with other children.

For the child who is afraid to paint boldly or to use his hands freely.

   Treatment: Find the cause of the child's fear; was his work ridiculed or thought funny? Is he timid? Has he been scolded for spilling paint? Help the child overcome his fear by praising something he does well, even if it is "painting one beautiful color all over the paper." Stress the magic of color, such as new colors that appear when two or more colors run together. Encourage new discoveries.

CHAPTER III

The Primary Classroom

A WELL DESIGNED ROOM for young boys and girls must fill the needs of active, imaginative children to insure their growth and development.

Each child needs adequate space for his art activities. Most small children work with comparatively large materials, and all children are continually moving while they are using most art materials; thus space is needed for freedom of self-expression.

THE ROOM MUST BE COMFORTABLE AND PLEASANT

1. *Well ventilated,* with a clean, fresh current of air, and the temperature kept between 65° to 70° (not above).
A place provided for wet garments.
Animal cage designed for sanitation and easy cleaning.

2. *Well lighted* with even, well-diffused light of 35-foot candles minimum recommended, without glare.
Children seated so as not to face the light in their library corner or listening area.

3. *Windows* should be below the eye level of the children so that they may observe more about their environment.

ACTIVITY AREAS IN THE CLASSROOM
(Group materials according to their kind and use.)

PLACE MATERIALS TO BE USED by the children within their reach.

I. The sink area should be on an inside wall at a height correct for the children.

1. A counter on either side of the sink made of formica or a similar plastic to be used as a working space for clay modeling, fingerpainting, and painting.

2. Materials that need the use of water should be stored near the sink:
powder paint, fingerpaint, clay in bins, clay boards, rags, brushes, containers for paint and water, and sponges.

II. A work bench with a vise for sawing should be on an inside wall.

1. The design of the work bench may

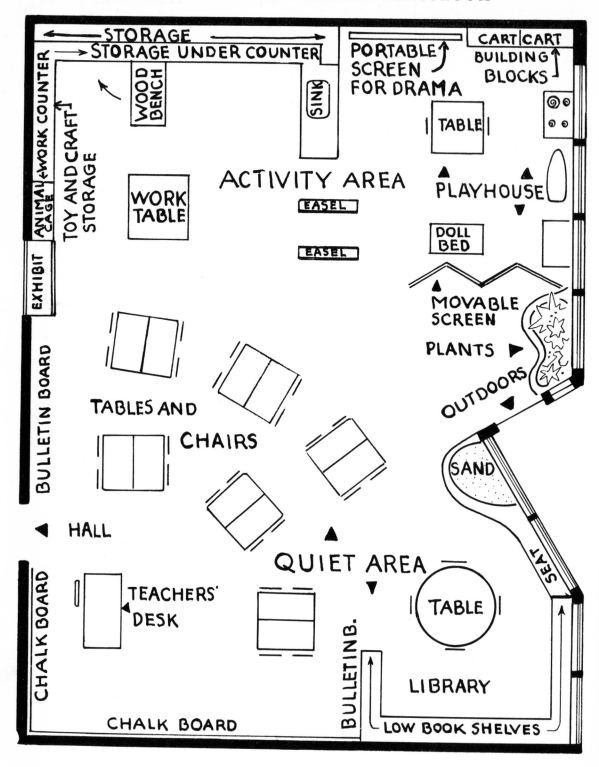

include space for the storage of scrap lumber.

2. The tools and nails are stored in a closed cupboard with doors. The shape of each tool is painted on the back of the storage cupboard to identify the correct place for each tool.

    a. Hammers, saws, planes, nails and drill.

III. Low shelves for toys and games within reach of children. Used for toys, puzzles, word and number games, and labelled boxes each containing materials a child needs for a given process.

IV. Wall storage space for movable cart for storage of large building blocks. Mobile wheel toys are also in this area which is removed from the passageways.

V. Corner for playhouse with one wall a window wall.

    1. Wall dividers for the playhouse.
        a. Screens.
        b. Back of bookcase (right angles to the wall).
        c. Back of the piano.
    2. Housekeeping properties.
        a. Table and chairs for eating.
        b. Bedroom with bed and cupboard for storage of doll clothes.
        c. Kitchen with stove, cupboard for storage of utensils and pans.
        d. Living room for conversation, enjoyment of books and music.

VI. Library for enjoyment of books.

The book shelves placed at right angles to the wall furnish a wall partition. The opposite side might have shelves for dishes for the playhouse.

The shelves need to be low. The top is an excellent place for plants, an aquarium, clay figures or other objects of beauty.

The library corner needs to resemble a comfortable, home-like living room.

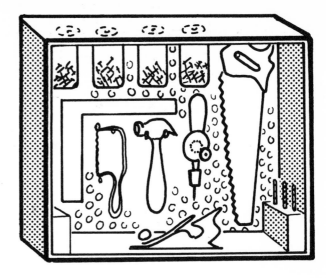

TOOL CABINET

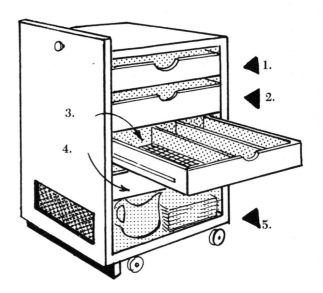

PAINT CART

1. **Watercolor boxes.**
2. **Dry powder paint containers.**
3. **Brushes stored and dried on screened shelf.**
4. **Water containers.**
5. **Miscellaneous storage with metal drip pan on shelf.**

The Primary Classroom / 19

VII. Space for group of chairs for stories and dramatic play.

1. Face a solid wall, a blackboard, chart easel or wall board.

2. Door is convenient to the right or left for dramatic play.

3. Away from the sink area.

4. Room to move freely about for dramatic play.

VIII. Science area combined with items children wish to share with the group (away from movable toys).

1. Pegboard with shelves on the wall for three- and four-dimensional objects.

2. Bulletin board for pictures relating to display.

3. A table for display of shells, birds' nests, seeds, rocks, and other natural or man-made items.

4. An animal cage or other provision for observation of living things — a cocoon, a squirrel, ants, or baby animals.

IX. Free space for rhythmic play.

X. Space for resting, either on cots or rugs.

XI. Movable tables, which may be moved together when added floor space is needed.

Table tops are needed for:

1. Cutting paper and pasting.

2. Painting.

3. Drawing with crayon.

4. Solving puzzle games.

5. Working with reading-readiness and writing materials.

6. Box and wood construction.

XII. Sand-box near activity center away from passageway.

1. Near storage of small wheel toys such as trucks and trains.

2. Near containers for sifting and measuring.

XIII. Painting easels are placed at right angles to the light; near the paint storage and sink.

XIV. The piano placed at right angles to an inner wall makes a room divider. Wall board covering the back will be useful for display, or as the background for a beautiful arrangement.

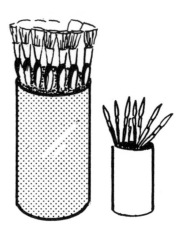

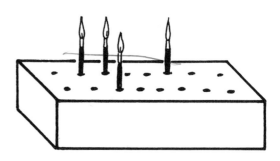

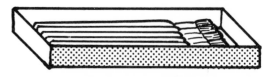

PROPER STORAGE FOR BRUSHES

CARE AND STORAGE OF MATERIALS

LABEL EACH CONTAINER with a symbol for the material and its name in large block letters. Keep dry brushes in rustproof cans, in boxes, or jars. Separate each kind of brush, and allow a space between the brush tips and the box.

Pour liquid paint into baby-food jars or juice cans for classroom use (wooden cheese boxes or shoe boxes are useful containers for these jars or cans). Place three in pound coffee can for class use. These may be stacked for storing.

Keep liquid fingerpaint in a large open-neck jar with a lid that closes tightly, and keep a wooden spoon beside the jar to use as a ladle in dipping out paint.

Store crayons and chalk in separate boxes; put warm colors — yellow, orange, red, red-violet — together, and cool colors — blue, green, blue-violet, violet, brown — together. Put white, gray and black together in a third group.

THE PLAYHOUSE

The playhouse experience provides opportunities for learning habits of order, cleanliness, good conduct and how to take responsibility. Children make choices in selecting things to combine and colors to use in the furnishings of their playhouse.

PLANS FOR THE PLAYHOUSE

THE CHILDREN, with the teacher's guidance, plan the size and location for their playhouse. A good way to help them visualize the area needed for each room is to place appropriate furniture on the floor in groups as it will function in each room. The children may then use chalk to mark the floor plan for the playhouse. The available classroom space determines the number and size of playhouse rooms, which need to be large enough for the children to move easily around the furniture. Use a corner of the schoolroom for two walls, and an outside window for light and warmth. Low screens may be placed to form a third wall, as well as to partition separate rooms. Movable screens permit easy changes of shape, size, and arrangement of rooms as desired.

FURNITURE CHILDREN CAN MAKE

Chairs from apple boxes or nail kegs; doll bed may be made from a banana crate or a wooden box. Shelves added to a wooden box make a cupboard. Attractive book shelves can be made by placing wooden boards on top of bricks.

Painting furniture (Rubber base paint is satisfactory.) It is advisable to use one color for all the furniture in one room. A few suggested color combinations follow: With light lemon-yellow walls use light grayed-green or turquoise blue furniture; with apple-green walls use ivory furniture; with light peach walls use light gray-blue furniture. When patterned wallpaper is used, solid colors are best for all the furnishings, and one of the wallpaper colors should be repeated in the furniture.

PLAY HOUSE
(A Group Project)

Art processes in the playhouse above completed by first graders include:

1. Painting or staining the wooden furniture. (Eighth-grade boys made all furniture except the dressing table, chair and table, which first graders made with help.)
2. Fingerpainting used for wallpaper.
3. Pictures painted in powder paint.
4. Potato-print border designs on the table-cloth.
5. Stick print all-over pattern on chair cushion.
6. Braided rag rug.
7. Blown dye-stencil design on the lamp-shade.
8. Fruit and bowl modeled in clay.
9. Clay figures and animals on shelves.
10. Illustrated booklets on shelves.
11. Tie dye square on dressing table.
12. Hand-dipped candles.
13. Crayon border design on curtains.
14. Patch quilt on bed.
15. Large rag doll.
16. Small stocking doll.
17. Border with stitches on the dressing-table skirt and bedcover.
18. Woven bag on chest.
19. Decorated paper plate on chest of drawers.

Selecting Cloth for Furnishings

COMBINE MATERIALS which are related in design, in color, or in texture.

Choosing colors. The color of the wall needs to be repeated as one of the colors in the pillows or slip covers. Cloth should be slightly lighter or darker than the furniture. The colors of the pillows should relate to the slipcover color or the wood color, whether natural or painted. For example, yellow and yellow-green pillows harmonize with a green slipcover; brown and orange also are related to green. These two colors add an accent because of the red they contain.

Combine cloth of one color with cloth having a pattern, and have the plain color material repeat a color in the patterned material.

Avoid combining many materials of different designs in one room.

Choosing textures. In choosing materials, relating the textures or weaves is important; materials which give the same feeling seem to belong together. Materials without a gloss, rough textured — nubbly knits, tweeds, woven hemp or burlap — combine well with woven straw mats. Materials with a gloss, such as silks and satins, do not combine well with cottons. Cotton and native materials such as woven straw mats are best for use in a playhouse. Their appearance harmonizes with the work of children.

Articles Children Can Make for the Playhouse

For wallpaper — Decorated papers made by fingerpainting, stamping, or using a brayer.

For shelf paper, place mats, or napkins — Border designs made by stamping, a stencil or with wax crayons.

For place mats or table covers — Threads or yarns woven with a needle into a coarse material such as burlap or onion bags; yarns, reeds, raffia, or jute woven on cardboard or wooden frame.

For rugs — Woven or braided rags.

For pictures — Paintings, drawings with crayon, or monoprint.

For dishes — Modeled clay, fired and glazed.

For pillow covers and upholstery — Designs applied to fabrics with wax crayon, stamping, or stencil.

For bed quilt — Large simple shapes of cotton cloth sewn together with a running stitch.

For beauty — Plant or flower arrangements.

DISPLAY AND BULLETIN BOARDS

Bulletin boards serve many useful purposes in the classroom. As teaching aids, they make facts tangible. Illustrative material gives meaning to words by allowing the observer to form a mental image of the subject. Boys' and girls' interest is increased to a greater extent if they contribute material for the bulletin board.

The teacher discusses with the children the making of choices in grouping ideas, in selecting illustrative material for these ideas, and in the way the material selected is to be placed on the bulletin board. Well arranged bulletin boards increase the attractiveness of the schoolroom. Material should be arranged to make the ideas clear to the observer.

Materials for Bulletin Boards

A bulletin board may be made of cork or wall board attached to a wall of the classroom; a lathe fastened across the top and bottom of a sheet of heavy paper with the top strip suspended from the molding; small mesh chicken wire fastened securely to a wooden frame either hung on the wall or placed on a trough along the lower part of the wall — "S"-hooks like picture hooks fasten over the wire for attaching heavy cardboard or plywood; a strip of wood or rod fastened to the wall and paper, burlap, or straw matting hung from the strip, or a window shade or the back of a discarded

1. Heavy folded paper with flap pinned to the bulletin board is used to make parts stand out from the background.

2. Pieces of heavy cardboard, wall board or wood are laced together with a heavy cord and suspended from the molding or top of chalkboard.

3. Clothesline rope is fastened to the edge of a piece of wood or wall board and stretched to nails, upholstery tacks or hooks on the bulletin board shelf.

4. Heavy paper or cardboard is folded in and out and placed on a table for display on both sides.

5. A picture frame fastened to the front of a box to use for a shadow box.

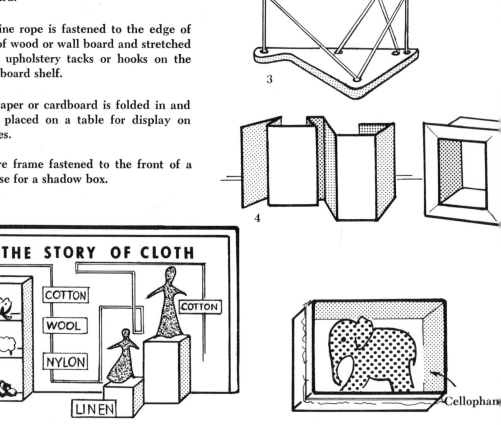

EXAMPLES OF BULLETIN BOARD ARRANGEMENTS

Informal balance creates interest, movement and variety.

Third dimension with informal balance. Boxes (for depth), lids (for projection), dowel or stick and string (for suspension of planes). String is used to hold the grouping together. Formal balance (static).

Three-Dimensional Display

A large box may be fastened to the wall or hung from a molding. Objects modeled from clay, papier-mâché or cut from cardboard may be arranged in the box. String or rope stretched from top to bottom across the front or a transparent material such as cellophane, adds an element of surprise or a desire to look inside.

Pegboard

A pegboard is fastened to the wall. Pegs or golf tees inserted in the holes can be used to support string and wire. Cards or a box may be hung from the pegs. A shelf can be placed across pegboard brackets to hold three-dimensional objects.

rolled map may be rolled down for display.

A screen with a wooden frame covered with burlap, wire or wall board with two, three, or more panels will make a standing bulletin board.

Sheets of chipboard or pieces from corrugated boxes can be taped together like an open book to stand on a table or can be fastened to a corner wall.

Suspended Objects

Wooden or cardboard shelves may be supported by a heavy cord, clothes-line, rope, or wire for the display of three-dimensional objects. Cord is fastened to the ends of the cardboard or wood and tacked to the bulletin board.

A bent coat hanger may be used for suspending puppets, birds, mobiles or other objects. The hook of the coat hanger may be fastened to the front or the back side of the top edge of the bulletin board.

Using Materials for Two-Dimensional Display

Two-dimensional display includes arrangements having height and width only. The materials listed below furnish a variety of textures and ideas for backgrounds, which may separate areas, group ideas, add interest, and make the whole display more attractive.

Useful papers for backgrounds are: colored poster or construction paper; corrugated cardboard; newsprint from want-ad section for gray value; oatmeal paper; sandpaper; parchment; cellophane. Due to the transparency of cellophane, one color overlapping another makes a third color, and words and illustrations are visible.

Useful cloths for backgrounds are: felt; flannel; tweed; net; quilted padding; onion

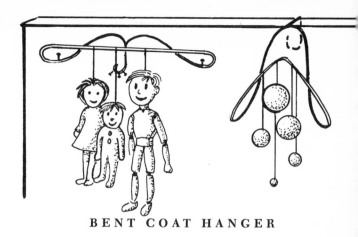

BENT COAT HANGER

PEEP SHOW
Modeled clay figures representing Indians grinding corn and making pots are grouped beside their pueblo.

The Primary Classroom / 25

Lines used to enclose a group of related ideas. ▶

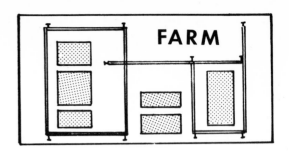

Lines used to direct the eye from one area to another.

▼

Lines that point directly to an important part.

▼

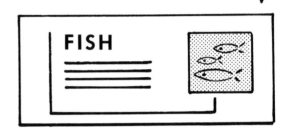

ORGANIZATION OF BULLETIN BOARDS

sacking; burlap.

Ways to make a textured background: Cover heavy paper or cardboard with glue or a good adhesive paste. Place materials — such as seeds, sawdust, shavings, small gravel, sand, pine or fir needles, grain, cereals, leaves — on top of the adhesive to cover the entire surface.

Other material for texture include wire screen and woven straw matting.

ORGANIZATION OF BULLETIN BOARDS

Planned lines direct the eyes. Make lines directly on the paper with a lettering pen and India ink, crayon, or paint; with such materials as yarn; thread; string; cord; rope; raffia; reed; strips of wood or colored cloth; tape; braid; covered electric wire, copper, brass or bailing wire; chain; rubber bands; straws.

SPACING AND MOUNTING ILLUSTRATIONS

GROUP CLIPPINGS TO FORM a square or rectangle; do not scatter them all over the bulletin board. Keep explanatory captions parallel in rectangular form. Various attractive ways of mounting material are: a wider margin at the bottom, with the top and side margins equal; equal margins all around; side margins wider than top and bottom (which should be equal); strips of related colored paper edging top and bottom or both sides of the illustration. One piece of paper may be used as a mat for a group of pictures, or pictures may be grouped to form a square or rectangle, with related subjects having a common background to tie them together. Do not overlap illustrations, for this is confusing to children.

To PLACE A fairly heavy object in front of the bulletin board, attach it to a wooden block, the thickness of which will determine the distance the object should be from the board. The size of the wood block should relate to the dimensions of the object, thus if the block of wood is smaller than the object, the block will be hidden from view.

Steps to follow in one method of doing this are: Glue each wooden block to the center of a firmly woven piece of cloth, which extends approximately two inches beyond the outside edge of the block on all sides. Pin the cloth to the bulletin board; tack the object to the block of wood. The object may be *real* such as a car, doll, machine, food product, or craft object. A picture made by a child or cut from a magazine may be mounted on cardboard and made to stand out from the background by tacking the cardboard to the wooden block.

Another way to accomplish this is with the lid of a cardboard box. Boxes may be placed on a table or shelf in front of a bulletin board, with objects inside or on top. The display material on the table can be unified with the bulletin board material by repeating colors, or by using lines of yarns, string, rope, or wire.

Paper sculpture used for three-dimensional designs. Forms of paper add life and interest to the total display. They may be used with boxes or alone with flat illustrations or other three-dimensional material. The paper should have body and take a good crease, as does construction paper. Variations of forms are made by cutting, folding, and rolling. See paper sculpture page 207.

A *peep-hole box* focuses attention on one theme without distractions. From a large deep box a peep-hole is cut in one end. Suitable subjects for a "peep" show are animals in their natural environments; story-book characters illustrating part of a story; people in their homes, such as Navajo Indians or Eskimos. The animals or people may be made from bent wire, clay or papier mâché.

When the objects are inside the box, an electric light globe or flashlight may be used for lighting the inside. The lid is placed on the box. When a child looks through the hole he turns on the light and enjoys the surprise inside. Colored cellophane used over the light adds interest.

SUBJECTS FOR PIN-UP BOARDS

PIN-UP BOARDS ARE ASSEMBLED from work boys and girls have done on a given theme, either by drawing or by the real object. Headings are simple words that the boys and girls understand. Each area with its heading may be separated by a line or by different color background paper.

Group related items under each heading. Subjects suggested for pin-up boards for primary-grade children which come from things in their home, school, and immediate environment are: toys with wheels; dolls; forest animals; vegetables and fruit; clothes we wear in the winter, in the spring, and in the summer; farm animals; things mother uses in the kitchen; things baby needs; different kinds of trees; tools used by the carpenter, the plumber, the electrician, or the painter.

Materials for sharing may be placed on a table or on shelves on a pegboard: a bird's nest; feathers; evergreens; leaves from different trees grouped by color and kind; a two-dimensional object sent from some other place; seeds grouped as to kind; different kinds of cloth; decorated papers; shells.

Newspaper. News shown by symbols or pictures combined with words. Suggested subjects include: weather—sun, rain, clouds; how choice of clothes depends on weather; how growing things are influenced by weather; "things we are going to do today"; things that happen at home; a trip.

Caring for ourselves and others would include: crossing the street safely, putting wheel toys away, learning good habits in playing games and proper eating habits.

Real objects explain subjects in visual form. How tools and machines are used is interesting to a child. The real tool or machine is placed opposite a picture for its use: hammer, saw, drill, shovel, rake, hose, fork, knife, spoon, meat grinder, measuring cup, egg beater. Use pegboard with hooks for this display.

Buildings children go to for a purpose. Opposite the picture the use of the building is written: My house is where my family lives. A grocery store, where we buy our food. The library, where we read books.

The children use folded paper to make their buildings stand out from the bulletin board. (See buildings, page 208.)

Group machines that people use according to their use. Farm children will know the ones the farmer uses. City children see the machines used by builders, street cleaners, and the workers in the park. Miners' children may have seen machines used in mines. Families use machines in the home and for transportation.

Seasons of the year are easily adapted to group participation in bulletin-board arrangements, such as, changes in games children play, changes in clothes children wear.

Wild flowers, spring flowers, or small branches from plants may be displayed in small test tubes, fastened to the bulletin board with wire or tape, and each one labeled with its name and a few descriptive words. Fill the tubes with water. These may be grouped according to color or kind.

Second-grade bulletin board. Cut-outs illustrate a story. The Little Red Hen.

Third-grade bulletin board to direct the study of animals.

ARRANGING PLANT MATERIAL

A FLOWER IS one of the greatest wonders of creation. You can awaken children to its beauty, its fragile petals, patterned centers, and variations in color and form.

Arranging flowers, leaves, dried plant material, branches, or driftwood are all forms of art expression. A trip to a garden, a wooded area, a vacant lot, a beach are all enjoyable and valuable experiences for children, provided you guide them to see the varied beauty in nature and to select plant material.

SELECTING MATERIAL FOR ARRANGEMENTS

FLOWERS SHOULD BE SELECTED and grouped according to color, size, and quality. Cutting stems at different lengths permits varied placement, as well as massing.

Fruit branches — ripe, green, or in blossom — such as quince, cherry, crab apple, gooseberry, strawberry, plum, mountain ash, blackberry, snowberry, add fine color and texture.

Suitable plants for making dried arrangements include horsetail, milkweed, seed pods with stems, sumac, dandelion seeds, sour dock, hollyhock, onions, thistle, tall grass, wheat and other grains, scotch broom, teasel, poppy pods, everlasting and pepper berries.

Graceful lines are made by tall grasses, ferns, virginia creeper, yellow yarrow, onion, brake, silvery grass, goldenrod, cedar, scotch broom, corn leaves, grain and poppy pods.

Choosing Containers for Flowers

Choose containers that enhance the beauty of the foliage and flowers, and that are appropriate to the spirit of the flowers as well as the surroundings.

Sturdy stemmed flowers such as zinnias, geraniums, or marigolds suggest round, squat pottery, brass bowls, baking dishes, or bean crocks, and each one of these harmonizes with hand-woven cotton or straw mats.

Light colored, slender-stemmed, feathery flowers and leaves, such as sweet peas, roses or lily of the valley are best in a vase of light color and weight — glass, china, or pewter. The amount of water and length of stem influence the height of container.

Suitable Containers Found in Most Homes

Glass bricks, glass fishbowls, shells, bottles, mixing bowls, pitchers, baking dishes, bean crocks, pottery bowls, teapots or ice buckets are among the many suitable containers found in the home. Tin cans or fruit jars may be placed inside a basket or covered with paper or painted a suitable color such as green, to blend with the foliage. Woven baskets or wooden mixing bowls are attractive holders for dried material or autumn leaves. A glass placed in a clay flower pot to hold a miniature tree.

Flower Holders and Other Supports for Stems

A forked branch of a woody tree or shrub, trimmed at both ends, so that it fits snugly wedged to both sides of the container makes a good support for flower stems, inserted through the forked end. A branch can also be split and used to support stems.

Needlepoint-type holders with long needles are best for the arrangement of a few flowers. These need to have a lead or other heavy weight on the bottom. To secure the holder firmly, place four lumps of plasticine on the bottom of a *dry* container, and place the needlepoint holder on top of the plasticine and twist until firm.

A hairpin holder has wire bent in loops like hairpins. These are higher than needle holders and hold flowers stems in position. Fasten this type of holder to the base with plasticine.

Wire mesh such as chicken wire crushed in the vase opening is helpful for an irregular shaped container, and is needed for large, massed, profuse arrangements. Wedge vertical stems of brake or sword fern or small-stemmed foliage such as huckleberry compactly through the wire mesh to hold the flower stems in balance so they will not tip. The wire holder will be completely covered by the arrangement and becomes a part of the whole design. This method will support stems in any direction needed.

Sword fern, privet hedge, evergreen, or hemlock massed in an upright position and cut even with the top of the container makes a fine firm holder for fairly long-stemmed flowers.

A container filled with fine sand or clay will support the stems of dried material. This container does not have to be waterproof. A wooden bowl is attractive.

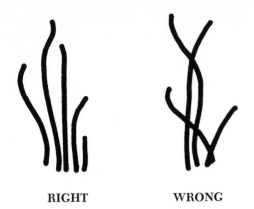

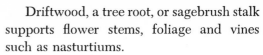

Driftwood, a tree root, or sagebrush stalk supports flower stems, foliage and vines such as nasturtiums.

Stones placed in the bottom of a container for heavy material, such as branches of trees, helps hold them in place.

For a heavy stem use a narrow strip of sheet lead; curve one end around the stem of the plant and bend the other over the edge of the container.

A perforated potato can hold small-stemmed flowers.

RIGHT   **WRONG**

A Guide for Choosing and Arranging Plant Material

Color considerations. Combine light and dark of one color, and various kinds of flowers for size and texture, making a dominant tone, rather than even divisions of color. Mass flowers of each color value together, rather than scattering them here

WRONG

RIGHT

RIGHT

RIGHT

SUGGESTIONS FOR ARRANGING FLOWERS

Avoid crossing principal lines of stems. Stems make line directions which must form a rhythmic movement. Avoid massing blossoms on a level line. Vary the length of stems, and be willing to cut flowers and leaves.

◀ Avoid crushing flower stems compactly into a container.

The plant needs room to breathe, as well as to show the graceful lines of stems. ▶

A line design becomes lost in front of a patterned background.
Place a line design in front of a plain background of one color or a woven screen.

RIGHT   WRONG

and there in a spotty arrangement. Use a light colored flower against a dark leaf or the reverse. Combine tones of one color, such as pink, red-violet, or different values of violet. Use smaller amounts of the more intense colors because of their power.

Group flowers. Low flowers balance higher ones. A large flower balances a group of smaller flowers or leaves. Larger flowers should be placed low and near the center. Combine open flowers with buds for variety. A few flowers well placed creates beauty.

SUITABLE BACKGROUNDS FOR FLOWER ARRANGEMENTS

THE BEST BACKGROUND for plant material harmonizes with the container and flowers in color, spirit, and texture. A solid background of one color — a wall or cloth — is best for most flower arrangements. Graceful stems cast a lovely shadow on a wall.

Textured materials such as a woven straw screen or a woven hanging of bamboo, wheat, corn husk, reed, snake grass, pine needles or burlap, bark or cork, combine very well with flowers and leaves of gold, reds, browns and yellow.

A mirror used for a background enhances the beauty of the arrangement by adding space and giving the viewer the opportunity to enjoy all sides of the arrangement. Avoid things seen in the mirror which compete with the beauty of flowers.

FLOWER ARRANGEMENT IN SCHOOL

FLOWERS GROW in the fall and spring, and these are the times to group and arrange flowers as to sizes, shapes, and textures, leaving dried materials and indoor plants to arrange during the winter.

Primary-school children love to bring flowers to their teacher, and often bring large quantities. A few very large containers which will hold many flowers can be placed at the entrance to the school, or at suitable places in the hallways against a plain wall. A screen or folded cardboard may be placed behind the arrangement to separate it from unrelated materials.

Flower arrangements in the classroom. Experiment with the boys and girls by holding flowers in different groupings to find the ones that go together best, and choose a container that enhances them.

Different materials appropriate to flower arrangements harmonize in spirit and shape and complete the arrangement — such as a woven mat, a wooden form, or a piece of glass. The base should repeat a needed color and add a variation in texture. A clay figure or animal modeled by a child makes an accent, as do things from nature — coral fans, bark, weathered wood that is bleached and polished by the wind and sun, plant roots, rocks, shells.

Backgrounds for arrangements of plant material primary-grade children can make. Selected colors that harmonize with the color of the plant material and that always remain in the background. Some backgrounds are: corrugated paper left its natural color and folded or curved to make a screen; small, straight twigs woven or tied together with jute or twine; egg crates fastened together make a pleasing texture; decorated paper, made by crayon batik or printing with stamps in an all-over pattern, may be pleated, folded or left flat.

Arrangements appropriate for the library table, playhouse table, or for individual tables. Buttercups and pansies are attractive floating in a shallow dish on a table low enough for the children to look into

CONSTRUCTING ROOMS FOR A DOLL HOUSE

I

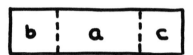

I

A. *Material for walls.*

Double-faced corrugated cardboard or chip board (heavy enough to be stood up). Approximate size: (a) 10″x13″ (b)-(c) 10″x 8″.

————Represents fold.

B. *Materials for floor* (d).

Cardboard either folded or attached separately and hinged.

II

A. *Material for walls.*

Double-faced corrugated cardboard box. Approximate size 10″x13″x8″.

B. *Materials for floor.*

Cardboard or construction paper or table top.

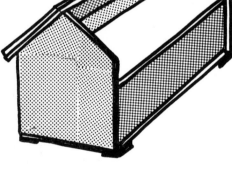

II

III

A. *Material for walls, roof, and floor.*

Wood construction, hinged roof. Approximate size:

Height — 2′

Width — 3′ 1½″

Length — 3′

B. *Hardware*

Double-acting hinge

IV *Separate cartons.*

(Allow for flexibility in room arrangements.) Each child plans one room. Group rooms to make doll house.

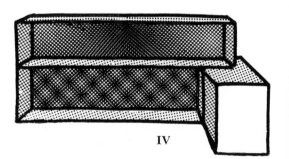

IV

BOXES USED FOR DOLL-HOUSE FURNITURE   *(Cut out all striped areas)*

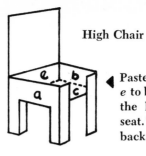

High Chair   ARMS

Paste *a - b* to arms; paste *e* to back; *c* is the seat. Use the lid of the box for the seat. Tape to the sides and back. Cut *d* out.

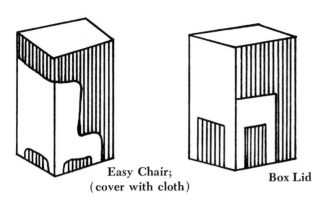

Easy Chair;
(cover with cloth)

Box Lid

Lid of Box

Cut out on dark line. Fold along dotted lines to make the seat and the back. Tape sides and the bottom edge of the back to the back edge of the seat, cover with cloth.

Bottom of box:

Glue bottom to top of box. Cut legs from top of box.

fold down
to form back

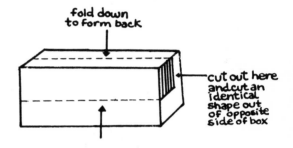

cut out here and cut an identical shape out of opposite side of box

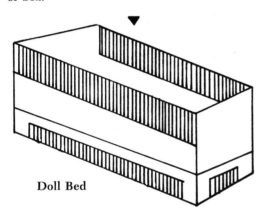

Doll Bed

A box shape cut from cardboard may be used for a cupboard, stove, television, or sink. The child paints the details necessary to explain the important parts.

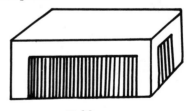

Table

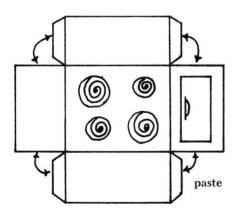

paste

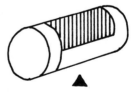

Cradle cut from salt or oatmeal box.

the faces of the flowers. Ferns beginning to uncurl, combined with woodland flowers make charming, intimate arrangements; a piece of driftwood, bark, moss, lichen or rock adds interest.

A flower committee may be selected from each classroom, and given the responsibility of providing a lovely arrangement each week. The committee should be changed periodically so that all the children contribute to the beauty of their room.

Children enjoy making and arranging furniture and accessories for their doll's house. Classrooms with a limited space do not have room for a playhouse. A Doll House may be placed on a table shelf, bench or on the floor. Thought is given to the kinds of materials children combine as well as to their appropriateness for their surroundings and for their use.

ONE OF THE FIRST art experiences of a five-year-old child is the making of interesting arrangements of varying sizes and shapes of building blocks. He finds he can express ideas with blocks and that as his ideas change he can make new combinations with blocks.

Children lift and carry blocks, place them one on top of another, and stand on them. There are many factors to consider in selecting building blocks, among them the following.

Kinds. Blocks made of durable, sturdy, smooth hardwood, will not splinter. The surface should be sanded and varnished, and the corners true right angles. Blocks can be solid or hollow but must be light enough for five-year-olds to lift. Hollow blocks need a reinforcing brace on the inside. Solid blocks are used for walls and foundations as well as for children to stand on.

Select blocks that are perfectly balanced to insure against undue falls.

Sizes and shapes. Large blocks are used for building walls for a train, playhouse, or store that is usually shared by a group of children. Small blocks are used as loads for trains, trucks, or for building by an individual child. Variety in lengths, widths and

BUILDING BLOCKS

shapes increases the child's chances for invention.

Assortment of sizes and shapes suggested for a kindergarten.

Large Blocks
12 blocks 12″ x 6″ x 6″
12 blocks 12″ x 12″ x 6″
12 blocks 12″ x 12″ x 12″

Other suggested sizes.
8″ x 8″ x 8″
8″ x 4″ x 8″
8″ x 4″ x 16″
8″ x 8″ x 16″

Smaller Blocks
Square and Rectangular shapes.
35 blocks 1½″ x 3¼″ x 3¼″
45 blocks 1½″ x 3¼″ x 9¾″
35 blocks 1½″ x 9¾″ x 9¾″
20 blocks 3″ x 9¾″ x 9¾″

Triangular shapes
12 blocks 1½″ x 3¼″ x 5″

Cylinders
12 blocks 1½″ diameter, 3¼″ tall.

Playing with blocks enlarges the child's experience.

1. The child uses small blocks for loading and hauling in wagons, trucks, trains, and boats. This gives him a conception of the volume needed to fill a certain three-dimensional area.

2. The child places one block on another in a vertical pile. He learns to place smaller and lighter blocks upon heavier and larger ones. This experience can be compared to a house's need for a strong foundation.

3. Children work together to build a structure they all will use, such as: walls to divide rooms for a playhouse, walls to divide stalls for animals, a wall for the front of a store, walls to enclose cars for a train.

Children enjoy building a train, with blocks, large enough for them to ride in. Useful discarded materials to combine with building blocks are a barrel, spools, film boxes, cans, lids, and boxes. A diner with a table and chairs, a sleeper with a bed and section for reading or conversation, are all parts of a train children can build and use for activities.

Children's imaginations supply the necessary additions to block structures so that they become very real trains, houses, bridges, stores, or ships.

LEARNING TO BE GOOD HOUSEKEEPERS

THE CHILDREN should learn to pile their blocks, according to sizes, in a designated place away from the passageway. Suitable storage places are under a table or shelf, in a frame container on rollers, on low shelves, or along a wall.

DEVELOPMENT THROUGH BUILDING BLOCKS

THE CHILD'S HANDS are strengthened by lifting, by carrying, and by placing the blocks in a structure. The child learns balance, by the first simple placing of one block on top of another; that wood is strong and will not break when it is dropped on the floor, and that a large building block will hold the weight of a child's body.

BLOCK CITY

Tall blocks are placed on a flat piece of wood to suggest office buildings in a city. This child selected television tubes, a cube of large-headed pins, and a group of rings to combine with the tall buildings. The child's imagination supplied a use for each structure.

CHAPTER IV

Wood Construction

WOOD CONSTRUCTION is used in building and imaginative play by small children. Suitable for their development are nailing, sawing, gluing and finishing of wood, all of which are used in constructing things of use.

To make a tool cabinet, fasten a packing box securely to the wall near a low work bench; or build a shallow cupboard with a pegboard back and door.

Arrange the tools to facilitate correct placing of tools by the children. Tools may be divided into groups such as:

a. *Tools which hang* — saws, hammer.
b. *Tools which may stand in grooves* — twist drills, files, screw drivers.
c. *Tools which stand on their sides to avoid dulling of sharp blades* — planes.
d. *Small compartments or glass jars with lids for different kinds of nails and screws.*

TOOLS FOR PRIMARY-GRADE CHILDREN

A MACHINIST'S VISE with a three-inch jaw, on the end of the work bench; a twelve-inch saw for cross-cutting and ripping wood; a twelve-inch steel-edge ruler or carpenter's square; a nine-inch plane; a sturdy hand drill with twist drills $\frac{1}{8}''$, $\frac{3}{16}''$, $\frac{1}{2}''$, and $\frac{3}{32}''$; a nine- to ten-ounce claw hammer with a sturdy pounding surface.

Work bench. The height of a sturdy solid hardwood work bench should fit the height of the child. The work bench should be placed to provide ample space for the saw's movement back and forth, as well as space around the table where several children can work at one time. Improvised working spaces — such as a sturdy chair on which to saw and hammer; wood placed between two saw horses for sawing; a long, low, sturdy bench; a packing box well braced; a kitchen table — must be the correct height.

Pre-Construction Experience with Wood
(Kindergarten and First Grade)

The Kindergarten or first grade child's entire interest is in the act of pounding.

1. *Materials for pounding nails*
   a. Large sheets of fibrous material or soft pine.
   b. Large-headed nails — shingle nails, 4-, 6- or 8-penny nails or roofing nails.
   c. 9- or 10-ounce claw hammer with a sturdy pounding surface.
2. *Position of child for pounding nails*
   a. The child should sit on the floor with the wood between his legs when he pounds nails, to give him control of his materials.
3. *Habits to form in the use of a hammer*
   a. *How to hold a hammer*
      Children get the best results when they grasp the handle far from the hammer head so that the handle acts as a lever. The weighted head is designed to force the nail into the wood. Explain the meaning of lever.
   b. *How to drive nails*
      The child should hold the nail between his thumb and forefinger, place the nail point in position on the wood, and then tap the nail lightly with the hammer to start the nail into the wood. He then strikes the nail with the center of the hammer to force it into the wood. He keeps his fingers away from the pounding of the hammer.
   c. *How to pull out nails with the claw of the hammer*
      The head of the nail must be above the surface of the wood. Place the claw under the head of the nail and pull until the hammer is straight up; if needed, place a block of wood under the claw of the hammer to increase the leverage.

First Experiences in Construction with Wood

Materials. Miscellaneous sizes and shapes of wood provide opportunity for inventiveness in building and stimulate the imagination.

1. *Sources for wooden scraps* are the home, a carpenter's shop, lumber yard, wrecking yard, school shop, grocery store.
2. *Useful discarded wooden materials* are spools from thread and wooden ends from rolls of paper towels; small boxes, such as cheese, chalk, or cigar; apple, orange, or banana crates; packing boxes from furniture or mattresses; barrels.
3. *Discarded materials to use with wood are* rings from adhesive-tape dispensers, fruit jar lids, corks, funnels, barrel hoops, tin film boxes, door knobs, coffee-tin lids, metal rollers, tongue depressors, binding wire, brushes, wheels, and tin cans. Bells, whistles and clappers add sound.

THE CHILD CONSTRUCTS A FORM WITH WOOD

1. First a child discovers he can nail a small piece of wood to a larger piece. After this he pounds nails for the purpose of making something.

2. The child nails a block of wood to each end of a long piece of wood to make a bridge. He discovers that the two pieces of wood on either end must be the same

distance up from the floor. He constructs his bridges to go over a river, a canyon, or a roadway in his play experience.

3. The child nails long pieces of wood close together along a piece of wood to make a floor for an animal's cage. He also makes a tabletop and a back for a chair for the playhouse.

4. A fence is needed around the animal cage. The child nails strips of wood with a space left between each long piece of wood.

5. The child makes a carrier for a load. He nails a box such as a cheese, cigar or chalk box to a larger piece of wood used for the base.

Children enjoy loading the box with gravel, spools, sand, small blocks, or other cargo.

Some children add a pole to the cubical form to represent a mast. This structure suggests a boat. The child desires a pointed bow to help the boat cut through the water.

Children have a reason to saw when one piece of wood must fit another, or when its shape must be changed.

Habits to develop for the safe use of saws.

To place the wood in a vise or on a saw horse for sawing.

To remain a safe distance from the child using the saw.

Not to hold the wood which is being sawed.

To carry a saw by the handle with the blade away from the body.

Not to walk around the room carrying a saw.

To place the saw in the tool cabinet as soon as he is finished using it.

To treat the saw with proper respect.

A Sample Project: a Boat: Grade 2
The Child Makes a Plan for a Wood Construction

INTRODUCING THIS project, the teacher might say:

"Where are boats used? Since all boats are used to go through the water they are built with the front of the boat tapering to a point to enable the boat to cut through the water with increasing speed.

"All boatbuilders first make a plan for the boat they are going to build. Boats are many different sizes. Today you have a piece of paper 6″ by 12″, the same size as the wood for the bottom of your boat. Since both sides of a boat are the same you fold your paper in the center to make the pattern for the bottom of your boat."

The child places the paper pattern on the wood. On both sides of the pattern, he marks the slant of the bow, with a pencil on the wood, and removes the paper pattern. He then places a steel square along the slant of the bow, first on one side then on the other, and draws a dark pencil line on the wood along the edge of the square. He places the wood in the vise ready for sawing the diagonal lines. He saws toward the point on one side, first drawing the saw lightly back and forth on the pencil line to make a groove. The child continues to saw with long strokes, in an even motion until near the end; then he takes slower, shorter strokes. The other side is sawed the same way.

The child has made a basic shape for a boat. From here he adds details to make the kind of boat he chooses.

Suggestions:

Teaching a child to drill a hole. The block of wood to be drilled is fastened securely in a vise. If the wood is placed on the table, a piece of wood must be placed under the area to be drilled to avoid drilling into the table. A pencil mark indicates the place to be drilled.

The child places the point of the drill on the pencil mark. He holds the drill straight up and down without pressing the point of the drill into the wood. The child turns the handle of the drill like an egg beater until the hole is as deep as desired.

Making a mast for a sailboat. The child drills a hole in the center of the base for a mast, which may be made from a wooden dowel. The length of the mast will determine the length of the cloth for the sail.

The sail. A triangular shape is cut from cotton cloth. A straight edge of the cloth is glued, tied, or tacked to the vertical pole.

The cabin. A wooden cheese box or other wooden box serves for a cabin nailed or glued to the deck. Smoke stacks may be made with spools.

The child's imagination adds the sound effects and various mechanical devices. The boat may be for sailing, fishing, passengers, or freight. Rails around a deck may be made by pounding nails in a row and using string from one nail to the next, or by boring holes and inserting meat skewers, small dowels, or twigs.

BOAT SHAPES MADE FROM A FEW BASIC PIECES OF WOOD

USEFUL THINGS CHILDREN CAN MAKE FROM WOOD
(Five- six- seven-year olds)

Steps in making a Spool Holder. A wooden base may be a rectangle 6½" by 3½" by 1", or a circular base 5" in diameter.

The child paints the wooden base a neutral gray or white, using rubber base paint, or powder paint shellacked after drying. A neutral tone will harmonize with the varied colors of thread. A border design may be added after the base color is dry.

The child cuts out a paper shape the

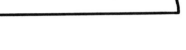

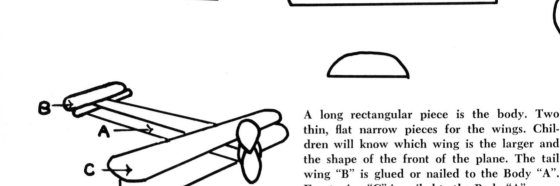

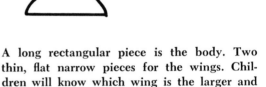

A long rectangular piece is the body. Two thin, flat narrow pieces for the wings. Children will know which wing is the larger and the shape of the front of the plane. The tail wing "B" is glued or nailed to the Body "A". Front wing "C" is nailed to the Body "A".

same size as his wooden base. Then he makes dots around the paper shape: 1) One row of dots 1½″ apart, 1″ from the edge of the rectangle all the way around; 2) One row of dots 1½″ apart, 1″ from the edge of the circle all the way around. (The circle may be folded, with small holes cut one inch from edge.)

A hole is punched through each dot on the paper. The child fastens the paper pattern on to his wooden base with masking tape. The child places a dot with his pencil in each hole. The pattern is removed.

A long nail with a small head is pounded on each dot as marked; the nail extends above the base one and one-half inches. The center of the spool of thread is placed over the nail.

"A Train"

Children join wooden boxes together to make cars. Wooden cars may be held together by using open screw eyes in the back of each car with closed screw eyes on the front of each car. Children use spools, wooden disks, or tin lids for wheels. A hole is drilled through the center of the round disk as well as into the wood at the place the wheel will be joined, where the screw or large-headed nail is to be inserted. Room should be left for the wheels to revolve.

Each car has a specific use. Children can model clay figures for the dining and sleeping cars. Baggage and freight may be made from discarded materials. Miscellaneous sizes and shapes of wood coupled with discarded materials encourage children to invent new forms. Children grow in inventiveness as they discover ways to hold parts together.

A few other things children can make are furniture for a doll house; items for a store; bird houses; docks; bridges and buildings for play towns, as well as new imaginary shapes which may be toys or objects to use in arrangements.

CHILD DEVELOPMENT IN THE USE OF WOOD AND TOOLS

The child learns that:

1. Tools are designed to help us with our work. They are not toys.

2. A saw is used to cut different sizes and shapes of wood.

> Wood is placed in a vise for sawing, planing, filing, and sanding.
>
> A saw must not be twisted or leaned upon.
>
> Saws are stored so that the blades will not become bent.
>
> He must stand away from the bench when he is not using the saw.

3. Vises are kept closed when not in use.

4. Pieces of wood are held together with nails.

> Small nails are used to join thin pieces of wood.
>
> Large nails will cause thin wood to split.

5. Pieces of wood are held together with glue.

> The two surfaces of wood to be glued together must be smooth and flat, touching each other at all points.
>
> The two pieces of wood are pressed close together in a vise or under a weight until the glue is dry.

6. To keep metal tools free from rust they must be kept dry and oiled.

7. A plane is moved with the grain of the wood to smooth a surface.

> The child places the wood in the vise with the edge of the wood to be planed in a horizontal position, extending above the vise. He grasps the handle of the plane with his right hand and the knob on the front of the plane with his left hand. The child pushes the plane with the grain of the wood from one end of the board to the other.
>
> Caution children to examine the wood they are going to plane to be sure there are no nails on the surface of the wood.
>
> When not in use blades are removed from planes, oiled, and packed separately so as not to injure the blades.

8. Sandpaper is wrapped around a block of wood. It is rubbed over a rough surface to make it smooth.

9. Each tool has its own place in the tool cupboard.

10. Only one tool is taken from the cupboard at a time.

11. As soon as work is completed with one tool, the tool is placed back in the tool cupboard. Tools are never left on the work space, floor, chairs, or table. A responsible child helps by checking the storage of tools.

THE CHILD DISCOVERS THE QUALITIES OF WOOD

Wood is strong. Wood is used for floors. The child walks, runs, or jumps on wooden surfaces. Wood is used for railroad ties and beams to support floors and roofs of houses.

Wood is hard or soft. It is more difficult to saw or hammer nails into hardwood than soft wood. Soft-wood floors wear away much faster than hardwood floors. A child can make a dent with his fingernail into soft wood; he cannot make a dent in hardwood.

Wood has grain. Children finish a piece of wood to see the pattern in its grain. First, children move a plane over a rough wood surface with the grain. Second, sandpaper is rubbed over the surface to make it smooth. The children see the true beauty of the grain of the wood. They will enjoy feeling the smooth surface with their hands.

Wood splits with the grain. Nails that are too large will split the fibers of wood apart. A thin nail will slip between the fibers of the wood.

How to retain the beauty of wood. The smooth surface and beauty of grain in wood is most enjoyed when it is oiled or rubbed with wax, which brings out the deeper tones in the grain with a velvet appearance.

CHAPTER V

Materials for Children to Explore

MATERIALS FOR TOUCHING, seeing, and manipulating are placed in appropriate containers on a table accessible to the children. Boys and girls learn to handle materials in a new way by first selecting the ones they like, then grouping and arranging the materials they have chosen. This experience is a form of play because they are stimulated by the feel, form, and color of the various materials.

Through feeling and experimenting the child discovers things made of wood, things that are rough, things that are smooth, things that are prickly, things that are slippery, things that are cool or warm. Through holding objects the child feels differences in shapes, such as round, square, irregular, and differences in sizes, such as large and small. Children see colors alike, colors bright or dull, and colors together in patterns. Children find objects that will float on water. They find many different kinds of cloth, each with a different feel. Some materials

they can see through.

By choosing, arranging, re-arranging, changing the form, sorting and returning each material to its place, the child gradually develops his faculty to see and understand the qualities and possibilities of materials around him.

Materials for children to explore are listed below according to kind. Each kind of material should be in an open container that children can look into closely.

From Animals: bones from chickens, hair, chamois, shells, feathers, fur, skin of snake or fish, sponge.

Buttons of many sizes, colors, shapes, and materials; buttons of different designs, such as open work, painted surfaces, or materials applied to the surface; buttons with different surface finishes such as matt, lustre, sparkle, or transparent.

A few kinds are bone, celluloid, glass, leather, metal, pearl, synthetic, wood. A few colors are red, blue, violet, and green.

CLOTH

USE CLOTH OF DIFFERENT weaves, colors, and threads. Cut the cloth into different sizes and shapes to include long strips, varying from one inch to four inches in width for easy manipulation by children. Clothes for puppets and dolls require larger pieces of cloth.

Buckram, burlap, cheesecloth, chenille; cottons, plain and patterned; eyelet embroidery, felt, flannel, monk's cloth, mop with cotton strands, mosquito netting, net, oilcloth, onionskin bag, organdie, rug scraps, satin, silk, stockings, taffeta, tweed, veiling, velvet, voile, wool.

METAL

Bottle caps, boxes from scotch-tape rolls, bolts and nuts, boxes from films, chains, coat hangers, film reels, keys, keys from coffee can, lids of various sizes, meatgrinder parts, nails, paper clips, perforated metal sheets and ribbon, screens of various mesh, wheels from discarded clock works.

Wire: bell wire in colors, soldering wire, colored pipe cleaners, gardener's wire, fine wires in copper and brass, from 18 to 30 gauge; heavier wire for standing structures, such as wire from 10 to 16 gauge; chicken wire. Wire in coils like springs and coat hangers.

NATURAL MATERIALS

Bark of birch, cedar; beans, pine cones; grain, wheat, rice; grasses, leaves and veins of leaves, pine needles, pebbles, reed, sand.

Seeds: nasturtium, squash, sunflower, watermelon, birdseed. Shells: walnut, acorn, chestnut, hazelnut, almonds.

PAPER

1. Opaque papers of one color such as colored construction and poster paper in sheets 9″ by 12″; varying shapes may be cut in different sizes — circles, long strips, triangles, rectangles, and irregular shapes.

2. Thicker papers for construction are cardboard and option bristol.

3. Translucent papers such as tissue, wax, or very thin writing paper which children can see through. (See "Synthetic" below.)

4. Patterned papers in different colors are found on paper napkins; envelope lining and wall paper; on wrapping papers for gifts, candy, gum, and cosmetics; on magazines and newspaper sheets. These papers may be shiny or dull.

5. Paper pressed into shapes such as paper plates, and cylindrical cups.

6. Papers with a texture surface are sand papers, crepe paper, corrugated paper and cardboard, molded packing papers such as found in crates of fruit and eggs and crepe-like papers for packing breakable materials or furniture.

7. Open cut-out designs in paper doilies.

SYNTHETICS

Cellophane (transparent), celluloid (transparent) film — photo, x-ray (transparent); copper mesh pot cleaner, hardware cloth, laminated materials, plastic (transparent).

MAKING STABILES

First-graders find out about materials through manipulation. Wire can be bent into many different shapes. Braids and ribbons may be looped, tied or stretched from one part to another. Some materials are light in weight and others are heavy. Net, cellophane, and x-ray paper are transparent. Coil spring. Designs in space look different from every side.

WOOD

Clothes pins, dowel sticks, ends from paper-towel rolls, golf tees, meat skewers, pegs for pegboard, picnic spoons and forks, sticks, spools, tinker toys, tongue depressor, toothpicks in colors and natural, twigs. Embroidery hoops, button molds, venetian blinds.

MISCELLANEOUS MATERIALS

Artificial flowers, beads of all kinds, braid, bulbs (small flash and electric light), cellophane straws in colors, china (broken pieces), confetti, corks of different sizes, cotton, earrings, foil of aluminum and tin, ribbons of varying widths and colors; rings in metal, wood, and rubber; rolls from toilet paper, towels, wax and foil papers; rope, rubber bands, rubber jar rings, tapioca (whole), foam glass, foam rubber, lace, linoleum scraps, macaroni, marbles, mirrors, ornaments (Christmas), paper straws, pipe cleaners of different colors, pins with large colored heads; sparkle, used at Christmas time; sponge, steel wool, stickers of various kinds, straw, string, tapes, tile scraps.

FIRST EXPERIENCE IN USING MATERIALS FOR TOUCHING, FEELING AND SEEING: A STABILE

A STABILE (OR SPACE DESIGN) is constructed from different materials attached to a base which stands in an upright fixed position. Designs in space which children can observe include:

The jungle gym on their playfield.
Aerials for radio and television.
Television towers.
The steel frame for a building.

Various aerial frameworks for rides in an amusement park, such as the ferris wheel with its large upright wheel rotating about a fixed axis with seats suspended at intervals around its rim.
The high bridge suspended from cables forming graceful curves to high towers.
The branches of leafless trees silhouetted in dark lines against the sky.

THE CHILD CHOOSES MATERIALS FOR A STABILE OR "STAND-UP" DESIGN

Materials for the base. A plastic material such as clay or plasticine the size of a tennis ball used for the base, makes it possible to insert material into the soft base for his space design. The base may also be a block of wood with holes bored into the surface to be used as holders for upright sticks or wire. Wire may also be stapled to a block of wood. Other suitable materials are foam, a container filled with sand or holes punched into a cardboard box lid.

Since the child fastens materials to upright pieces which he inserts into the base, the supports must be strong enough to hold up the weight of the material. A variety of lengths used for the uprights add interest as well as help to balance the whole.

Materials for uprights are: pipe cleaners, colored bell wire, wire 10 to 16 gauge, coat hangers, twigs, dowels.

Materials the child fastens to the up-right standards (must be light in weight): beads, brightly colored paper, buttons, cellophane, Christmas ornaments, feathers, foil, jar rings, lace, macaroni, paper cups, pieces of cloth, plastic mesh, ribbons, seed pods, spools, string or colored yarns, strips of corrugated paper, wheels from clock works.

Materials the child uses to fasten one material to another: glue for wood; paste for paper and cloth; thread or yarn for beads, buttons and macaroni; airplane cement for metal, wood, or plastic; stapler for cardboard or other material that is difficult to fasten with an adhesive; clips; clothes pins. Other helpful materials are scissors and a punch.

The Child Makes a "Stand-up" Design

THE CHILD'S IMAGINATION, coupled with his curiosity and desire to put the things together he sees on his work table, furnish ample stimulation. The child chooses materials for his upright. The teacher asks, "Which things will stand up in a clay base or which ones can be inserted into the holes in a wooden base?" The child discovers that he can easily insert things that are stiff and rigid into the soft clay in any direction. If the holes in the wood are too large to hold a smaller dowel stick or wire in place, the child presses plasticine, cotton, or paper around the stick to fill in the holes. The child finds he can bend flexible wire.

The child chooses materials to place on the uprights. The teacher asks, "Which materials are light enough in weight to use with the upright supports; which ones used together will make a beautiful design to enjoy from every side?" The child finds he can extend bright ribbons or colored yarns from one upright to another, from these he can hang light objects such as feathers or beads. Some children cut coils of paper and

glue one end to the top of a stick. Others fasten pieces of net and brightly colored silk between two wire uprights. The child finds he can easily press things like bottle tops, beads, or buttons into the soft clay base, and that he can insert toothpicks and golf tees. The space design the child has made can be enjoyed from every angle.

The teacher asks, "When you think you are finished with your stabile or stand-up design walk all around it and see if each side makes you feel happy. Put your stabile on a chair seat or on the floor and look down on the top. Do you like looking down on your design? Does your space design need anything added to make it more beautiful? When you are all finished place yours in the center of your table."

If the child intentionally puts materials together with something in mind he will, no doubt, name his creation. For the very young child, this experience is like an adventure which is purely the result of joy in manipulating materials. The child discovers differences in weight and balance of materials.

A MOBILE SPACE DESIGN

A MOBILE IS A SPACE DESIGN constructed from a variety of materials in such a way that it will be put into motion with currents of air or by touching. Mobiles are usually suspended from the ceiling, a wall bracket, or a standard.

Forms suitable as frameworks for mobiles which can be suspended

A. Metal Jar rings.
B. Colander or lampshade frame.
C. Clothes hanger.
D. Wooden dowels.
E. A suspended hoop.

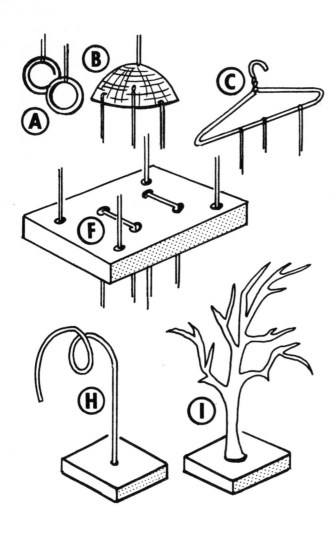

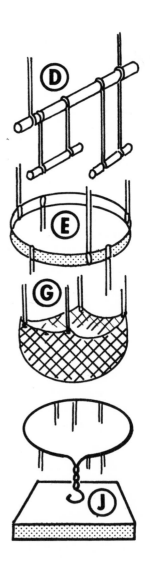

F. A box, cardboard, or disc with punched holes. Objects may be hung from strings looped through the holes.
G. Chicken wire or mosquito net.
H. Wire fastened to a base and bent.
I. A spreading tree branch fastened to a base.
J. A coat hanger may be shaped and fastened to a base.

Things children see in their environment which move in space include: revolving sprinklers, kites, a bird swinging on a perch, balloons, airplanes and rockets, a merry-go-round, speedboats, cars, fireworks, soap bubbles.

Children themselves enjoy motion — swinging, turning round and round, jumping, running, and going up and down on a teeter-totter.

Mobiles may also be suspended from a clothes-line rope or wire stretched across the room above the work tables but within the children's reach, or a cord may be stretched between tables or chairs. This provides a suspended line to which children can tie their mobile designs.

Suitable materials to hang on mobiles must be very light to move with the circulation of air. Some examples follow:
beads, buttons, cellophane, Christmas ornaments; cloth of varying kinds, colors, and sizes, some in long strips; corks, corrugated paper cut into strips, feathers; foil in tin, aluminum or copper; forms modeled from sawdust and paste or paper mâché; macaroni, colored and plain; metal filings, metal or celluloid rings from curtains, metal jar rings; paper shapes curled, folded, or cut in varying sizes and shapes; paper clips, paper cups, pine cones, pipe cleaners or telephone wire bent into shapes, ribbon, rolls of film, nut shells, sea shells.

Materials for fastening parts together include: needle and thread, stapler, paste, yarn, string, wire, paper clips, airplane cement, glue, tape, ribbon, thin pliable wire.

A supply table accessible to the children should contain these materials.

Before the children start making mobiles, the teacher might say:

"You have made a stand-up design you can see on all sides. Another kind of design you can make is one to hang above your head that will move around. Think of how things change as they turn and move." A long strip of curled paper is held up and turned around for children to observe.

"Materials are on your supply table to use for your hanging design. Materials to help you to fasten parts together are on the center of your table. You may fasten your hanging designs to the frame nearest to your table."

Children invent new forms by lacing ribbons, straws, or yarns through holes; by joining several together; by sticking things like toothpicks into foam or corks; by hanging beads, balls, or buttons inside other forms — such as a paper cone or a drinking cup; by cutting paper to represent animals, people, fish, birds, or leaves, or by folding and curling it to make designs.

Shavings from wax crayon placed between two sheets of wax paper and pressed with a warm iron, on the top surface of the paper, result in a bright, variegated transparent paper appropriate to cut into simple shapes for a mobile.

Children learn how to balance objects. When children tie a hanging object on one end of a suspended dowel stick they discover that something else must be tied to the opposite end. Some objects are heavier than others. Several objects may be needed on one end to balance a heavier object on the other.

Place finished mobiles high where air currents circulate. Children may blow or tap them lightly to make the mobiles move.

Uses for mobiles. Mobiles can be party decorations or simply as beauty in the room. Mobiles may also have a specific theme — sea life, a circus, or a season of the year. Spring can be shown with birds, or fall with leaves.

A COLLAGE (OR DESIGN TO TOUCH AND FEEL)

Introducing collages, the teacher might say:

"You have painted pictures we can all see and enjoy. This time you have different kinds of materials to use instead of paint for your color and shapes. You are making a picture to touch as well as to see. Each new kind of material feels different. Find materials you like together. Try different ones. It is fun to have a surprise when you touch a material that has a different feel. You may change the shape of cloth or paper by cutting a new shape or the length of ribbon, yarn, or rope." You can fold paper, loop and tie ribbons.

MATERIALS FOR COLLAGES

Base or frame may be the inside of a box lid or the bottom of a shallow box, or a stiff cardboard approximately 9″ square, or a 14″ by 17″ rectangle.

Adhesives needed are airplane cement for metal; glue in a small bottle with dispenser for cloth or wood; library or wheat paste for paper; a stapler for papers, ribbons, cloth.

The child combines materials that are pleasing to see and touch, with variety in size, shape, texture, and color, such as: something rough and something smooth; something sparkling and something dull; cloth or paper with a pattern and some of one color; something big and something small; long pieces like string, beads, yarn, or ribbon that he can move in and out and around to make a pathway through his design.

THE CHILD ARRANGES MATERIALS TO MAKE A COLLAGE

LET EACH CHILD ARRANGE material on a piece of paper the same size as the background he will use. This experience helps him visualize the size of materials he can combine within a given space. Materials of different kinds are grouped together. Transparent materials may overlap to make a new color or texture surprise. A repeat of buttons or seeds make a variation in pattern. The child enjoys trying different combinations of things. When he is satisfied with his arrangement he is ready to place it on the cardboard background. The child often changes his idea with each arrangement.

THE CHILD FASTENS THE ARRANGEMENT HE HAS MADE TO THE BACKGROUND

THE CARDBOARD BACKGROUND should be covered with adhesive. The child places the material on top of the adhesive and lightly presses it down. More adhesive is applied to materials that overlap. For materials like corrugated paper that do not touch the background cardboard at all points, a staple may be needed. A small stick can be used to push pieces in place to protect the child's fingers from glue.

When the material is dry and fully adhered to the background, the children can have the pleasant surprise of both seeing and feeling the different textures on the collages each child has made.

The children have discovered that some things feel good and that others do not. Weavers know that it is important for bedding, rugs, upholstery, and clothing to feel pleasant to the skin.

Examples of materials with different kinds of "feel" would make a good subject for a sharing and discussion period, such as prickly thistle, soft down, or rough sandpaper.

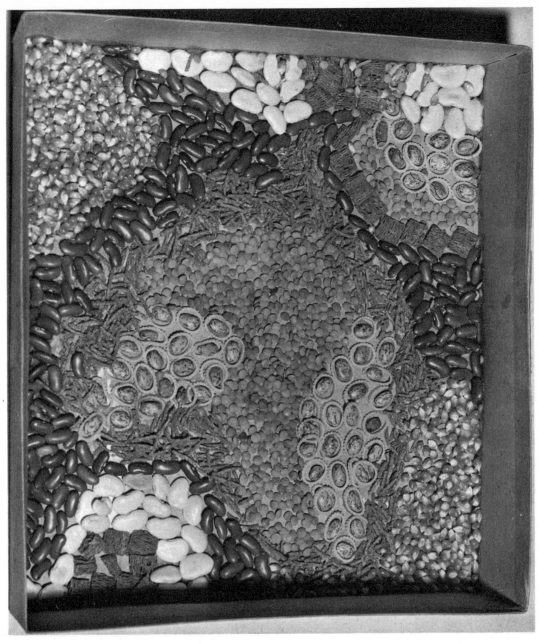

A PLEASING TEXTURE DESIGN IN GROUPING OF
MATERIALS AND COLORS

A TEXTURE DESIGN varies in roughness, smoothness, fineness, glossiness, dullness, and in shapes, and colors of the materials used.

Materials for a texture design include: Grains — barley, bran, grit, oats, rice, wheat; *Seeds from plants* — birdseed, squash, sunflower, watermelon; *Miscellaneous* — macaroni (elbow, shell), pebbles, pencil shavings, sand, sawdust, split peas, whole tapioca, wood shavings.

Material for a background may be a piece of stiff cardboard, wallboard, or plywood approximately 10″ by 12″; glue bird, elmers glue, or wheat paste.

Procedure. The child spreads a thick layer of an adhesive over the cardboard background until it is completely covered. This is the surface on which the child places areas of different materials listed above. Minute particles — such as sand, grit, or finely ground sawdust — are more easily spread over an area if they are poured from a small can. The child should choose materials for his design that vary in coarseness — such a selection would be rice, wheat, squash seeds, and wood shavings.

The child fills one area of the cardboard with one material such as sand. The child chooses a second material such as sawdust to fill another area. The child repeats one kind of material in different parts of the cardboard. A variety of one kind of material might be used for the entire design, such as different kinds of seeds or different kinds of grains. When the cardboard is entirely covered, the child presses over the top of the materials with something flat as a pancake turner, bowl of a spoon, or cardboard. The texture design is allowed to dry. The child turns the design upside down over a piece of newspaper to allow the loose pieces to fall down on the paper. The child adds more adhesive to bare places, then adds the appropriate material to cover the open spaces. The design is finished when the entire surface is covered.

Texture designs are appropriate to combine with driftwood, rocks, plants, or ceramics as well as to enjoy just for itself. This is one way children can add beauty to their surroundings.

A SAMPLE PROJECT: A SEEING AND TOUCHING PICTURE TO REPRESENT A PLACE OR TIME OF YEAR
(Suggested for the Third Grade)

"THE FALL"

A WALK IN THE FALL in a park, in the country, or through a vacant lot interests a child who is seeing how many different things he can find for his seeing and touching picture.

A few delightful things seen in the fall which children may assemble for their Fall Panel:

Leaves in greens, yellow, oranges and browns as well as in various sizes and shapes.

Round brown burrs with their prickly needles are usually found in clusters.

The winged seeds from the maple tree are a new kind of shape.

The many different sizes and shapes of seeds on dried plants are a variety of brown.

Corn with its kernels, tassels of silk, and long wide leaves can be used in several ways.

The hazelnuts, walnuts, almonds, and many other nuts are ripe in the fall.

The stalks of grain — the bearded barley and the long cattail, and bamboo leaves — are graceful, narrow, spear-like shapes.

A SEEING AND TOUCHING PICTURE TO REPRESENT FALL

The background is a vertical piece of cloth: natural colored burlap approximately 12″ by 18″; 16″ by 29″ or 8½″ by 19″ for individual panels.

Procedure. The children choose materials they like together — because of shapes, colors, or sizes. Small things like seeds may be grouped together or repeated in rows. Long grain, reeds, or cattail stalks make line designs. Leaves add shapes of different sizes and colors. Each child places his material on his burlap panel which is on a flat surface.

Suggested ways to fasten the materials to the burlap. Heavy yarn, the color of burlap, is threaded into large-eyed needle. Simple stitches back and forth over the ends of stems and grain stalks will hold them in place. A stapler is needed for some.

A hole is drilled into nuts, and a thread inserted. Pine needles may be laced in and out of the warp. Glue may be needed for things that cannot be sewn or stapled.

A "Textures" collage or panel might contain *seaweed* in many different greens and browns; *roots of sea plants* that are delicate or bulbous; *sea animals,* small and large, with fins, tentacles, scales, a few legs or many legs, with claws, with webbed feet; *driftwood; shells;* and *rocks.*

The sea, woods, and earth abound with textured materials which can be combined in delightful collages.

A Sample Project: A Place the Child Has Been — "The Seashore"

Press wet plants found at the seashore between blotters to dry. Use a piece of plywood or woven straw 16″ by 29″ as background, and use airplane cement to adhere shells and other material to the background.

Materials such as rocks, shells, and driftwood may be pressed into freshly poured cement or plaster.

Procedure. The children test different materials from the seashore together to find the combinations they most enjoy, and try to arrange the material so that each part can be easily seen and its beauty enhanced by its simplicity and variety.

SHELLS OF VARYING SHAPES, PATTERNS AND TEXTURES

Shells of varying shapes, patterns, and textures combined with weathered wood worn and shaped by sea and wind are full of interest and beauty to children.

CHAPTER VI

Beauty in the Child's World

THE BEAUTY OF GROWING things, of the earth, sky, and weather, as well as of things made by man, can be appreciated by children. Children who look for beauty on their way to and from school, at home, and when they go on trips have many pleasant memories. During the first hour of school in the morning or afternoon, a few minutes can profitably be spent listening to members of the group tell their classmates what they saw that day that to them was beautiful.

Reserve a table or a shelf for things the children love because of their beauty. The method of display can enhance the true beauty of the object (see Display, page 24).

From the classroom windows children observe changing conditions of weather, such as:

Make-believe pictures in the sky — of fleecy sheep, of animals with feathery tails, of cream-puff clouds, of islands of soft thistledown where fairies live, of boats sailing on a sea of silver, of deep caves piercing black clouds, of a rain-

bow with many-colored ribbons, making a jumping rope;

Sunlight shining through the green leaves making dancing shadows on the wall;

Smoke from the chimneys curling upward, then floating gently away;

Wind swaying the branches back and forth;

Rain washing the dirt off the leaves and flowers.

While taking a walk outdoors children see:

Many kinds of green in leaves on different sizes of trees;

A young colt curled up beside its mother;

New ferns like curled plumes;

Beautiful colors of rocks under the water.

Observing growing things and the care that is provided for all living things helps children appreciate the world. Many more examples may be added to these:

Some seeds are like parachutes and others have wings to help them to sail in the wind;

In the spring fruit trees are covered

with flowers; in the fall the same trees are covered with fruit;

Animals that live where there is snow and ice have fur coats to keep them warm;

The rain gives the plants and animals water to drink so they will grow;

The sun keeps us warm and gives us light in the daytime;

Frogs have long hind legs to help them jump.

Through seeing, children learn things which belong together. They combine these in their designs and pictures.

A cat and kittens.

A dog and puppies.

A hen and chickens.

A fish in water.

Different kinds of fruit — apples, oranges, and pears.

Different kinds of vegetables — carrots, peas, and beans.

A tree or house and ground.

Leaves with flowers or trees.

Lumber or bricks with a house.

A boat with water.

Unfolding the Child's World

Ideas for pictures come from the child's whole field of experience. The way children feel added to things they see, like to do, imagine, and read about are all subjects for their pictures.

Many experiences give children the feel of things: they perceive the quality of things by touching them; they feel a closeness to the earth when they touch the ground or the grass; wet sand feels cool to their bare feet and hands; they feel the softness of fur as they stroke a kitten or a rabbit.

Children feel hardness as they touch smooth metal, slate, cement, or rocks; roughness when they touch the bark of trees or sandpaper. They may see as well as touch the uneven stubble of grain, pine needles, or the top of a wire or picket fence.

As they hold things in their hands children can feel differences in shapes: the squareness of building blocks, the roundness of a ball or an orange, the changing contour of an animal's back as they stroke its soft fur.

Children are emotionally affected by things in their environment. Gentleness is experienced by a child when he feels a soft

Looking into the heart of a flower.
7-year-old child.

breeze blowing against his skin or hair. A feeling of abandon and freedom is felt as he runs with his hair flying out behind him. Children feel the power and force of wind and rain as they walk. They see and feel the intensity of a storm as the wind bends trees or as waves pound against the shore.

A child feels the warmth and protection of a mother's love when he sees a mother cat lick her kitten, or his own mother care for him. A child feels full of joy when he dances and sings to the rhythm of music.

EXPERIENCES THAT HELP CHILDREN BECOME CONSCIOUS OF RHYTHMIC MOVEMENTS

MOVEMENTS EXPERIENCED IN DRAMATIC PLAY ACTING:

1) A child moves his arms up and down to interpret the flying of birds. 2) Children quiver their arms and hands in a downward movement to represent leaves falling. 3) Children sway their bodies back and forth as branches in a breeze. 4) Children feel a quick movement as they jump like frogs or grasshoppers.

MOVEMENTS EXPERIENCED IN PLAY:

An easy flowing movement is felt in swimming.

A steady movement up and down is felt in jumping rope.

A swaying motion from right to left comes with even strides in skating.

A sweeping, uplifting movement is felt when children swing high into tree tops.

A pulling movement is felt as children run forward drawing a kite string or pulling a wagon.

A revolving movement of the arm comes with the turning of a jumping rope.

An upward and downward motion is experienced as children toss and catch a ball.

A pushing motion is experienced in moving doll carriages and toy cars.

Watching his pet hen eat from his hand.
5-year-old child.

The music of rain tapping on a roof.

Small fountains rising with each drop of rain on water.

Bright, fresh colors outside after everything has been washed clean with rain.

Flakes of snow dropping from the sky and sprinkled over all outdoor things.

Tumbling in soft snow, rolling and building snow people and houses.

Running through fallen leaves; gathering them in heaps and finding many different beautiful colors.

Walking along paths in the woods, through grass in the field, or along the seashore.

Seeing growing plants, where animals live, and how they take care of their young.

Seeing a hummingbird suck nectar from a flower or a squirrel holding a nut in its front paws.

Seeing a beautiful flower open its petals.

CHAPTER VII

Art Materials and Their Use

A CHILD'S FIRST experience with art materials should come when he can use them constructively.

IN A NONCONSTRUCTIVE USE; a child uses fingerpaint as he would any thick liquid — to stir, to pour, to play in with his hands, or to daub on his face and hair. Used constructively, a child enjoys the feeling of moving his hands through the slippery soft paint. He is interested in watching the new designs made with each movement of his hands.

NONCONSTRUCTIVELY, a child plays with liquid paint by pouring it from one container to another or stirring it round and round. The child in the scribble stage is not ready for paint — and should be given a large crayon for scribbling lines. In a constructive use, the child's purpose is to discover what he can do with brush and paint on paper. He is ready to paint when he can manipulate a tool for painting, such as a brush, a stick, and piece of cardboard or other suitable tool.

NONCONSTRUCTIVELY, the child is not interested in manipulating clay. He may run around with it, try to eat it, use it in his truck, or throw it like a ball. Constructively, he manipulates clay as a plastic material with an aim in mind. He may roll, punch, squeeze, pull, or twist the clay. He builds with clay balls and rolled worm-like forms. When his purpose is to represent a specific thing he will name the form he has produced.

The child who has not developed sufficient coordination between his eye and hand muscles to cut with scissors effectively simply slashes paper with no purpose in mind. Constructive use occurs when the child handles scissors well enough to cut the shape he has in mind, and can direct the scissors to move in the direction he desires.

INVITING MATERIALS arouse children's curiosity and encourage them to explore. Through handling, children find out what each material is like. Some materials satisfy a child's ideas, others develop his imagination.

During this period of discovery the child works with energy and interest, as long as the material is intriguing to him. He needs time to feel assurance and confidence in himself or to feel "at home" with the material.

During the time their main interest is in the material children are not concerned about what they have made as something to be named, but are likely to give a different name each time they explain what they are doing. Frequently named are: up and down lines, a design, me, a big hole, round and round or just rolling balls.

FINGERPAINT

INTRODUCE FINGERPAINTING to children through rhythmic movements — have them move arms and hands through the air feeling and interpreting the movements of birds flying, of leaves and trees blown by wind or of waves on the shore. Have them interpret the rhythm of slow and quick movements they hear in music.

MATERIALS

Fingerpaint (see page 279): approximately one quart for thirty children. A dark color is best. Fingerpaint for grades 1, 2, 3 should be the consistency of thick cream. Paint that is too thick forms ridges which disturb the child as he makes designs with his hands.

Paper: A nonabsorbent paper with a glazed surface on one side permits many movements over the paper without disturbing its surface. Appropriate papers are: glazed butcher paper, wrapping paper, book paper, shelf paper, magazine sheets, tag board, finger-paint paper.

Size of paper: 16″ by 22″ or 15″ by 20″.

Working surface: A table, bench, or floor with a smooth washable surface such as porcelain, enamel, oilcloth, marble, masonite, varnished wood, or two coats of shellac on three-ply wood.

Containers for water (large enough to submerge sheet of paper): roasting pan, sink, baby bath tub, or dishpan, or a sponge to wet paper instead of submerging it in water.

Newspaper to place under finished fingerpainting when set to dry.

Pieces of cardboard to scrape designs through paint: sizes 1″ by 4″ or 2″ by 4″.

Aprons for children.

PREPARATION FOR FINGERPAINTING

PLACE A CONTAINER half full of water over oilcloth on a low table, chair seat, or the floor, or use a sink as a container for water.

Then give the following instructions to the children:

To put their aprons on and roll up long

sleeves to protect clothing.

To cover their working space if necessary;

To place a newspaper over the space designated for drying the finished paintings;

Helpers give each child one sheet of paper, which the child places flat on the work surface in front of him;

To roll their paper, then using both hands to pick up their roll of paper holding it at both sides.

About six children at a time go to the pan of water holding their roll of paper. You must demonstrate the way to submerge the roll of paper in the water, at the back of the pan, then drawing the paper through the water and lifting it out from the front side of the pan, thus allowing surplus water to run into the pan. The paper is held a moment over the pan to allow remaining water to run off and the paper to become smooth. Each child submerges his own paper into the water with one hand on each side of the paper, then carries the wet paper to his work place and puts it down, the *glazed surface on top.* To remove bubbles or wrinkles he lifts the edge of the paper to allow air to escape.

Using a wet sponge instead of the method above: first wet the working surface. Place the paper over the damp area then rub the wet sponge over the surface of the paper. Smooth the wet paper free of air bubbles and wrinkles. *The sponge method is best for children to use during a free period when they work independently.*

The children should stand with their feet flat on the floor, a short distance from the table; they should not lean against the edge of the table while they paint. Children working on their knees on the floor should kneel with their paper in front of them.

The teacher places a tablespoonful of

Going round and round.

fingerpaint in the center of each child's wet paper. If colorless fingerpaint is used, the child dusts powder paint on the paint solution and mixes the color into it with a circular motion of both hands (this method uses much more paint).

The children place the palms of their hands together over the fingerpaint; the left hand should move from the center to the left edge of the paper, the right hand from the center to the right edge of the paper, and repeat this back and forth movement until the paper is free from wrinkles and air bubbles and the fingerpaint is spread smoothly over the entire surface of the paper, going outside the edges.

The moist surface is now ready for the child to discover the many different designs his own hands can make.

The teacher should encourage the children to use their whole hands in making big movements up and down, across, and round and round, covering the whole paper. After each design the child smooths the fingerpaint with strokes across his paper from left to right or up and down with the palm of his hands. His paper is now ready for a new design. The fingerpaint should be slippery and moist for easy flowing movements. When the paint becomes too dry, water should be sprinkled over the surface with a spray or clothes sprinkler. The child continues making new designs with his hands, as long as his interest lasts or until he has made a design he wishes to keep.

VARIATIONS OF HANDS AND FINGER POSITIONS

THE FOLLOWING variations are suggested, and children discover many of these and more:

Going round and round in rows like wheels of a train or the letter "O";

Making arcs like waves, shallow or deep, varying in widths and groupings, using the padded parts of fingers opposite the fingernails, or the fleshy part of the side of the hand;

Making upward flame-like movements with the side of the hand;

Making loops or continuous circles across the paper;

Patting paper with the palm of the hand; making a lovely texture like fine ferns or like snow crystals on the window — this may be used for a background. Over this texture a large swinging movement combines well;

Zigzag movements like mountain tops, lightning, a flame, or letter "Z";

Making wiggly lines like a worm or a tadpole swimming;

Using both hands together to make a growing tree reaching up and out.

Children enjoy experimenting. Every new turn of their hands will make a new form. Their imagination added to the stimulus of the quickly changing images, produces a new and exciting design.

Movements to music in fingerpaint. After the first experimental stage, when children have learned what they can do with fingerpaint, music may be used to inspire rhythmical movements. A simple repeated phrase is best.

Before using fingerpaint to music, young children need to make patterns with their hands and arms to music in the air or on the table tops. The following records are suggested:

"Snowflakes Dancing" by Debussey from *Children's Corner Suite* (quick movement suggests dance rhythm).

"Meditation" by Massenet from *Thais* (continuous movement)

Fingerpainting over wax crayon designs that cover the entire paper. The design may be movements, or areas of color. Colors of crayon are chosen to contrast with the color of the fingerpaint, such as light colors of crayon with a dark color of fingerpaint. The child spreads thin liquid fingerpaint over the finished wax crayon design. Finger movements are made in the fingerpaint which reveal the crayon underneath.

Drying finished fingerpaintings. The child places the finished finger painting on newspaper or cardboard to dry on a flat surface. If possible tape or tack the painting around the edge to a board to keep it from shrinking. Approximately an hour is required for drying. When dry, if a smooth surface is desired, press the finger painting with a hot iron on the reverse side. Finger paintings that are well stretched before drying will probably not need pressing.

To preserve the surface, paint or spray a plastic, clear shellac, or spar varnish over the pressed, dry surface. This is desirable for items that need washable and dustproof surfaces, such as wastebaskets.

Habits to encourage in children. A smock or apron is worn to protect the clothing. Hands are used only for fingerpainting until the painting is finished. The child closes his hand to make a fist if he needs to walk away from his work surface.
Hands are washed if the need arises to touch anything.
After the finger painting is finished and placed on a flat, covered surface to dry, the child cleans his work surface, washes his hands, removes his smock and puts it in a designated place.

Time required for lesson in fingerpainting. One-half hour is needed with ten min-

Making upward flame-like movements.

Making a tree.

utes added for cleaning the children and the working area. By giving the lesson just before lunch, recess, or afternoon dismissal, the teacher can dry the paintings by leaving them on the tables or desks on top of one another until thoroughly dry.

USES FOR FINGERPAINTINGS

As decorated paper: for wallpaper for the playhouse (a light color is suggested, such as yellow, light blue, or light green); for shelf paper in a cupboard for the playhouse, the school, or the home; for place mats for under plants or flower arrangements; for folded or accordian-pleated backgrounds for beauty spots; as covers for scrapbooks and telephone books, or for booklets children have made for spelling, language, or social studies; as covers for tallies, score pads, or calendars; to cover containers to be used for knitting boxes, gift boxes, or wastepaper baskets.

For cut-paper shapes: to represent ground, flowers, or trees; for murals, dioramas, or puppet-stage backgrounds.

USE OF FINGERPAINT FOR SEATED WORK PERIOD

MOST CHILDREN are ready to work without help after two lessons in fingerpainting. The following materials should be kept on a cupboard shelf accessible to the children:

A covered quart jar containing liquid fingerpaint.

A wooden spoon for taking paint from the jar.

A sponge inside a low bowl, into which the child can pour a little water. Use striped design as a background for stamping.

Glazed paper in sheets ready to use.

Newspaper.

A panel of masonite which can be used as a working surface.

When children are finished fingerpainting they should clean their working surface, wipe the fingerpaint from the rim and outside of the jar, place the lid on the jar, and return the jar to its place.

VALUES OF FINGERPAINTING

THE CHILD'S HANDS are his tools. He has no mechanical tools to learn how to use or that hinder his success. The child feels the soft, slippery paint as he moves his hands easily over the smooth paper. The free rhythmic movements in fingerpainting help the child coordinate his arm and hand movements.

The use of different parts of the hand strengthens the child's fingers. Every attempt is a new adventure and a surprise which changes with each hand movement. Many successive trials may be made quickly on the same sheet of paper. The child is happy as he sees new designs emerge.

WAX CRAYON

WAX CRAYONS come in small and large sizes, in wrapped or unwrapped sticks with 8, 12, 16, 24, or 48 colors to the box. They are round, hexagonal, or half-round. Large round sticks with eight or twelve colors to the box are suggested for kindergarten, grade one and two. Small crayons are suggested for third grade. Wrappings help to keep sticks from breaking. Unwrapped sticks give children the opportunity to use the side as well as the point.

Criteria for judging good crayons: the crayon should not flake off on to the paper when it is rubbed back and forth; the crayon should glide easily and smoothly over the paper; the color should be clear and full strength.

Characteristics of wax crayons. Wax crayon has a glossy effect when it is rubbed on the paper in a solid area. It is water resistant. It can be dissolved in turpentine to make a thick paste-like substance which can be used like oil paint on wood or cardboard. Wax crayon may be melted in a container over heat and poured into a mold.

WAYS TO USE WAX CRAYON

Drawing includes expressions of ideas about things seen or imagined. Use scraps of unwrapped crayon about one and one-half inches long, on the side, varying the pressure. Greater pressure is possible if the child works directly down, on the paper, instead of reaching out to the paper. Darker colors result when repeated pressure is applied. Experiment with different pressures, starting with heavy, gradually becoming lighter, then heavy again.

Use end of the crayon for lines.

Overlap one color over another color to make a new color.

Strokes of crayon can suggest texture and direction, such as fur on an animal, hair on a child's head, bark on a tree, lumber on a house, waves on the shore, or rain pouring down. Such strokes should follow the direction of the surface of objects.

Turn the crayon different ways with strokes to make different edges, straight and curved. With each one try different lengths and different pressures. The result can be

Ann, Grade Two, has made strokes with the end of a crayon to define a bird, a house, and fence. Movement is also produced.

Rhona, Grade Two, used the side of a crayon for her train and the end of the crayon for the hills. The train looks important because it is a darker color.

Art Materials and Their Use / 67

Carolyn, Grade Three, used the side of a crayon to draw a bear.

used for texture in plain spaces, in designs, or for patterns on imaginary animals.

Rubbing *(Kindergarten, First, Second, and Third Grade)* is a process which brings new discoveries and surprises. Fairly flat-textured, hard materials which make the design are placed on a hard surface. A smooth, strong light-weight paper is placed over the materials. The child rubs in one direction with the side of a dark color wax crayon over the surface of the paper. Like magic an image of the materials under the paper comes to view on the paper.

Materials to use for rubbing (do not overlap materials for the first rubbing), include: coins, wire screen, shapes cut from light-weight cardboard or heavy paper, back of clam shell, grained wood, bark, woven straw mat, coarse sandpaper, pine needles, leaves, ferns, grass, cedar, grain, crushed cereals, buckram, grater, corrugated cardboard, string.

Variations. The child rubs over a few simple shapes. He lifts his paper up and moves his shapes or adds a new shape, then makes a second rubbing. Experiment with different pressures and colors of crayon.

Scratched wax crayon. Use a paper with a pressed surface such as butcher, finger-paint paper, or tag board, about nine inches by twelve inches.

The child covers the entire surface heavily with light colors of wax crayon such as yellow and orange. The same color should be repeated in different areas.

The child completely covers the first layer of light colors with a dark color of wax crayon such as black, brown, violet, or blue; (in place of a dark color of wax crayon, a dark color of tempera paint may be used to cover the light layer of wax crayon).

The child uses a sharp instrument to scrape away the top layer, in places desired, thus uncovering the light colors which make a design.

Tools for scraping away the crayon or paint: pocket knife, nut pick, bobby pin,

Linda, Grade Two, enjoyed turning the side of her crayon in different directions to make forest animals.

fingernail file, pen nib, blade of scissors.

Discoveries. Textures result when small shapes are repeated such as dots, checks, star shapes, lines like thistledown, pine needles, or bird tracts. Scraped-away areas can be varied in color value by scraping lightly in some places and heavily in others.

Appropriate subjects. Trees with spreading branches, a child with patterned clothes, a portrait, tropical fish, or a beautiful design made from new kinds of shapes and lines.

Watercolor with wax crayon or crayon resist. The child makes a drawing or design with wax crayon leaving parts of the paper exposed. The crayon lines must be firm and strong in color. The child paints over his crayon drawing using contrasting colors of watercolor paint. For example, he paints blue or green — which are dark and cool —

Alan, Grade One, cut one animal from construction paper for his design. He moved the shape around under a sheet of mimeo news each time he made a brown crayon rubbing.

over crayon colors like yellow, orange, and red — which are warm and lighter in value. See color illustrations, Imaginative Shapes in a Dream World and Taking a String for a Walk, following page 98.

Wax crayon may be used to stain wood by covering the surface of the wood with crayon, then rubbing the surface with a rag or brush saturated in turpentine or banana oil. Color wood with crayon, keeping the strokes in one direction. Rub the surface to polish.

The crayon-resist method may also be

Scratched crayon: Black tempera paint covered bright crayon colors. A bobby pin was used to scratch away the clown.

used on wood. Shellac the completed piece.
Wax crayon on cloth. Children make line designs with textures using symbolic shapes of houses, people, plants, or imaginary shapes on paper. A piece of pressed cloth is placed on top of the crayon design. The cloth is pressed with a warm iron thus transferring the crayon design onto the cloth.

The child may add more crayon to the cloth or may call the work finished. In another method, the child draws with crayon directly onto the cloth using firm, even strokes making clear, deep colors; the strokes should follow the weave of the cloth.

To set the color: place paper over the ironing board; place cloth with crayon design down, facing the paper. Remove all specks of crayon, or they will melt and make spots; place a damp cloth on top of the cloth with the crayon drawing; press with a hot iron to steam the color into the cloth by lifting the iron up and down as each part is pressed. Do not *rub* the iron back and forth.

Things to make with cloth include: place mats, wall hangings, curtains, napkins, laundry bags, costumes for plays.
Wax crayon batik on cloth. Choose an absorbent light-weight cotton, white or a light color. Remove all sizing by washing.

Previous work combining watercolor with crayon will have given the children the experience of choosing a color contrast. A similar contrast will be needed for crayon batik. The child uses light colors of crayon and draws with a firm, heavy stroke. Designs similar to South Sea, New Guinea, and Indian ones are appropriate for crayon batik.

Children can use repeated shapes like those found in letters or combine circles, squares, and triangles with stripes. After the design is completed on the cloth it is soaked in cold water. Then it is dipped into

C R A Y O N   O N   C L O T H

A third-grader made this design on cloth. It has been pressed with a warm iron.

a dark-colored dye, and hung to dry. The cloth not covered with crayon strokes absorbs the dye. Next, place the crayon batik between papers and press with a hot iron. The crayon melts into the cloth making a pleasing design.

Melted wax crayon transparencies (Third Grade). Shavings are scraped from crayon by moving the crayon over a grater or knife blade. Use a separate sheet of paper for each different color of crayon shavings. One sheet of wax paper is placed on a flat surface, with the wax side up and a few crayon shavings are placed on the surface to make a pleasing pattern.

A second sheet of wax paper is placed on top of the materials with the wax side down. Press with a warm iron by placing the iron flat on the top sheet of wax paper, lifting it up and down until the surface has been covered. The wax melts and laminates the two sheets of wax paper together.

Other materials which may be combined with the crayon shavings are: confetti; small shapes of thin, colored tissue paper; threads, yarns, or braids; feathers; glitter such as copper or silver dust. Nature supplies ferns, leaves, thistle down.

CHALK

CHALK IS A SOFT, sensitive material which glides easily and rapidly over the paper. Heavy pressure on chalk results in deep, intense colors. Light pressure results in a light color value. Such changes in color values occur because chalk is sensitive.

Chalk is transparent: one color overlapping another mixes with the first color, making a new color — i.e. red over blue makes violet.

Chalk smears and dusts off the paper if rubbed back and forth.

Materials to use with chalk:

Rough paper such as: bogus, screening, craft, manila, oatmeal, paper towel, sandpaper, construction, mimeograph news.

Fixative (if work is to be handled or saved). Apply fixative with a spray or atomizer over the surface of the chalk drawing or paint the fixative over the back of the chalk drawing with a brush.

Any one of the following may be used as a fixative:

  (a) Fixative made from 7 parts alcohol to 1 part shellac;
  (b) Thinned paste spray;
  (c) Plastic spray;
  (d) Dip chalk drawings in water in which glue has been added. This sets the color more permanently;
  (e) The paper is coated with liquid starch, buttermilk, or liquid paste. The chalk drawing is made over the wet surface.

Kneaded eraser or wall-paper cleaner is used to remove areas or lines of chalk.

Storing chalk and classroom use: Separate colors, one to each container. Match boxes, paper cups, or muffin tins are appropriate. Place small containers filled with crayons in a larger box or tray.

Habits to encourage:

1. The child wears a smock and rolls up long sleeves.
2. A sheet of newspaper is laid under the paper upon which the child is drawing with chalk.
3. The child stands to work, slightly away from the table or desk.
4. The child does not lay his left hand over the chalk drawing while working with his right hand.

5. The child does not rub the chalk with his fingers or rub the chalk back and forth in one place making a dust.

6. The child avoids picking up his chalk drawing and shaking the paper to remove excess chalk. If it is necessary to remove chalk dust shake gently over newspaper away from the other children.

7. The best way to use chalk is for the child to stand and draw at arm's length with chalk on a paper fastened to a stiff board placed in an upright position on an easel or on the chalk rail.

FIRST EXPERIENCE DRAWING WITH CHALK ON WET PAPER

Place materials for four children to share:

a. large sticks of red, yellow, blue, green, violet, and turquoise chalk;

b. sponge in a pan or bowl with a small amount of water to which a little wheat paste or laundry starch has been added;

c. four sheets of newspaper;

d. four sheets of *absorbent paper* such as paper towel, oatmeal paper, or manila paper.

Preparing the work space. One sheet of newspaper is placed on a smooth surface in front of each child. Rough absorbent paper is placed on top of the newspaper. The child dampens the paper with a sponge moistened in water. (If sponge is not available the child dips the paper in water.)

The child stands to make his design, drawing freely with bright colors, using dark colors with light ones, gray colors with bright colors.

He invents new shapes and colors. He

A MARE AND COLT
Karen, Grade Three, has freely drawn, in chalk, a mare with a colt resting among the flowers. She has made the colt a dark color to stand out next to the light color of the mare.

A TREE IN CHALK
Larry, Grade One, has drawn a tree in chalk, with outstretched branches on a stormy day, with a small boy running home.

makes one form grow from another. He makes shooting out parts. He makes beautiful patterns with dots, whirly lines, curls, and many more kinds of lines and shapes. He uses all the colors he likes together. He makes imaginary pictures about fairies, dragons, goblins, and other things only he knows about.

Through using chalk the child finds out what materials are like: that wet paper tears easily, therefore he must not press too hard or rub back and forth, and that strokes with chalk glide over the paper; that colors seem brighter when they are wet — there is no chalk dust when chalk is used over wet paper; the color runs slightly on the edges where paper is very wet.

Other ways to use chalk: the child can draw with chalk over paper soaked with buttermilk, which keeps the chalk dust from flying in the air: he uses a large brush to dampen the paper, in the area where he is drawing.

The child first covers dry paper with deep colors of chalk, then takes a small amount of wallpaper cleaner or a kneaded eraser and wipes away parts of the chalk. Imaginary forms like smoke people are easy to make this way.

The child makes a stroke with the broad side of a piece of red chalk. He makes a second stroke partly overlapping the first, thus attaining a darker color. The child chooses blue for a second color and makes a stroke in the opposite direction partly overlapping the stroke of red. He sees a new color, violet. Thus he continues to overlap colors and to create new colors. Sometimes he uses the side, and sometimes the end of the chalk.

The child places shapes cut or torn from heavy paper on top of his desk or table. Over these shapes he lays a sheet of newsprint. Using the side of a piece of chalk he

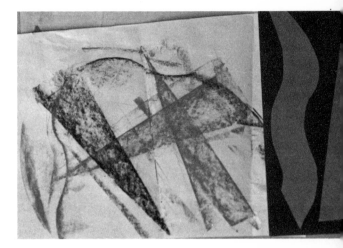

CHALK RUBBING

By Carol, Grade two.
Carol rubbed chalk over the newsprint which she placed over the two cut paper shapes on the right. She moved the paper shapes to make new shapes.

Art Materials and Their Use / 73

makes broad strokes over the surface of the newsprint. Like magic he sees the shapes come to life. He discovers that new designs are made if he moves the paper shapes or adds new shapes and makes a second rubbing with the chalk on top of the newsprint. He should make all strokes in one direction.

The child cuts out basic shapes such as long strips, circles, and irregular shapes out of mimeo-news or drawing paper. He draws a line of chalk about ½ inch in from the edge of one shape. He places the shape on a piece of newsprint and rubs the chalk on to the newsprint with cotton or a soft cloth. He moves the shape and repeats the process. He adds new shapes, overlapping some. The child discovers a new kind of design. He may add a second or third color. His imaginative thinking develops new forms. It is good to make the entire design by rubbing the chalk from the chalk line over the edge of the paper shape to the paper underneath. This project is full of surprises. The cotton rubs the chalk dust into the paper. See repeated stencil trees for rubbing chalk, page 191. Use chalk to interpret rhythmic, flowing movements heard in music.

TEMPERA AND POWDER PAINT
(For all grades)

ESSENTIAL COLORS ARE yellow, red, blue, black, white. *Supplementary colors are* red-orange, magenta, turquoise blue, green, brown.

Tempera, poster, and show-card are names of liquid, opaque water-soluble paints. Opaque paint is not transparent: one color covers another color, giving a mat finish. Liquid opaque may be purchased in two-ounce, half-pint, pint or quart-size jars.

Powder tempera paint comes in pound cans and costs less than liquid tempera. Leading art supply companies have two grades of powder paint. Number one quality has more color pigment and less filler. Number two quality has more filler and less color pigment. Both quality paints have a binder which makes it adhere to the paper, and a preservative which keeps it from spoiling. Dirty water will spoil the paint.

Materials to mix with inexpensive powder wall paints such as kalsomine, which is like chalk and does not adhere to the paper:

For binder add glue or flour or wheat paste to keep paints from rubbing off.

For preservative for paint kept for a period of time add a few drops of oil of cloves or sodium benzoate.

Mixing powder paint (an amount for 30 children):

Place 1⅓ cups powder in covered jar or aluminum shaker (rustproof).

Add ⅓ cup of water and stir vigorously or cover and shake.

Add ⅓ cup of water and mix again until dissolved and the consistency of thick cream.

Stroke paint over print on a newspaper. If the print is visible the pigment is too thin and more should be added. The paint should flow easily from the brush for the length of a stroke across a paper approximately 18 inches. If the paint feels sticky, or gives a dry brush effect, it is too thick and water should be added.

The amount of paint needed for immediate use can be mixed, or a larger quantity can be mixed and kept in an airtight container.

COLORS TO COMBINE TO MAKE A THIRD COLOR CALLED RELATED COLORS
(Powder paint or tempera)

FIRST MIX EACH COLOR separately, then combine the two liquids.

yellow
plus
red
} orange
(slightly grayed)

yellow
plus
red-orange
} orange
(clear orange)

yellow
plus
turquoise blue
} green
(bright green)

yellow
plus
blue
} green
(slightly grayed)

red
plus
blue
} violet or purple
(slightly grayed)

magenta
plus
blue
} violet
(clear violet)

Brown is a mixture of the three primary colors: red, yellow, and blue.

White mixed with any color will make it lighter and less intense.

Place white *first* in container, then add small amounts of the other color until desired lightness is reached.

Mixing two parts of one color with one part of another results in one color predominating; in the listing below the stronger color is named first:

2 parts yellow
+
1 part red or
1 part red-orange
} *yellow*-orange

2 parts red or
2 parts red-orange
+
1 part yellow
} *red*-orange
or
(vermilion)

2 parts yellow
+
1 part blue or
1 part turquoise
} *yellow*-green
or
(chartreuse)

2 parts blue or
2 parts turquoise
+
1 part yellow
} *blue*-green

2 parts blue
+
1 part red or
1 part magenta
} *blue*-violet

2 parts red or
2 parts magenta
+
1 part blue
} *red*-violet

2 parts blue
+
1 part red
+
1 part yellow
} *blue*-brown
or
chocolate brown

2 parts yellow
+
1 part blue
+
1 part red
} *yellow*-brown or
golden brown or
mustard brown

2 parts red
+
1 part yellow
+
1 part blue
} *red-brown* or
brick color or
terra-cotta.

Colors grouped according to value (meaning the degree of lightness or darkness). Each color listed below is full intensity.

Light colors:
white
yellow
yellow-orange
yellow-green
orange

Middle value colors:
red-orange
red
green
yellow-brown

Dark colors:

blue-green	red-violet
blue-violet	red-brown
blue-brown	brown
blue	violet

Colors grouped according to warm and cool

Warm	*Cool*
yellow	blue
yellow-orange	green
yellow-green	blue-green
orange	blue-violet
red	blue-brown
red-orange	
yellow-brown	
red-brown	
red-violet	

Yellow and red and any mixtures predominantly yellow or red are warm colors, associated with sun and fire.

Blue is cool. Any mixture predominantly blue is cool, associated with blue ice, sky, water.

Grays made by mixing one color with a small amount of its color opposite or complement.

Complementary colors are pairs of colors which when mixed in equal proportions produce neutral gray. To determine the compliment of a color start with the primary colors red, yellow, blue. Together these make complete color. Take one away, for example blue. Red and yellow are left which make orange. The complement of blue is orange.

Place the color to be grayed in a container. Add its complement in a very small amount then stir or shake until well mixed. Repeat until desired gray is attained.

The following approximate gray mixtures are given for the teacher to use if subdued colors are needed as for backgrounds or painting modeled pieces of clay.

½ tsp. blue 1 cup orange	grayed orange
½ tsp. orange 1 cup blue	grayed blue
½ tsp. red 1 cup green	grayed green
½ tsp. yellow-green 1 cup red violet	grayed red violet
½ tsp. violet 1 cup yellow	grayed yellow

WATERCOLORS

(Recommended to begin in the second semester of the Third Grade.)

THE TRANSPARENCY and fluid quality of watercolors make them most suitable for painting atmosphere, feelings, or moving forms with indefinite shapes, such as clouds or imaginary forms. The young child with a desire to paint his individual concepts may easily lose confidence in his own ability to paint if the paint runs or if he is unable to control the wet, soft watercolor brush. Many delightful and expressive watercolor paintings begin with a happy accident. For the child who is not ready to use the running color to paint definite forms, opaque tempera paint — which is more easily controlled — is preferable. The esthetic quality of watercolor can be understood more easily by a twelve-year-old than by the third-grader, whose satisfaction will come mainly from discovering new colors by mixing colors.

Characteristics. Watercolors are transparent — the paper is visible through the watercolor paint, one color shows through an overlapping color and every movement of the brush is visible. Watercolor is a very sensitive medium. Sparkling, fresh color results when the paint is applied directly on the paper in one application. Watercolors are brighter when wet and become duller when dry.

Materials.

Brush. Long-handled, soft-bristle brush that will come to a good point when wet, with ½″ or ¾″ ferrule and 12″ handle.

Paper. Absorbent paper in white drawing, cream manila, or mimeo news, 14″ by 17″, 15″ by 20″, or 12″ by 18″. One piece 6″ by 12″ for trial brush strokes.

Paint. Watercolor box with whole pans containing red, yellow, blue and black; or whole pans in magenta, scarlet, yellow, turquoise, blue, and black.

Container for water: plastic dish or enamel water pan.

Other materials. Cellulose sponge, paint cloth of absorbent cotton in muslin or outing flannel approximately 5″ by 12″ folded.

Suggestions for classroom use of watercolor paint in Third Grade. Each child should have the materials listed below: paper for trial strokes, water, brush, paper towel, paper for painting.

Have each child arrange his painting materials so he can use them easily and efficiently.

Watercolor cakes must be clean at the beginning of each painting lesson. After the painting materials are in order, the child dampens the surface of each cake of paint by stroking it with a brush laden with water. This gives time for the dry cake of paint to soak during the discussion period preceding the painting.

The child adds one color to another color on his brush to make new colors. Many different colors can be made before washing the brush. He may fill his brush with yellow, then paint an area. Then he may stroke the yellow brush over blue and paint on the paper with a new color, green, resulting, and so on.

The child makes lighter colors by adding water to his brush. He dips his brush in water and fills the tip of the brush with a dark color, such as blue. He strokes the brush full of paint across the paper from left to right. He sees that the beginning of his stroke has a deep color, and that the color becomes lighter as it continues across the paper.

The child sees light and dark values of a single color change with the amounts of paint and water he has on his brush. These are very exciting experiences for a child who is trying to see how many colors he can make.

The child finds that different parts of his brush attains different effects. The brush should be filled directly with paint from the cake of color. This permits variations of color within a stroke as well as clearer, more intense color: for example, one side of the brush is stroked over red paint, the opposite side of the brush over blue paint, with the tip of the brush dipped in black.

The child lays the bristle end of the brush down on the paper to see the variations of color. The child tries turning the brush over in a rolling movement. He strokes with the side or the tip of the brush. As the color becomes thin or is used up, he adds more color.

All-over repeated designs of strokes can be attractive.

The child paints the way he feels the gay colors he sees in a circus or parade, the movements of the cool water he feels in swimming, the deep dark colors he experiences in a storm, or he paints a dream he has had.

Other ways to use watercolors. Have children paint over wet paper; wet part of the paper with a sponge and leave part dry; paint over the entire paper and see how the paint changes over wet paper.

Let the child use crayon to draw a picture or a design using all warm colors. When the space is well filled he paints cool colors, darker in value than his crayon colors, over his crayon drawings.

Another time the child draws with cool or dark colors in wax crayon which resists the watercolor, thus the paper absorbs the paint only where there is no crayon mark.

The child paints over different kinds of paper, such as paper towels, packing papers, light-colored construction paper, oatmeal paper, and tissue.

The child wets his paper and drops watercolor paint on it. He picks the paper up with both hands and moves it around, watching the paint run to form shapes. The child's imagination is stimulated and he adds to the moving shapes, lines, shapes, or textures.

The child interprets music with color such as: *Clair De Lune* by Debussy, *Moths and Butterflies* by Elgar, "Snow is Dancing" from *Children's Corner Suite* by Debussy.

Cleaning up. Clean water is essential for cleaning the cakes of paint. A brush full of clean water is drawn over the surface of one color at a time. The brush is cleaned and stroked over the cake a second time. This continues until the cakes of color are all clean and clear in color.

Paintings are left flat to dry.

A painting lesson should precede recess, noon, or afternoon dismissal, for the teacher's convenience.

Brushes are collected and washed, with the bristles shaped to a point, and placed flat on a paper towel to dry.

Paint boxes, when clean and dry, are closed, collected, and placed in a designated container.

Have helpers carry a fruit-juice can or pitcher between the tables or desks to enable children to pour their dirty water out, close to their work space.

Teachers decide whether the paint rags are to be discarded or washed. Paint rags can be washed in a bucket of warm water, which is changed several times, by using a rubber plunger. Rags can be left on a wooden clothes rack to dry. Paper towels serve as a substitute for rags.

EASELS

Location. Place easels near a window with light coming over the left shoulder of the child. A strip of linoleum placed under the easel protects a wooden or cement floor from spilled paint or stains on the floor.

DESCRIPTION OF EASEL PARTS

1. ***Board for working surface.*** A wall board 24″ by 36″ placed at a slight angle. The center of the board should come to the child's eye level when the child is standing. Newsprint or other absorbent drawing paper, size 18″ by 24″ or 24″ by 36″ is tacked to the board at points A and B.

Clamps used on either side of several sheets of newsprint hold the paper firmly to the board, or a cork is placed over a dozen sheets of drawing paper at left and right sides. Drive a nail through the center of each cork, through the paper to the board. This prevents paper tearing loose as a child works.

2. ***Trough to hold jars of paint.*** Seven circular openings, four inches in diameter, are cut about one inch apart across the top for jars. The front is left open to make cleaning spilled paint easier. This part may also be used as a tray to hold chalk.

3. ***Container for brushes on right end of easel trough.*** Openings are provided for the handles of brushes allowing one brush for each color.

4. ***Leg length to trough.*** Length for Kindergarten and First Grade is 21 inches. Length for Second and Third Grade is 33 inches.

5. ***Joining the two sides of the double easel.*** A wooden or metal strip fits over a screw or like device to hold the two sides

DOUBLE EASEL

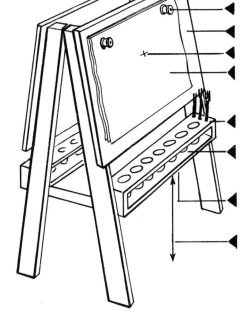

1. Mortised Hinge.

2. Cork or Spool.

3. 24″ x 36″ Board.

4. Eye level of Child.

5. Several sheets of 18″ x 24″ or 24″ x 36″ paper.

6. Holes to insert brush handles.

7. Opening to hold paper cup, cans, glasses or other paint containers.

8. Open for Easy Cleaning.

9. 21″ for 1st and 2nd graders. 33″ for 3rd grader.

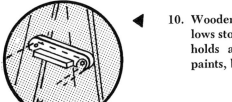

10. Wooden brace which hooks over pin allows storage. Wooden bar fastened to brace holds a removable shelf for paint rags, paints, brushes.

Art Materials and Their Use / 79

of the easel firmly together. When not in use the strip may be lifted and the easel folded to fit into a narrow space.

A solid triangular piece of wood may be used to fasten the front to the back. This kind is the most sturdy and firm but cannot be folded. A shelf may be added to the space between the legs or sides C and D to store the paint.

Avoid chains or hinges which may make easels collapse under slight pressure. One child paints on each side of the easel.

SUBSTITUTES FOR EASELS

A long wire screen (for standing or sitting). Fasten chicken wire with large openings securely to a wooden frame. Place the long wire screen on the chalk rail or on a long bench against the wall.

Drawing boards of wood, chipboard or wallboard, which have a hook on either side of the back at the top, are hooked on to the screen at the desired height.

A drawing paper is taped or tacked to the drawing board. A cheese box or other long, narrow wooden box, with a hook on either side of the back, at the top edge, is hooked below the board at the desired height for the child. The box is used as a container for jars of paint or chalk.

Paper hanging on the wall (for standing).

1. Cut two strips of wood 28″ long, from 1½″ to 2″ wide.

2. Place about 25 sheets of newsprint 24″ by 36″ in an even pile over one strip of wood. Match the center of the wood to the center of the pile of paper.

3. Place a second strip of wood on top of the paper, directly over the first strip of wood.

4. Pound one nail through the center of the wooden strips with paper between and nail three inches from each end.

5. The wooden strip extends out from the edge of the paper two inches on each side. One inch from each end of the wood cut a notch. Tie a strong cord around the notch on either end of the strip of wood.

6. Hang the above from the molding at the top of the blackboard or a similar place, at the correct height for a painting surface for the children.

One child paints at a time. Each finished painting may be removed or turned over the top of the wooden strip, leaving a clean sheet for the next painting.

Strips of wood used to hold mural paper (for standing). This method is used in rooms without chalkboards or bulletin boards. Murals may be painted in the hall, or in the classroom.

Place two long wooden strips the length of the mural paper on the floor. Fasten the top of the mural paper to one strip and the bottom of the mural paper to the other strip. Suspend the wooden frame from the molding with wire or heavy cord having the center of the paper at the eye level of the children.

Discarded maps and window shades. The backs of discarded maps or window shades are a fine proportion for large easel pictures. They may be suspended from a molding or be placed on the table or floor.

An inverted chair placed on a table top (for sitting or standing). The front edge of the seat is parallel to the front edge of the table. A piece of stiff cardboard or a wall board is propped against the inverted chair. The newsprint for painting is clipped to the top of the cardboard. A piece of plasticine pressed against the front of the board on the table will keep it from slipping.

A chair with a straight back (for standing). Cover the seat with newspaper. Place a board against the back of the chair. Tack newsprint or drawing paper to the board. Place paints in containers on the seat of the chair.

Double-table easel and bench easel made with portable display racks (for sitting). A piece of wallboard (not much larger than the rack) is placed on the rack. The paper is tacked or fastened with tape to the board. These are not so steady as two wall boards fastened with a brace.

PAPER FASTENED TO CHALK BOARD OR BULLETIN BOARD

Drawing paper 18″ by 24″, 12″ by 18″ or 24″ by 36″ is fastened to heavy cardboard, wallboard or wooden boards and stood in the chalk rail, or the drawing paper is fastened directly to the chalkboard with scotch or masking tape.

Cover chair seats or tables with newspaper for the paint supply.

Place chairs at intervals. One can serve four-to-six children.

Placing paint containers in a box or coffee tin helps avoid spilled paint.

MOVABLE TABLES MADE FROM PIECES OF CORK BOARD, WALLBOARD, PLYWOOD

Support for pieces of board: stools, screwed-down desks, or wooden horses.
Procedure.

The children stand or sit to work, depending upon the height of the working surface.

Cover the surface with newspaper.

Place paint supply in three baby-food

A BENCH EASEL

1) The top of the bench should be the correct width for the child to straddle. 2) The bench is as tall as the distance from the child's knee to the floor. 3) A vertical board is fastened to one end of the bench, extending above the seat A. 4) A strip of wood C is fastened to A one inch from B. 5) Drawing board rests against B and is held in place by C. The drawing paper is fastened to the drawing board. 6) The paint supply should be in a box on the bench in front of the child.

DOUBLE-TABLE EASEL

A and B — Two pieces of wall board, chipboard, plywood or scraps from wooden crates, approximately 24″ by 36″.

Join A to B on one end with book-binding tape. Lap tape over front and back edge at least one inch. If A and B are wood, use wooden hinges.) A brace is needed to hold A and B in a rigid slanting position. Paper is fastened to A and B.

tins. Place inside a 1-pound coffee can.

Place a supply of paint where as many as six children can share it.

Place the paper for painting flat on the table.

This type of movable table may also be used for making murals.

A long strip of wallboard may be placed along the chalk trough, or over one row of desks or stools.

A square piece of wallboard is convenient to use over four desks. This working surface may be used for smaller groups for working with papier mâché, puppets, or for painting glazes on clay.

The method above is planned for rooms with screwed-down desks and no space for work tables.

PAINTING ON THE FLOOR

THIS IS ONE WAY OF providing painting space for a number of children in rooms lacking tables or easels. One painting area for four children: Two large double sheets of newspaper are placed on the floor to form a square. One piece of newsprint 18″ by 24″ or 14″ by 17″ is placed in the center of each side. One jar of paint for four children is placed in the center. One long-handled, stiff bristled brush is placed to the right of each paper. Each child kneels with his knees parallel to one side of the square newspaper.

The following procedure is suggested for first- and second-grade children.

The example given is for three colors. The first painting experience should be with one color, later two colors, then three.

When three different colors are to be used — as red, blue, and yellow-orange, place one color in each painting area.

36 children will need nine painting areas (four children for each area), and 3 areas will have red paint, 3 areas blue paint, and 3 areas yellow-orange paint.

When each child is in his place ready to paint, brushes are placed with bristles in the center by the paint. Each child plans his picture, paints with the color in front of him, repeats the color in different areas of his paper, and balances the color he has on the paper. In a few minutes the children are ready for a second color. Each child picks up his painting, with one hand on each side (to keep wet paint from running).

The children move on, walking in an orderly fashion to the next painting area, where each child places his paper down on one side of the square newspaper, parallel to the edge. He picks up the brush in front of him and adds the second color. This color may touch the first color in places or not, and it may be repeated.

After the children have had ample time to use the second color, the brushes are placed in front of the child with the bristle end toward the paint container in the center. Each child picks up his painting, and the groups move as above to a third color area.

At the end, the group has used four colors — red, blue, yellow-orange, and white (paper color). After once or twice the children move automatically. They can be trained to walk on the right side to avoid bumping.

The advantages of this procedure are that each brush is used for only one color, so does not have to be washed until the painting period ends; that many children can paint at one time, and that few paint containers are needed. Place colors accessible to children with unfinished work.

CHAPTER VIII

The Child Encounters the Brush

During the manipulative stage, when the dominant interest of the child is in the movement of the brush, the following procedures are suggested:

a. The child enjoys painting on the chalk board with a large brush, using clear water, making strokes with his brush as far as he can reach up and down, across and around.

b. He should paint with a brush in each hand to experience simultaneous movement using both arms, with strokes starting low and springing from both sides of a given point. Long wavy lines like waves in the sea are made from left to right using a full arm movement. The child is intrigued by the way the dark fades when the water on the blackboard is dry —like magic to the child in the manipulative stage.

MATERIALS FOR THE FIRST PAINTING EXPERIENCE
(Each material has a designated place, well labelled and known by the children.)

1. Opaque paint the consistency of cream: tempera, show-card, poster, or 3 parts powder paint mixed 1 part of water).

2. Stiff bristle brush with ½" ferrule and 12" handle: stiff bristle brushes are easier for young children to control because they retain their shape and do not become limp when full of paint. They also feel firm when they are brushed over the paper.

3. Absorbent paper 18" by 24" or 14" by 17" or 15" by 20": unprinted news, mimeo news, construction paper, newspaper.

4. Containers for paint; jelly glasses

with lids, rustproof baby food tins, milk cartons or paper cups.

5. Container for water: a pitcher or a large fruit juice can pinched on one end to make a spout.

6. Newspaper.

7. Easel or substitute (see pages 79-82).

8. Absorbent paint rags: at least an eight-inch square per child.

9. Aprons.

10. Smooth, flat sticks 8″ to 12″ for stirring paint to keep in solution.

11. A shaker with a tight lid for mixing paint.

Choosing Colors to Use Together

Use dark colors with middle and light value colors. (Use warm colors with cool colors. Yellow is light, warm; chocolate brown is dark, cool; blue is dark, cool; green is middle, cool; orange is light, warm; red is middle, warm; yellow-green is light, warm.)

Use colors related to each other (see page 75, and try combining primary colors with black.

The child's experiences with paint give him the opportunity to: discover color differences; feel the movement of the brush; see his ideas take form; learn how to control his materials and experience the pure joy of creating his own colors and shapes.

Suggested Habits and Skills to Encourage

For the child to form good habits he must understand the reasons for given procedures. The children need frequent reminders before the following practices become a natural part of their painting experience.

Place the paper on the painting surface so that the center of the paper is at the child's eye level. If it is not possible for the child to paint on an upright surface he can stand by a table or desk or kneel on the floor, with his paper in front of him.

Amount of paint to use: pour paint into containers to the depth of the bristles of the brush, for if the paint does not cover the handle of the brush, it does not come off onto the child's hands. Also, paint is not easily spilled from this level.

Characteristics of powder or tempera paint: liquid paint will run. The brush full of paint is wiped on the edge of the container. Thick paint settles to the bottom of the container, leaving thinner paint on top.

A stick left in the jar of paint can be used to stir the paint, thus keeping it even and full strength. Tempera and powder paint become lighter in color when they are dry.

During the first few periods of acquainting the child with the materials of paint, paper, and brushes the teacher, who must allow sufficient room between children for free arm movements, guides them to form the following habits:

To wear aprons for painting.

To stand firmly on two feet.

To paint at a distance which does not necessitate stretching or reaching beyond arm's length.

To move the arm from the shoulder and the hand from the wrist in an easy flowing movement. Exercises in moving the arms up and down and around rhythmically to music, and flexing the wrist helps develop a relaxed feeling and helps relieve tension.

To hold the brush above the ferrule *lightly* so the spring in the brush can be felt. Pressing hard and scrubbing back and forth hinders rhythmic movements, ruins the brush, and gives a worn-out look to the painting.

To work directly with paint, with a color as dark as desired, insures brighter and smoother color. Painting several times in one place does not make a darker or brighter color unless the paint is very thin. Opaque color, the thickness of cream, gives complete coverage with one application, and adding layers of color only dulls the original color.

To wait until the first color is dry before using a second which overlaps the first if the second color is desired. Not to scrub or the first color will mix with the second.

To wash a brush clean between each different color that is used insures full intensity color. Using the same brush in different colors usually results in muddy color.

To have a brush for each color identified with a waterproof band of that color around the handle insures pure, clean color. The use of water for cleaning is not needed by the children during painting.

To share paint with other children.

To learn to wait for one's turn.

To hold a cloth in his hand to take care of dripping paint from the brush, if a child has to walk from the supply of paint to his work space.

To clean up paint when it is spilled. It is easy to soak it up with a moist absorbent rag when it is wet, but scrubbing is required after paint has dried. Paint left on the floor may leave a stain. A bleach or sandpaper usually removes the stain.

CARE OF PAINT MATERIALS

A SPIRIT OF COOPERATION during the clean-up period makes a happier group. Wet paintings are placed to dry. Paintings on boards or easels dry where they are. Each child discovers wet paint will run if the paper is held upright, and that wet paintings piled one on top of another will stick together and be blurred. Hence, paintings should be placed flat on a piece of newspaper beside each other (not overlapping) on the floor.

Monitors can be assigned for each different task described below. One collects brushes in a jar or large can.

Cleaning brushes. Fill a quart jar one-fourth full of warm soapy water. Move about six brushes round and round. Do not push bristles against the bottom. Rinse in clear water. Place brushes on absorbent paper towel to dry with bristles out straight. *CAUTION — Brushes dry just as they are left.*

Left full of paint, they will be dirty and stiff.

Left in the paint jar with the bristles pressed against the bottom, the bristles will be bent.

Left in water or in paint, they will become loose at the ferrule because water loosens the glue in the ferrule.

Storing brushes. Roll dry brushes in newspaper, 12 to a roll, and place them flat in a box. Avoid pressing the bristles against the end of the box. Moth balls placed with the brushes help protect bristles stored for a period of time.

Care of paint. Paint jars should be carried to one supply table which has been covered with newspaper. Scrape the paint that has collected around the inside of the jars into the paint and stir. Like colors are poured into one container, as all blues together, all greens together. Colors that mix together into a new color may be poured into one container. White may be mixed with any color. A small amount of many colors poured into one jar make a gray. Replenish paint for the easel. Place jars of paint in cartons ready for the next lesson. Cover the jars to keep the paint from drying. Keep enough water over paint to retain softness. Do not discard powder paint by washing it down sinks; put it in paper or in a tin can in the waste container.

Cleaning paint jars. Scrape color from emptied jars with a knife or rubber scraper. Soak jars in water then clean with a bottle brush.

Newspaper. Pile unused pieces of clean newspaper neatly in a designated place for the next lesson. Put spotted or wet newspaper in the waste container.

Paint on clothes. Powder paint is soluble in water and washes easily from cottons. Allow paint to dry on woolens, then rub cloth together to remove the paint.

It is important for children to learn right away that materials are not wasted or lost if proper care is taken of them; that materials should be kept in good condition, in the right place ready for use when they are needed.

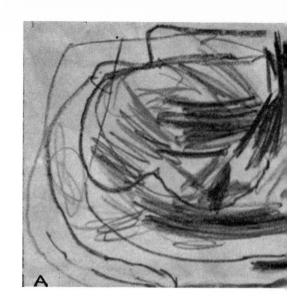

EVIDENCE OF GROWTH IN TWO PAINTINGS

Evidence of growth and that the child is better organized: the lines are clear and direct; he names his scribble (B).
"Running all around."

DISCOVERY

THE CHILD FINDS OUT WHAT happens when paint of different colors is applied to paper. He is stimulated by handling this new material. He finds he can make many kinds of marks and movements with his brush full of paint. He discovers that paint will flow from the brush across the paper with one stroke, provided:

    a. he does not press too hard,

    b. the paint is a creamy consistency,

    c. the bristles are full of paint.

He tries all the colors, daubing one after another on the paper. Each new color is a

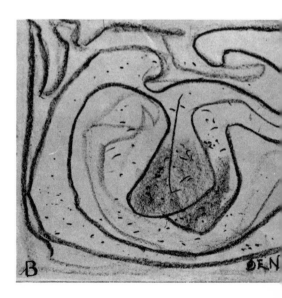

surprise. His enjoyment comes from the color itself. The clear pure colors may suggest to the child a jewel-like pattern, a light streaming through a stained glass church window, the faces of flowers in a garden, or many other things. See color illustration, Little Girl surrounded by jewel-like colors, page 98.

The child paints over the whole sheet of paper with one color because he loves the movement of the brush. He may paint one color over another for the same reason. Some children stir the paint round and round because they enjoy the movement. If they use more than one color they see a new color appear, and deep pools, caves, or tunnels as a result of vigorous movements.

The child paints a second color over the first color while it is still wet and produces a new color. The child paints blue on his paper. Before the color has dried he puts his brush in red and paints on top of the blue. He sees the new color, purple or violet, which has resulted from the mixture of blue with red. Occasionally the excited child dips his brush first in yellow and then in red. When he paints he sees neither yellow nor red, but orange. These are a few ways children observe how new colors are made.

SUCCESSIVE STEPS IN DEVELOPMENT

AN EARLY STEP COMPRISES scribbling or lines going in many directions, when the child's interest is in the track made by the movement of the brush. Encourage free big, rhythmic movements. In the beginning stages of scribbling a large black wax crayon is best used on a smooth large sheet of paper. This material gives the child the

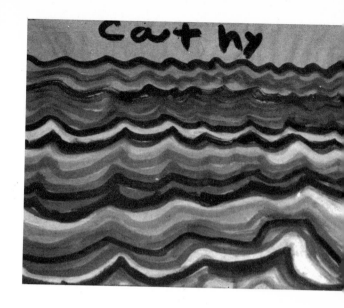

MAKING STRIPES WITH A PAINTBRUSH

Making stripes: stripes vary in width and in distance apart. Strokes start at the top. One brush-full of paint will last from the beginning to the end, in one continuous movement.

opportunity to move easily and freely over the paper and to make clear, unblurred lines.

At this stage the interest is in the path the child can make all over the paper. The child has control over the brush. A five-year-old may consider his brush, crayon, or chalk as an object, such as an animal, and the line he puts on the paper is the direction taken by the running animal.

To make plaid designs, stripes are made in two directions, first from the top to bottom, then with a second color from left to right. Select two colors which contrast. As one color passes over the other color, a third color is made. The finished design will have four colors; for example where vertical stripes are red, and horizontal stripes are blue, where they cross will be violet and where there are no lines the white of the paper will show.

Two colors such as yellow and green might be used for vertical stripes with one made important by being repeated more times, or made wider, and a third color, brown, could be used for the horizontal stripes.

Papers decorated with these designs would be appropriate for box or book covers or for place mats.

Observation of Design. Experienced teachers know that children are more interested in things other people do when they are doing the same things. At the time the children are repeating units in all-over patterns and making striped and plaid designs, examples of this type of design can be observed in wallpaper, dress goods, drapery materials, linoleum, blankets, and children's clothing. Children enjoy finding how many times one unit is repeated.

With experience, the child acquires better control. He organizes material, makes definite shapes, and connects his motions with imaginative thinking by naming his shapes — a tree, a man, a house — he is making symbols for his idea. Encourage the expression of new ideas by elaborating on some key idea, such as "Where is your puppy?" "Does your puppy have a house to sleep in at night?"

Enjoyment of color is separate from the object. A child chooses a color because he likes it, not because it is the real color of the object he has in mind.

The child progresses by adding new shapes or colors for each new idea. See color illustrations, Buildings, Land and Boat by Eddie, Grade 2 and A Boat With Shooting Guns, Grade 3, page 100. Eddie used many colors to interpret sound.

CHAPTER IX

The Beginning of Representation

THE YOUNG CHILD TELLS IN words far more than he represents with art materials. He makes symbols for his ideas by combining his imagination and his emotion with what he knows. He expresses what is actively important to him during the time he is creating. This is why art material should be used at the peak of the child's interest to attain the best expression of his ideas.

THE CHILD'S PERCEPTION

1. The child may not relate objects to his environment or observe relative sizes. People, trees, and houses may all appear the same height to him. He makes the part most important to him the largest.

2. Realistic meaning is not understood by the child. All different kinds of trees are the same to him, and all trees grow tall and have branches spreading out all around.

3. Proportions within an object are not compared, understood, or of any significance to the five- and six-year-old. People need a head to think, eyes to see, a mouth to speak and eat, legs to move about. This much is all that matters. Man, to the child, is symbolized in a simple form. Mother, father, baby may all be the same size. When the child needs arms and hands for carrying or making something, they will be added.

4. Distance is not seen or represented. The first indication of it in a child's work is the placing of one object above another on the paper.

The Beginning of Representation / 89

The teacher needs to:

Encourage the child to make more things.

Give children a chance to explain their work.

Encourage them to try things they have not done before.

Leave them with further ideas which they are eager to express.

Use questions such as: "What is the pattern like on the turtle's back?" "Where does the train go?" "What toys does your baby brother have?"

Supply colors the child needs to express his ideas.

Stimulate the child's imagination.

Encourage children to fill the picture plane with clean, clear color areas.

Remember, subjects do not change (such as houses, trees, people, animals, ground, weather, and machines). How people think about subjects does change. Personal experiences and perceptions change as the people grow older. Know what a little child sees, how he thinks and reacts to what he sees.

GRADUAL DEVELOPMENT OF CHILDREN'S ART EXPRESSION

THE FIRST REPRESENTATIONAL pictures are child-centered. The child makes the thing most important to him the largest, and spends all his energy on this one part. Other parts may be barely indicated or omitted. When the child's interest ends he stops painting.

The child may enlarge hands with outstretched fingers because they are used to catch a ball or for some other purpose. When the hands do not serve a purpose the child paints them like clubs or with a mere stroke of the brush.

As the child grows, symbolic shapes are added based upon the parts or characteristics the child considers important.

The child puts many ideas down, feeling his way. He is not concerned with any organization or plan or relationships. The teacher praises his many ideas. Which ones does he like best? He might make a picture of this one.

The child puts things together that belong together. He begins to associate ideas and group them together. The child loves

repetitions making rhythmic movements with fine design qualities.

The child considers the entire space. One part belongs to the other with the shapes and colors balanced. The child has made his idea important by placement and color contrast.

The child makes forms with solid color, no longer only single lines.

The child says more in a picture. He places emphasis on things or ideas that go together such as a horse and wagon with a driver placed on the ground or base line.

The child uses dark colors over light and light colors over dark to make his ideas stand out.

The child observes and represents children and many things with a front, back and side.

Children are very matter-of-fact. They paint the essentials of things the way they are to them. Above their heads is the sky. Under their feet is the earth. The air they breathe is all around them, around houses and airplanes. In the child's world all things

Jim, Grade One, has painted building like blocks, a bulbous tree form and other simple shapes for machines. He has painted directly with assurance.

Barrett, Kindergarten, painted lines to represent a house. He enjoyed making the smoke moving in and out and around.

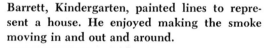

Teresa, Grade One, first made an outline with crayon to represent a child's body. Then she added strokes for the dress and hair.

Cathy, Kindergarten, has painted the parts important to her. Eyes for seeing, a mouth for talking and eating, and long hair with a ribbon on each end. The blue line across the bottom makes it complete.

Judy, Kindergarten, called this fine pattern a man. The projecting parts are the arms, legs, and ears. She loved painting with bright colors.

Yvonne, Kindergarten, has painted her mother taking care of her brothers and sisters. A few simple shapes tell her story.

"Boys and Tree."
By Ullrick, Grade Two

Roberta, Grade Two, has painted the bottom
of the ocean as she imagines it to be.

happen between the earth and the sky.

The child tells us all he knows about one thing in his picture. He paints the inside and outside of buildings. He shows two sides of one building on one street. He shows one tree in bloom and one with fruit. He emphasizes one idea. He paints objects within his experience in the order he thinks.

CLASS DISCUSSION ABOUT CHILDREN'S PAINTINGS AND DRAWINGS

THIS IS A PERIOD OF appreciation, when each child tells the group about his own picture and what he likes about the other children's pictures. The teacher should encourage constructive ideas that suggest good thinking and the best use of materials, and remember that children enjoy color apart from an object, that their imagination often changes the visual form of the object and that the child should express his own idea.

Following is a suggested basis for discussion:

Are the colors clear? If not are the brushes dirty or was the paint scrubbed on the paper.

Has the child painted with assurance and confidence, using strong, direct strokes of the brush?

How many ideas have been expressed? Are the symbols for each idea easily seen or all mixed up?

Has the child worked large in big movements?

Has the child filled the whole space?

Are the parts of the picture or design connected by movement or repeated color which are balanced in shape and color?

Are colors too close in value, thus preventing us from seeing the separate parts? Does pattern cover all the shapes, making our eyes jump about?

Has the color been used to emphasize the part the child considers important?

Positive comments are useful, such as:

Symbols for ideas are easily seen when they have simple contours with shapes separated, not overlapping.

Colors that touch each other should have a different value, with light against dark and dark against light.

Pattern should be surrounded with plain areas.

Emphasize seeing the beauty of color and rhythmical movements. Let the child discover color relationships.

A Second-Grade child has painted the inside of his house to show what happens.

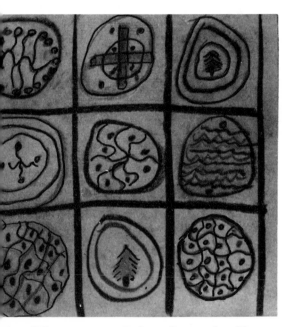

jewel-like pattern made by a first-grader. "I ke pretty colors."

Sandra, Grade Two, "I like birds. This is my own picture with my bird."

The Beginning of Representation / 95

CHAPTER X

Observing Color in Things Children Know

COLORS IN THE CHILD'S WORLD

COLOR COMBINATIONS FOUND in the classroom and in children's painting offer a basis for class discussion. The principles concerning the effect of one color another provide a guide for the teacher in selecting and evaluating colors.

Examples of matching colors or repeated color.

A ribbon in a child's hair matching a color in her dress.

Socks which match a sweater, blouse, skirt, or pants.

A blouse or sweater chosen to match a color in a plaid or patterned skirt or pair of pants.

Birthday candles on a white cake selected to match the flowers on the cake.

A green vase which is the same kind of green as the leaves in a bouquet.

Window shades or venetian blinds the same color value as the wall.

Light and dark of the same color look well together: a light blue sweater with a dark blue skirt or pants, a golden brown shirt with dark brown pants, light brown blotter on a dark brown desk.

Yellow, in buttercups, daffodils, lemons, grain, the sun, canary birds, a hair ribbon, clothes, autumn leaves.

Blue, in the sky, water, children's eyes, bachelor buttons, bluebells, clothes.

Red, in flames, apples, strawberries, cherries, tulips, poinsettias, autumn leaves, cranberries, clothes.

Green, in grass, leaves, trees, lettuce, peppers, frogs, rugs, clothes.

Brown, in sand, tilled soil, bark of trees, children's hair, fur on squirrels, rabbits and bears, shoes, purses, clothes.

Dark colors:
Blue of a stormy sky
Shadows in water
Purple of grapes
Black of hair or fur
Green of pine trees
Brown of bricks, rocks, earth
Blue-black of night
Gray-black of smoke
Light colors:
Yellow of the sun
Golden hair
Orange of pumpkins

Sunsets
Pink of children's cheeks
Blue of water
Blue of baby's blanket
White daisies

Warm Colors: red of fire, red cherries and apples, yellow of the sun; gold, red, and violet of flowers.

Cool colors: green of the grass, blue of the water, green of trees, blue of ice.

Grayed colors: squirrels and elephants, rocks, sand, a foggy day.

Colors that are both light and dark: light blue and dark blue, like the stripes in a sweater; lavender and purple, like vari-colored sweet peas or pansies.

Color combinations in nature:
A sunflower with yellow petals outside and brown seeds in the center.
Red tulips with deep blue violet stamens.
Red apples surrounded by green leaves.
Pansies with purple petals and yellow centers.
Animals with two-color spots: leopards, fawns, turtles, certain dogs, fish, and snakes.

BACKGROUND COLOR KNOWLEDGE NEEDED BY THE TEACHER

A light value color placed next to a dark value color makes that part stand out, as yellow touching blue, yellow-green touching violet, or light orange touching dark brown. The greater the difference in value the more a given part will become important.

Colors close in value do not stand out, for example, yellow touching white, blue touching violet, purple touching black.

Base the choice of color for the painting surface upon contrast of light and dark.

a. White or light colors such as yellow, yellow-orange, pink, are more effective painted on dark paper. (Snow pictures are an example.)

b. Dark colors such as blue, violet, brown and medium colors such as red and green are more effective painted on white, cream or other light-colored paper.

A group of colors with one color in common look well together (these are called a color family or related color). An example of the application of related color is a flower arrangement of white daisies (which have yellow centers) grouped with orange marigolds.

To give variety to a group of colors use ones which have different values, ones warm and cool and related colors as in the following: Each of these related colors contains yellow: orange has a light value and is a warm color; green has a middle value and is a cool color; chocolate brown has a dark value and is a cool color.

To unify a group of colors a predominance of either warm or cool colors is needed. Green, which is cool, is the predominant color in the following group: yellow-green, blue-green. A small amount of yellow, orange, or red, which are warm colors, give a contrast in hue which is a relief. The spot of red becomes important, serving as a surprise surrounded by its opposite, green, and needs to be repeated for balance.

CLASS DISCUSSION ABOUT SELECTING COLORS

WITH THE ABOVE IN MIND, the teacher should discuss with the children the color choice for a given lesson, and hold one color up before them. Ask them to find a color they would like to combine with this color, such as a color that makes it look happy or bright

A Color Portfolio
of Children's Paintings

ARRANGEMENTS OF COLORED PAPER SHAPES
ILLUSTRATING COLOR RELATIONSHIPS

TOP LEFT: Yellow is one ingredient of each color here — thus they are all related colors, mostly light and middle value. The small cool green triangles add interest and variety to the predominant warm yellows and oranges. Variations of a triangle have been used to make related shapes. TOP CENTER: Cool-colored, symbolic fish shapes touch each other, making a pattern of fish. Dark green and blue outline very light colors making these shapes important. There is variety in kinds of green. One small bright red fish serves as a surprise; it tends to stand out because it is surrounded by cool green colors. TOP RIGHT: A yellow-orange sunburst with a saw-tooth edge stands out because it is placed on a square which is a darker color, red-orange. The straight edge of the square accentuates the jagged circle. LEFT SIDE: In the panel, each blue animal has the same basic shape and color. Two rectangles of different colors placed behind each blue animal result in color variations and contrasts that illustrate colors that make other color areas important as well as colors that subdue other color areas. MIDDLE CENTER: The warm red fingers reaching out into the warm violet are subdued because of the red in both colors. The red is more pronounced along the bottom curve because there it contrasts with dark cool blue. The red shape stands out more than the dark green to the right because the green and blue are close in value and both are cool. BOTTOM CENTER: A yellow circle is shown on three different backgrounds. Each one has a different carrying power. The yellow on blue is the greatest contrast of light against dark, therefore it is the strongest. The yellow on white has the least carrying power because the values are close. The second yellow circle on white is accented by a black outline, which makes it more important. LOWER RIGHT: Related warm colors are combined in dark tones. Small shapes of dark blue close to the value of red add interest and variety, and balance the warm red. The lightest shapes stand out most because they contrast most in value. MIDDLE RIGHT: An arrangement of shapes with warm, gay colors varying in light and dark contrasts. The small green shapes appear very intense because they are not related to the red in color. They are related to the large yellow shape, which helps to unify the whole.

ARRANGEMENTS OF COLORED
PAPER SHAPES TO ILLUSTRATE
COLOR RELATIONSHIPS

"Imaginative Stars," *crayon and water color,*
by David, Grade Two.

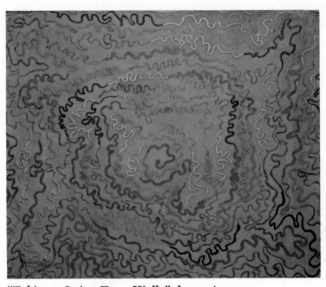

"Taking a String For a Walk," drawn in crayon
then painted in blue watercolor,

by Donald, Grade Three.

"A Little Girl Surrounded by Jewel-like Colors," *painted by Joyce, Kindergarten.*

"Day and Night,"   *painted by Ginny, Kindergarten.*

"A Little Girl With Her Pet,"   *painted by Debra, Grade One.*

"Mother Hen With Baby Chickens," *painted by Elizabeth, Grade One.*

"My Friends," *painted by Judith, Grade Three.*

"Birds Singing,"   *By Karin, Grade Three, in crayon.*

Karin has spread the wings of her birds to
show how they fly, making a delightful design.

"Going For a Walk in The Park,"   *By Doreen, Grade Three, in chalk.*

"A Boat With Shooting Guns," with exploding movement in the sky, water, and boat.

By Paul, Grade Three,

"Buildings, Land, and Boat,"

By Eddie, Grade Two.

"A Bird in a Bed of Flowers,"   *By Janice, Kindergarten.*

"Mother Bird With Baby Birds in a Nest,"   **"A Clown Doing Tricks,"**
By Linda, Grade Three.   *By Dean, Grade Two.*

"A Lion Where It Likes To Be,"   *By Marlene, Grade Three, crayon.*

"Springtime,"   *painted by Marie, Grade One.*   **"Playing Indian,"** *painted by Lynda, Grade Two.*

or that seems to belong. After the choice is made, hold the two colors up together while the children choose a third color.

Another day ask each child to choose a color he likes, then find a second and third color which are "happy" with his first color. Have members of the group tell what they like about the colors together.

Encourage children to cover their whole paper with color. When children name the colors they have used in their picture, they should include the color of the paper as one of the colors, if they have not covered all the paper.

Suggested number of colors for five-year-old children to use at first. For children learning to use their brush one dark color is best. Two or three colors at one time are best for small children in the symbolic stage. Often, when a picture is nearly finished, a child desires another color for a specific reason. Keep a variety of colors in a box for this purpose.

Importance of variety in color selections. Different color combinations are used for each new lesson, giving the children experiences with a variety of colors and hues. Often colors suggest ideas to children. Other times something children have seen or heard about inspires them to express their ideas in color. Children with a definite idea of the color they need should have access to that color. Color choice may be emotional rather than the actual color of the object.

A Sample Project: "A Sparkle Picture"
(Grade Three)

The teacher to the children:
"A sparkle picture makes you happy. Many bright colors dance on the paper."
"You may take this for your subject:
"In the blue-black darkness of night rockets shot higher and higher into the sky piercing the blue-black darkness — behind them a trail of sparkling diamonds left a pathway in the sky; or this:
"A little girl and a little boy turned shining sparklers round and round. Little sparks flew out from every side making big circles of sparkling light in the dark night."

"Use dark blue, violet, or black paper."
"Paint with pure colors of red, blue, yellow, orange, violet, and white opaque paint with jewel-like colors close together to make a sparkle picture."
"Another way to make a sparkle picture is to rub bright colors of crayon over a smooth paper (like tagboard). Repeat your colors to make the movement you want your sparkle picture to have."
"Cover the entire paper with black crayon, or a dark India ink. Scrape the dark color away to show the sparkling lights.
"Your first picture will help you find out what happens. Try several until you have colors which dance on the paper."

CHAPTER XI

Stimulating Ideas in Children

THE FRESH REACTIONS AND wonder of small children should not be dimmed by adults. Children should be allowed to satisfy their curiosities.

Descriptive words used by the teacher and found in books reveal the appearance and nature of objects and initiate appreciation.

The size of things

Building blocks

A block as *high* as it is *wide*.

A block that is *tall* or *high*.

A *low, long* block.

This block is smaller than that block.

That block is taller than this block.

Trees

Which tree is the tallest?

Find trees with branches reaching up to the sky.

Which tree is the shortest?

Find trees spreading their branches out on all sides.

Find trees with drooping branches.

Things that have similar shapes. Building blocks are long and short, large and small. Similar shapes:

A truck is shaped like a long building block and like a box car on a train.

A train is like a number of long blocks in a row.

A store may be like several blocks in a row or like one block on top of another.

A house may be like one long building block or like several different shapes of blocks together, such as, a square block with a long block.

Apartment houses usually have several stories, like one long block on top of another.

Office buildings usually have many stories, like many blocks one on top . of another.

Some things have more than one kind of shape: a truck, a train, and a car have bodies like boxes or like building blocks with four round wheels.

SUBJECTS FOR CHILDREN'S PICTURES

Things of interest in the home. The child's first experiences are in the home with his family, and his thinking is influenced mainly by family and teachers, by things that are said about things that they see or imagine.

The Home: "What I like about my home." "The rooms in my house." "Things I do at home before and after school."

The Family: "The members of my family." "Things our family do together." "My favorite person."

Things mother does for the family.
Teacher:

"What does your mother wear?"

"What does your mother use to help her with her work?"

"In what room does she do each different kind of work?"

Things the child does with his mother or father, or things father does for the family. The parents of twenty-five or more children represent many different kinds of employment.

Things of which the child is a part are important to him, and offer subjects for pictures.

"Things I like to do best."

"Funny things."

"The happiest time I can remember."

"What I would like to do when I grow up."

"What I like to do best after school."

"A dream I remember."

"What I would do if I could do as I please."

"Things I like to see."

"My favorite toy or game."

"What I like for a treat."

"The most beautiful thing I know."

"My party."

"My doll."

"Mother Working in the Kitchen,"
By Wayne, Grade Three.

"My Family,"
By Sandra, Grade Two.

Stimulating Ideas in Children / 101

CARL A. RUDISILL LIBRARY
LENOIR RHYNE COLLEGE

"My train."

"Picking flowers."

"How I help others."

"The pet I would like to own."

"Being all dressed up."

"Things I am thankful for."

See color illustration, "A Clown Doing Tricks," following page 98.

Answers the child can give to "Where? When? What? How?" provide subjects for art.

Where?

"Where do you sleep?"

"Where does the robin build its nest?"

"Where does your puppy sleep at night?"

"Where do you eat your dinner at home?"

"Where are the fire engines kept?"

"Where do you get your groceries?"

When?

"When do you wear your snow suit?"

"When do you wear your swim suit?"

"When do the stars come out?"

"When do you feed your pet?"

"When do you go to bed?"

"When do you help your mother?"

What?

"What did we do today when we went to the auditorium?"

"What did we do today when we went to the park?"

"What did we do today when we went to the bakery?"

"What did we do today when we went to the pet store?"

"What does mother use to make cookies?"

"What do you do on a picnic?"

"What do you do in Sunday School?"

"What do you do when you visit your grandmother?"

"What do you do after school?"

See color illustration, Going for a Walk

"A Clown Doing Stunts,"
By Jimmy, Grade Two.

"In the Auditorium,"
By Mary, Grade Two.

in the Park, following page 98.

How?

> "How do you play on the jungle gym?"
>
> "How does your mother take care of your baby brother or sister?"
>
> "How do you take care of your pet?"
>
> "How does the farmer milk the cow?"
>
> "How does the mother hen care for her chicks?"
>
> "How does daddy mow the lawn?"

Play in its many forms is very real to the child, and is another source of subjects.

Toys

> Toys with wheels, that children ride, such as wagon, tricycle, car, bicycle, scooter.
>
> Toys with wheels that carry loads, such as cars, trains, trucks.
>
> Toys children hold, such as dolls and animals.
>
> Toys children play with together, such as balls, games, dishes, jumping ropes, ring toss, checkers, marbles, teeter-totters.
>
> Toys used for building, such as blocks, erector sets, tinker toys, logs.

Games. Games children play together, such as "Cat and Mouse," "Indian," "O'Leary" and "Ball Toss."

See color illustration, Playing Indian, following page 98.

Tools children use for a definite purpose: garden tools to prepare the ground for planting, such as a hoe, rake, shovel, wheelbarrow; carpenters' tools for making something, such as a hammer, plane, saw, vise.

Machines children see in their homes:

The wheels of the sewing machine that go round and round while mother sews.

The flour sifter and the egg beater with

"Games We Like Outdoors,"
By Paul, Grade One.

double wheels that the child can turn with his own strength.

The sprinkler used to water the lawn.

The vacuum cleaner with its revolving brush, and the handle with which the child can push it.

The washing machine mother uses which revolves round and round making dancing suds among the clothes. The electric beater spinning around in the bowl.

THINGS CHILDREN SEE OR DO WHICH PROVIDE A SUCCESSION OF IDEAS

THE FOLLOWING IDEAS ARE suitable subjects for murals or moving pictures. The teacher discusses each subject with the children. A working plan is made with each member of the class assigned to a definite part which interests him. The subjects may be in chronological order or grouped according to related ideas.

1. *A picnic* (related ideas are grouped in chronological order).

"How did you prepare for your picnic?"

"How did you go to the picnic?"

"What did you do at the picnic?"

A picnic will vary in different localities and different families. Picnics are usually fun that children remember, and they respond with enthusiasm to the idea of picturing in color all the things that happened. Since most picnics are on warm days, sunny warm colors should be suggested, to be used with cool green colors for the ground and plants.

2. *Habits of birds* (related ideas).

Birds build nests for their homes from twigs, straw, string, mud, or feathers.

A mother bird sits on the eggs in the nest.

The mother bird feeds the baby birds while they are in the nest.

Young birds learn to fly from their nest.

Since children accentuate their main idea

"Jumping Rope,"

By a Third-Grader.

by making it large, a nest and bird may fill the entire sheet. A branch or a few leaves may suggest a tree.

3. *Children having fun at a birthday party.*

> "What do children do at a birthday party?"
>
> "What did you do first?"
>
> "What did you play together?"
>
> "What did you wear at the birthday party?"

A "Happy Birthday" picture of gay colors would be charming painted on a large square shape and hung at the end of a hall-way; one subject could be Mary with her presents and many, many children all around her. Children will know how to paint a "Happy Birthday" picture.

4. *A child's day:* This subject is appropriate to be used in a booklet, giving each event a different page, or in a newspaper, with the important happenings to the child for each day told in pictures, with the teacher adding a few descriptive words related by the child.

5. *A typical school day* (chronological order):

> Dressing for school and eating breakfast with family.
>
> Saying good-bye to parents.
>
> Walking to school, perhaps with a group of children, or with a pet.
>
> Reading circle.
>
> Science experiment.
>
> All the children doing rhythms to music.
>
> Playing house.
>
> Modeling clay, painting, constructing.
>
> Sitting in the assembly room.
>
> Watching a moving picture about woods animals.
>
> Watching the kindergarten children play train or do rhythmic dancing.

A Clown

By Kathie, Grade One.

"Birds,"

By Barbara, Grade Two.

A Picnic

By a Third-Grader.

Eating lunch in the lunchroom, or going home for lunch.

Playing at recess.

Responsibilities in the classroom such as feeding and caring for the hen and her chickens in the pen; feeding and cleaning the water for the goldfish; watering the plants; putting the books in order.

Taking a piano, violin or dancing lesson after school.

Home with the family for dinner and the evening.

6. *Sunday:*

The family enjoying breakfast together.

Ready for Sunday School with a "best dress" or "suit."

Singing in Sunday School.

Going to Grandmother's in the afternoon.

All the family together.

Playing with the kittens.

Looking at the garden.

CHAPTER XII

Growth in Representation

CHILDREN WELL DEVELOPED in the symbolic stage can coordinate the handling of a tool with their thinking. They are ready for progressive steps within their understanding. Most classes have at least three groups of children at distinct phases of development.

Order of development in representing people. The child's first human figures are symbols for an idea, like primitive picture writing or sign language; symbols reduce a subject to its simplest form, without showing characteristics which differentiate it from others of its species.

First stage (five- and six-year-olds). The child considers the head most important. He sees with his eyes, talks and eats with his mouth. He makes the head important by making it a large round shape, bigger than any other.

Second stage (six- and seven-year-olds). The child becomes conscious of his two legs. He runs, jumps, climbs, and walks with his legs. He uses his arms for reaching

The two most prevalent practices which are cues to the teacher that a child needs to progress are a child's repeating of one form many times, and a dissatisfied child, who feels unable to put his ideas into the desired form. Repeating a symbol the child knows makes him feel secure.

DRAWING PEOPLE

and doing many different things. At first he draws arms and legs only as lines or loops.

Third stage (eight-year-olds). Hands are used to hold things, like a toy or food to be eaten. Hands catch a ball or grasp a jumping rope. The child often represents the palm of the hand as a circular shape with lines or loops, designating the fingers reaching out from the palm all the way around.

Feet are usually rounded forms or loops on the end of the legs. The child knows the foot is a long form starting at the end of the leg and extending out in one direction.

Each one of the above symbols represent growth in thinking. The child has progressed from meaningless scribbles and dabs to making meaningful shapes which have a definite character. They are honest, sincere representations of an idea. If the same type of rendering has been repeated a number of times, the children should be guided to think in terms of related ideas.

SAMPLE GROUP DISCUSSIONS

The following group discussions are suggested guides for the teacher for the period when children share ideas with each other. The purpose of discussion is to guide children to think while they see. You must never give the impression that a child's work is incorrect, or poorly done. Directing observation to details comes after the symbolic period, when the child desires realism in the third grade. Drawings of people should be of the total figure, not of single parts, except in portraits.

Suggestions for discussions for different days:

Discussion Number 1. Legs (Second Grade).

Teacher: "Why do we need *strong* legs?
"What do we *do* with our legs?
"How do our legs help us?"

Children answer (one at a time):
"I run fast."
"I play on the jungle gym."
"I kick a ball."
"I jump rope."

The children are given rhythmics to music in which they use their legs to swing back and forth for skipping, jumping, and running.

Teacher: "I'm sure the little child in Billy's picture likes to run and play. Do you think his legs will hold up his body?"

Billy: "I guess not. I'll make them wider."

Result of discussion of legs. Every healthy person has legs strong enough to support his body. In drawing or painting, wide spaces make stronger legs than narrow spaces.

Discussion Number 2. Arms (Second or Third Grade).

Teacher: "We have found out that we need strong legs to run and play. I wonder if our arms are important too. What can we do with our arms?
"Why do we need *strong* arms?"
"How do our arms help us?"

Children answer (one at a time):
"I carry my doll and sometimes hold my baby brother."
"I throw a ball."
"I can reach up high."
"My arms help me climb a tree."
"I put my arms around my mother."
"My arms go round and round when I turn the jumping rope."

To music that has a swinging movement the children bend their bodies, using their arms in a swaying motion, and swinging large wheels round and round with their arms.

Teacher: "Remember how we make things look strong?
"You will need strong arms to do all the things you have told about."

Discussion Number 3. Length of arm (Third Grade).

Teacher: "Now you are sitting down. I

see most of you have your hands in your lap. Mary said she used her arms to hold her doll. Mary, would you like to sit in this chair beside me and show how you hold your doll?" (Mary responds.)

The children see that Mary's forearm reaches from one side of her body to the other with her elbow coming to her waistline.

Teacher: "Each one of us can find out for himself how far he can reach if he stands up straight, with his arms close to his sides.

"See how far you can reach.

    A. "Above your head.

    B. "Out from each side of your body.

    C. "Down toward your feet.

"What did you find out today about your arms?"

Children answer in turns:

"They have to be strong to help us to carry things."

"They are long enough to reach above our head and down to our knees."

Teacher: "How do you make arms strong in your pictures?"

Child: "Make them wider."

Discussion Number 4. Shoulder (Third Grade).

Teacher: "Each day we have been thinking about how we can make some one part of our people stronger. One day we told all the things we do with our arms. I wonder where our arms are joined to our body? Harold thinks he knows. You stand up and show us, Harold."

"This Is Dolores When She Was a Baby,"
By Dolores, Grade One.

Growth in Representation / 109

(Harold points to where his arms join his shoulders.)

Teacher: "Billy, can you show us how long the shoulder is?"

(Billy runs his hand from his neck to the end of his shoulder to the place his arm is joined.)

Teacher: "Our shoulders are very important. They help our arms do things. How do you draw strong shoulders?"

Mary: "By drawing them thicker."

Teacher: "We do have a bigger bone in our shoulder than in our arm. We might say a wider shoulder, also.

"Does your shoulder come beyond your head?"

(The children observe a child's head and shoulder.)

Result of observation of shoulders. Our neck is joined to our shoulders. Our arms move from our shoulders. Our shoulders must be strong enough to carry the weight of our arms. We make our shoulders wider to make them stronger. Our shoulders extend beyond both sides of our head.

Discussion Number 5. Neck (Second and Third Grades).

Teacher: (Moves her head around with the children.)

"Do your heads feel heavy?"

"Do your heads feel tippy?"

"I wonder what you have to hold up your head?"

Mary: "We have a neck."

Teacher: "Let's all feel our necks to see how wide they are."

(The teacher places one hand on either side of her neck, directly below her ears and follows the line of her neck to its base at the shoulder.)

(The children do the same.)

The teacher observes that the younger the child is the shorter is his neck.

Teacher: "I wonder if the neck of the little girl in David's picture is strong enough to hold up her head?"

(David runs for his picture. Now he knows what to do to make it stronger.)

Things that are used for support must be strong. Everyone has a neck wide enough to support his head and long enough to turn his head from side to side. Our heads are smaller than the trunk of our body, so we do not feel tippy.

Comparing sizes and shapes (Third Grade). The simplest way for young children to paint or draw people is to use broad strokes for the masses or areas found in their clothing, head, arms, and legs.

Discussion Number 6. Relative sizes of different parts of the body (Third Grade).

Teacher: (The teacher uses a jointed doll for an observation lesson.)

"Mary brought her doll, Annabelle, to school today.

"Annabelle is just about the same age as the girls and boys in this room.

"Which part of Annabelle is the smallest; her head, her blouse, or her skirt?"

(The children answer, "Her head.")

The teacher chooses two boys and two girls to stand in front of the room for the others to observe their clothing.

Diana wears a white blouse and blue pleated skirt.

Suzanne wears a one-piece dress that hangs from her shoulders.

Jimmy wears a striped sweater with long blue pants.

David wears a leather jacket with long pants.

The children have on their desks colored papers 9" by 12" in cream manila, light orange, blue, brown, white, yellow and black, with a pair of scissors and paste.

Teacher: "How many have cut out clothes for paper dolls?

"Today instead of painting people you have colored paper to cut out clothing for the people you make. Each boy and girl in the front of the room wears a different shaped garment.

"Which is the larger shape — Diana's white blouse or her blue skirt?

"Which part of Diana's skirt is the narrower? The part around her waist or the part around the bottom?

"Skirts must be wide enough to give room for legs to jump and run.

"Look carefully to see the shape of Suzanne's dress. Find the part that is the narrowest and the part that is the widest.

"Jimmy and David have long pants. Will they be longer than the girls' skirts?

"Which part do you think the light orange paper is for?"

The children:

"The head."

Teacher: "You can cut different kinds of clothes for boys and girls. Think of colors that you like together. When all your clothes are finished, place them on the manila paper and paste them down. Add the head, then cut the figure out. A long strip of paper is on the bulletin board. This is for your finished paper people. When several are ready, you can move them about to make a nice group, then pin them to the paper."

Jane: "May we make hair and hats?"

Teacher: "Of course, you may use your colors for anything you need. See how big you can cut your shapes out of the paper you have. Remember the parts that are biggest and the ones that are smaller."

Legs and arms may be made of cut paper or painted onto background paper. The children add a background, also, of cut paper, to represent the place they would like the people to be, such as a city or park, or as spectators at a parade or game.

After doing this the children are more aware of related areas of sizes and shapes in people as well as of harmonious color combinations.

Drawing or painting the human figure (Third Grade). As an aid to focusing attention on large proportions, give children vertical sheets of paper corresponding to proportion of the figure from head to feet, about 8" by 18". They draw the figure the width and length of the paper.

The family. Members of the child's family are very close to him, and he is likely to exaggerate something that impresses him the most. It may be a flowered dress, a fresh curl from the beauty parlor, an apron, or a new coat. Perhaps the glasses their father wears, his bald head or certain clothing makes him seem very important to the child. The younger the child is, the more his attention is focused on one thing at a time.

Growth in Representation / 111

See color illustration, My Friends, Grade 3, following page 98.

Discussion Number 7. Position of legs (Second and Third Grades). The child knows legs come below a dress but not just where. The position of the legs is unimportant unless the child recognizes the legs in his drawing placed at the extreme right and left of the skirt are not like those of his classmates and he asks for help. In response the teacher asks Ruth and Jerry to stand up in front of the room. The teacher holds a yardstick from Jerry's chin to the floor.

"The Family,"

By a Third-Grader.

> *Teacher:* "Where are Jerry's legs?"
>
> *Mary:* "They are right under his chin."
>
> *Teacher:* (The teacher holds a yardstick from Ruth's chin to the floor.)
> "Where are Ruth's legs?"
>
> *David:* "They are in the middle, too."
>
> *Teacher:* "Ruth's skirt goes around her legs. See how far her skirt goes beyond her legs on either side."

Results of observation of placement of legs. When children have noticed that skirts go around the body and extend out beyond the legs they will draw them that way, if they are concerned about the position of the legs or their function. This does not need to come until the end of the third grade. You must be careful not to draw the child's attention to details before he is concerned with them.

Discussion Number 8. Walking (Second and Third Grades).

> *Teacher:* "It is hard for us to see running legs because they move so fast. Is the movement different for running legs than for walking legs?
> "The best way to find out is for us to watch children

walk and then watch them run. What parts of the leg do they bend? Does the position of the body change? What do they do with their arms?

"We need four boys who are good walkers."

(David, Jimmy, Harold, and Paul walk across the room.)

The children observe the following:

When the right leg is forward the left is back, the right leg is straight and the left leg is slightly bent at the knee and ankle. All the children walk in a rhythmic step across the room. They discover they feel better if they swing the whole body, including arms, with each step. The arm swings forward with the forward movement of the leg on the same side.

Children use the broad side of the chalk on a piece of newsprint to swing in the walking lines. One line starts at the neck and goes down to the toe. After their lines seem to move in a rhythmic way, they add width and make the lines into many walking people.

Discussion Number 9. Running (Second and Third Grades).

Teacher: "Yesterday we made walking legs. Today we will find out how to make running legs."

The children observe the body position of a running boy.

With each stride the body stays forward while one leg at a time is bent at the knee. Most runners bend their arms at the elbow. That helps them to push forward.

Teacher: "Today we will make many running lines. Remember we bend our legs much higher for running than for walking. Our body leans further toward the front. It

"Going for a Walk,"

By Deborah, Grade One.

is fun to run and feel the wind on our faces.

"You can make a nice border of people running."

Discussions coupled with observation of other positions of people doing things such as sitting, bending over and reaching are given as the need arises. A brief guide for observation of children of these body positions follows:

Sitting in a chair

Teacher: "See where Mary bends her body at her hip and at her knee to fit the chair. People usually sit in a chair for a reason, such as to read, to eat, to hold a baby or to watch television."

What they are doing is for each child to decide for himself.

Bending over

Teacher: "What things do people do that cause them to bend over?"

Response might be to pick up a ball, to pick a flower or to dig with a shovel.

Teacher: "To do these things you would have to bend a little way for some things and a long way for others. You can show in your drawing what the people bending over are doing."

Reaching

Teacher: "Think of all the things you do in which you reach for something. You can reach up high, down low or out to your side. Do you bend your bodies or your arm when you reach?"

A reaching picture needs to have something people are reaching for or perhaps holding like a painter with a brush.

"Skating,"

By Jennifer, Grade Three.

"PEOPLE DOING THINGS"
(Second and Third Grade)

The teacher might say to the children:
"People are made so they can do many things.
People are long so they can walk through
doors and see things above the ground. People have long arms to help them to reach
up high, to pick apples from a tree, or to
reach out in front, as to catch a ball. People
have long legs so they can run, jump, and
climb. If you watch people doing things,
you will see just where people bend."

***"Think about where you bend your own
body*** — when you sit in a chair, when you
hold a doll or kitten in your lap, when you
go up and down steps, when you touch
your toes. You have to bend your arms, legs,
and body to do all of these things. You are
made just right for doing many things."

People doing things in a picture. Suggest that the children represent in a picture
the people in their own families, themselves
and their playmates, or just of the child
alone doing something he likes to do.

Show the children how to push up with
the broad side of the crayon to make a
body, making it strong and wide, and how
to push out from the body for the arms and
legs. Point out that the direction of the
crayon stroke must change in the places
where people bend, doing things.

Suggest they try making many people
doing different things, all over the paper.
If they like one or two people very much,
suggest they fill the whole sheet of paper,
leaving no part empty.

Another day the people doing things
might all be in a row, one after another,
for a border.

Many children working together can
make a decoration for their wall on a long
piece of wrapping paper, of people doing
things. Each person may reach from the
bottom of the paper to the top.

"Pushing-out people," *with chalk.*
Second and Third Grade.

CUT-OUT PAINTING ON CUT-PAPER MURAL

Joyce, a First-Grader, is pinning the child she has painted and cut out to the cut-paper mural.
By a First Grade.

"A FUNNY MAN TO MAKE PEOPLE LAUGH"
(Second Grade)

The teacher might say to the children:
"*A funny man first must be a surprise —* someone no one has ever seen before. He must be big, so everyone can quickly see he is a funny man."

"*Some funny men do tricks* — stand on their heads, jump like frogs, waddle like ducks. No one is to see your funny man until you are all finished. Then he will be a surprise."

Pass out tall pieces of paper 12″ by 18″, and remind children that colors like bright green or red will make a funny man different in color than any real man.

"SOMETHING YOU LOVE TO HOLD"
(Second Grade)

The teacher might say to the children:
"You are holding something in your hands. Your hands have fingers that go all around what you are holding. Think of things you love to hold, so you can feel their shape or softness, like kittens."

"Sometimes you sit down and other times you stand up to hold things. Think of something you love to hold. If you keep it a secret everyone can guess what it is when they look at your picture. The paper will help you out, if it goes up and down.

Think about where you are and what is around you when you are holding something you love to hold.

"To make what you are holding so

everyone can see it easily, make it a different color from the background. Remember, what you are holding is a secret."

Place drawing paper 12″ x 18″ in dark and light colors, crayon and chalk, on the supply table. First choose your paper then the color of chalk or crayon you think is best to make you and what you are holding important. Choose those colors you like together.

CUT-OUT FIGURES ARRANGED FOR A BULLETIN BOARD

By a First Grade.
Cut-out figures arranged for a bulletin board. These happy, active children were painted by First-Graders. The animals in the merry-go-round express the same joyous feeling.

Growth in Representation / 117

CHAPTER XIII

The Community

A COMMUNITY SATISFIES people's needs in many ways. How families work together and help each other in the community provides subjects for individual pictures, border designs, murals, sand tables, booklets, or a community map.

A group discussion between the children and the teacher, about merchants, or workers for public services, before each art period stimulates thinking. Questions may be answered by pictures instead of words.

Trips help children form a visual image of things they wish to portray. They need stimulating experiences that give them the feel of things to awaken their vision. Seeing helps clarify the meaning of words, helps prove the reality of points discussed and adds many new experiences.

PREPARATION FOR A TRIP

THE TEACHER'S PLANNING for a trip should include:

A guide for the observation of important things of interest to the child.

A rough list of good questions to help the children understand how things work or are used. Suggestions for good conduct are given.

SUGGESTIONS FOR TRIPS OF INTEREST TO PRIMARY GRADE CHILDREN

Observation of how things grow: vegetable gardens, and greenhouses with their potted plants.

Observation of how things work: a bull-dozer with its large blade digging dirt; the bakery with its big ovens, kneading machines, and belt of moving bread; the newspapers going over big rollers; the canned milk plants with rows of bottles and big separators.

Observation of the way things are planned to fill our needs.

The barber shop with the chairs that turn around; the big mirror where children can watch the barber cut their hair; the counter in front holding vari-colored bottles.

Food stores.

"How many different kinds of food stores do you know about?"

"How does the storekeeper separate different kinds of food?" (Some need to be kept cold, some damp, some under glass.)

"In large stores a cart is furnished to help shoppers. Does your baby brother or sister sometimes ride in the front of the cart?"

Clothing stores.

"How are clothes separated in a clothing store?"

"What are some different kinds of clothing?"

Hardware stores.

"What tools are used by carpenters, plumbers, electricians, engineers, farmers?"

Ask questions about how things are made to do a specific kind of work, such as a shovel to dig and hold dirt, household appliances such as vacuum cleaners to suck up dirt; furniture, such as chairs needed for sitting.

A store as the subject for a painting.
The outside edge of the paper may represent the walls of one department or one kind of store, thus offering space for the child to clearly depict the contents to illustrate the kind of store. A few representative objects, clearly and simply made by the children, can explain the kind of merchandise sold in each different store.

"What I Saw at the Bakery,"
By Chris, Grade Two.

DIFFERENT KINDS OF PUBLIC SERVICE

EXPLAIN TO THE CHILDREN that railway stations are planned for people traveling from place to place by train, that bus stations are planned for people traveling by bus, that fire stations, fire trucks and firemen, are needed for fire safety and that in post offices men sort letters and packages from many different places into compartments and bags for the postman to deliver to people. All these are good subjects for pictures, as are banks, police stations, parks, and libraries and trips to any of these places provide stimulating experiences for children to draw upon for creative expression.

SAMPLE TRIPS

Houses.

Interest — Every child knows about houses because he lives in one. He has built walls with building blocks, cardboard, or sand. Conversation at home often concerns the construction or repairing of some part of the house.

Observation and discussion of buildings furnish ideas for pictures. Going for a walk in the immediate neighborhood gives the children the opportunity to see different kinds of buildings. The teacher should direct observation to the details on the outside of a building and to what they tell us about the building, such as:

The horizontal rows of windows can tell us the number of stories high a building is.

The exterior tells us some of the materials used in the building, which may be lumber, brick, glass, shingle, stucco, or others.

Chimneys tell us the location of the stoves and fireplace.

Doors tell us the number of entrances.

"At the Post Office,"
a sand-table project, Grade Two.

"Men Working at the Post Office,"
By Bonnie, Grade Two.

Roofs vary both in materials and in slants.

Buildings differ widely in shapes and sizes. Some houses are irregular in shape with parts extending out from the main section, or recessed back allowing rooms to have windows on both sides. Apartment houses and office buildings are much higher than they are wide. Large grocery stores are much wider than they are high.

Observation of the ways different buildings are planned according to their function helps the child think and express ideas in visual form.

A garage needs an entrance wider than a car or truck.

A service station needs a place beside the gas pumps for cars.

A library needs room for many shelves of books.

A church needs room for many people. Some churches have brightly colored windows.

A house needs a door large enough for people and furniture to enter.

Some houses have an inside court. In warm weather families enjoy eating outside. Children may safely play in this area, away from the street.

Additions may be added to a house for a woodshed, a garage, a play room, workshop, or extra bedroom.

Seeing a building being constructed is close to the child's play experiences with building blocks, dump trucks, steam shovels, and other mechanical toys.

The child sees all sides of the building as well as the machinery that is used in building, such as the steam shovel, derrick, hoist, crane, rivet gun, and truck.

The bulldozer scoops up load after load of dirt in its big mouth. It turns around to dump its load. Trucks carry the dirt away.

"Children Going to School,"
By Holly, Grade One.

The cement mixer turns round and round as cement is mixed and poured into forms.

Seeing the carpenter, bricklayer, and painter at work helps the child form a visual image of the way they dress and the tools they use.

The carpenter wears an apron with compartments for his hammer, nails, and ruler. He uses a level and square to be sure all his supports are straight.

The bricklayer places each brick very carefully one above another so the wall will be straight. Children have discovered this themselves when they have built walls with blocks.

The painter, in his white cap, sits on a long plank suspended by heavy ropes fastened to big hooks. His pail of paint is beside him as he strokes a large brush full of paint over the wall. The child feels an inward pride because he also can paint with a brush.

Class discussion following the trip. Children enjoy telling each other about their own house or one they have visited. Guide the discussion to emphasize the use of different rooms and the need for different parts, such as the windows, doors, roof, and chimney. The same material the children use for clay modeling is used for tiles and pipes.

BULLETIN BOARD

Well-labeled samples of different building materials are valuable to familiarize children with various kinds of wood, wall boards, plastics, and other materials.

The plan and building of the playhouse is suggested as a good activity to follow the observation of a building under construction (see pages 21, 22).

Using buildings as a subject for pictures

"Steam Shovel,"

By Mark, Grade Two.

"Tractor,"

By Carl, Grade Two.

in crayon, chalk, or paint. A house is one of the first representations a child makes. The house needs a door to enter, windows to see out, a roof to cover it, and a chimney for the smoke from the fire. These are the essentials to the child.

The preceding observations of buildings, if made by the child when he is mature enough to see differences of sizes and shapes, will gradually be added to his first symbol for a house.

The second-grader is ready to make houses along a street, with people, vehicles, and trees added.

Many third-grade children paint houses on either side of the street by first painting them on one side of the street and then turning their paper around, they paint the houses on the opposite side.

Practically all interesting activities are carried on inside a building. To enable the child to show what happens inside a building, suggest he leave the walls out, with the outside edge of the paper becoming the boundary of the room. In this space the child draws in detail things people do in the room.

The following guide for stroke direction is suggested for a group discussion (after children have full muscular control). Second Grade.

Teacher: "How does the carpenter build the frame for a house? Remember the way you built your playhouse?"

A child draws a frame on the blackboard. The first supports are up and down. (Strokes are easier to make from the top to bottom.)

Painting the walls. Strokes of the brush or crayon made from left to right, the same way the boards are nailed to the frame, make it possible for the child to see his brush and thus guide his stroke. Paper left

"The Bricklayer,"

By a First-Grader.

showing between the strokes shows how the house is built. Walls of stucco or cement may be one big area of color. The space is covered with paint using strokes from left to right or from top to bottom.

Windows and doors may be filled in with solid color, left the color of the paper, or outlined.

Helping children grow in expression. The child who repeats the same box-like shape over and over may be stimulated to grow in expression by such comments or questions from the teacher as these:

"What are the different rooms used for in your home?"

"Is there more than one room in the front of your house?"

"Why do houses have windows?"

"Are the windows different sizes in different rooms?"

"Do some rooms have more than one window on one wall?"

"Does your house have more than one story?"

"Where are the doors in your house?"

"What room do you enter through the front door?"

"Do you have to go upstairs to your front or back door or is it on the same level as the ground?"

"Is there a porch on one side of your house?"

"What trees and flowers will make your house more beautiful?"

"Why do people need fences?"

"Does your house have a garage?"

PEOPLE IN THE COMMUNITY WHO HELP FAMILIES

THE VISUAL APPEARANCES of people serving the community within a child's experience can be described, to serve as subjects for individual pictures, for a mural, or a moving picture.

The milkman stands in his wagon with rows of bottles of milk and cream. He carries the container with compartments for milk bottles to each house as he delivers milk.

The postman carries his mail sack over his shoulder delivering letters and packages to each house along the street. Some people have mail boxes on a post by the side of the road. Others have mail boxes by their front doors.

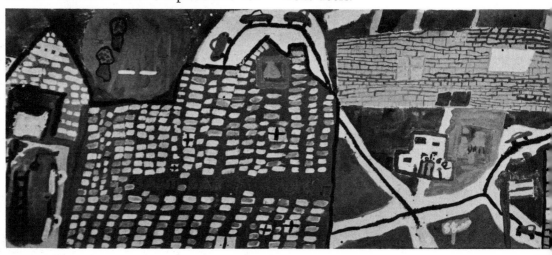

"Houses,"

By a Second-Grader.

The fireman wears a big hat while he drives his long fire truck which is filled with hose and long ladders.

The service station attendant uses a long hose to fill the gas tank.

The policeman may wear a belt and high boots while he directs traffic on a busy street.

The garbage collector dumps large cans of garbage into his truck. Sometimes wash tubs, dish pans, and shovels are fastened to the outside of the truck.

The moving men drive big vans full of furniture to the new family in the neighborhood. They move large pieces like pianos on rollers.

The workmen with big snowplows scoop up the snow on the streets and highways. Large cities have trucks with moving belts to carry the snow into a large truck. The large truck dumps the snow into a river or other place where it will melt.

The street cleaners sweep refuse into a cart with a stiff broom, along the street.

The bus driver drives a big bus full of people. Mothers hold children on their laps. Some people stand, their hands holding the bar above their heads.

The newsboy carries a bag of papers

"Our Neighborhood" (a mural painted in powder paint),

By a Second Grade.

PEOPLE IN THE COMMUNITY

A group project made by Third-Graders in connection with the study of clothing.
The people were cut from cardboard then colored with crayon. The children sewed cloth to make
the garments. Each child had a specific person in mind, such as their own father, mother, brother,
or sister. The painted houses were placed with grouped figures to make a unified arrangement.

from house to house as he delivers papers. Children know other people who help, such as those who come to their houses to fix pipes, lights, or furnaces.

PLAY EXPERIENCE
(Used as a Motivation)

A CAR, TRUCK, OR TRAIN

FROM BABYHOOD CHILDREN have been attracted by toy cars, trucks, and trains that run on wheels. Children make tracks in the sand, pushing their cars from place to place with loads of lumber, pebbles, or sand.

A train holds a fascination for a child, with its many cars joined together and pulled by a puffing engine that whistles at every station. Sometimes a group of children can buy their own tickets for a small amount and take a trip to the next town.

The train (Kindergarten, First and Second Grade). One day a new child named Joan comes to school. She tells the children how she came to town by train. A visit to a railroad station is decided upon so the whole class may see a real train and what happens in a station.

The railroad station.

Observations inside the railway station.

...he Fireman,"

By Jerry, Grade Three.

"At the Gas Station,"

By Ila, Grade Two.

...he Policeman,"

By Patty, Grade Two.

"The Postman Comes to Our House,"
By Jane, Grade Two.

gooseneck trailer

automobile carrier

snow plow

livestock truck

KINDS OF TRUCKS

By a Second Grade.

People are eating at lunch counters.

Toys, books candy and gifts are in glass cases in one corner with people looking at or buying them.

The agent sells tickets behind a cage-like window.

People put luggage into lockers for safekeeping.

People look at large maps to find the places they are going on the train.

Redcaps carry luggage for the people going on the train.

People read, mothers care for their children, and some people sleep on benches.

Observations outside the station.

A train comes in with smoke puffing and its whistle blowing.

A high fence has several gates, each one for a different train.

A conductor announces a train's arrival.

Children, mothers, fathers, grandparents, watch the train come in and wave their hands to people coming to see them.

Carts carry the mail and baggage for people going on the trains.

Redcaps push carts full of baggage unloaded from the train.

Subjects for dramatic play, pictures, and construction. After children have observed a train, they will enjoy building one with blocks and boxes, with perhaps a barrel for the engine. The children can sit in the train they have built, which may include a diner,

elgin sweeper

city bus

pick-up truck

cement mixer

KINDS OF TRUCKS

By a Second Grade.

sleeping car, observation, and baggage car. There are endless possibilities in this play experience. If space is limited, the cars may change names and functions every few days.

A mural (see page 130). A passenger train with many cars is a logical subject for a mural. Kindergarten and first-grade children enjoy painting the engine pulling many cars. The real-life order of cars influences their placement on the mural. First comes the engine at the far left or right, and heading toward the edge of the paper, next the coal car, the baggage car, tourist car, diner, sleeping car and lounge. To show how each car is used, the children leave the front wall off the car and fill the space in with what happens inside the car.

Freight trains have many different kinds of cars. They are built to carry lumber, animals, grain, fruit, and machinery. The child paints the framework for the front wall of each car, then paints the inside with its contents.

The delightful way children make the railway track, with the rows of wooden ties in a vertical position, adds to the design of the picture. Second-grade children may wish to show where the train is going, with buildings or landscape above and in front of the train.

The shapes children draw for their cars are the same as their building blocks, with the same basic strokes as the house. The interest span of the children determines the number of details the children add to their train mural.

MURAL
By a Second Grade.

A Sample Discussion: "Where the Train Goes"
(Second Grade)

The teacher might say to the children:

"*Have you thought about where the train goes?*"

"If you have taken a ride on a train you can show, in your picture, where the train went. Bridges help trains go over rivers. Snowplows help trains go through the mountains, covered with snow. Trains go under big cities in tunnels."

"*Trains go almost every place* — over mountains, over farmland, over water, through cities."

"A picture telling *where the train goes* may have the train with all its cars travelling through the places you know about."

"*Where the train goes* may fill all the picture without the train in the picture."

"A wide sheet of paper will give you room to make a train with cars joined together."

"First, paint the place the train goes. Use colors you like to see out-of-doors."

"When this part of your picture is dry, paint the train, with a dark color, where you want the train to be!" Trains have cars for sleeping, eating, and for baggage.

A Sample Project: Children Construct Their Community
(Third Grade)

I. Materials:

For the foundation or the ground (one of the the following).

A sheet of plywood, insulation board, wall board, or double-faced corrugated cardboard approximately four feet by five or six feet.

A sheet of heavy wrapping paper.

A sand table box.

For the construction of the buildings.

Boxes of different sizes.

Cardboard or heavy paper.

Blocks of wood.

For plants.

Twigs, dried plants, sponge, burlap, colored paper, wire, cloth.

For animals and people.

Modeled clay, plasticine, salt and flour or sawdust and wheat paste mixture.

Covered wire or pipe cleaners used for bodies with wooden beads or cork for heads.

II. Making the plan for the streets, and locating the buildings and park areas. The sheet of material to be used for the ground is placed on the floor away from traffic, or

MURAL

By a Second Grade.

on a table top. Strips of gray, black, or brown paper are placed on top of the ground to represent streets running north and south and east and west, one block apart. The teacher helps the children with the names of the streets.

III. The areas for different kinds of buildings are located on the map.

IV. Suggestions for grouping children to work on different sections of construction.

Buildings for residential area: homes, library, post office, park, school, church, fire station.

Buildings for business and shopping area: food stores, gas stations, clothing stores, business offices, hardware stores.

The ground and streets.

The park with its trees and play areas.

Have the children observe the characteristic shape of each different kind of building or the way it is built to serve a need.

V. Suggestions for colors of paint or colored paper.

Colors for buildings — The color of the buildings should be a lighter or darker value than the ground — in related colors such as orange-brown, yellow-orange, yellow, brown; or white, gray, and black with one primary color; or gray tones of middle value and lighter. Windows might be a lighter or darker value of the wall color.

Colors for ground — different kinds of green, such as yellow-green, green, apple green, blue-green; or different kinds of brown, such as golden brown, chocolate brown, red-brown, or a lighter value of the last two.

VI. The children place the finished buildings on the ground plan.

VII. When the areas are completed, details of landscaping, people, and forms of transportation are added.

"The Roundhouse,"

By Steven, Grade Two.

"Freight Trains,"

By Grant, Grade Three.

DIFFERENT WAYS TO USE ART MATERIALS

A Sample Project: "Our Neighborhood"

Paper background.

1. Cut-paper shapes to represent buildings and people are pasted to a paper background.
2. Details are crayoned in on colored paper shapes which are used for buildings, trees, and people.
3. Paint is used for the background, with cut-out painted people and trees made to stand out in relief in front of the buildings.

Felt background.

1. A neutral color of flannel or felt is used for a background stretched on a wooden board.
2. Streets are made with yarn or string stretched between pins on the flannel board.
3. Symbolic shapes for buildings, people, and trees are cut out of flannel or felt. These are placed on the felt board.

For each of the above projects the ground is made first, then the streets, buildings, plants and people are added.

Encourage use of a light color over a dark color and a dark color over a light color. Colored papers offer the opportunity to group colors and see them together before the details are worked out.

A cardboard box used for a community. Cardboard strips are extended from one side of a box to the other to show buildings one behind another. This construction gives a feeling of objects standing in space. It occupies little space, making it a desirable project for a small classroom.

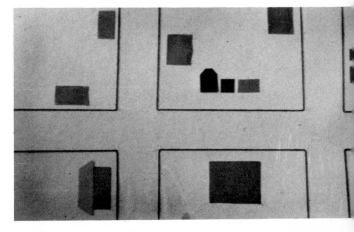

"A Community Map,"

By a Second Grade.

A. Detail to show the way a box is cut.

B. Stiff cardboard is cut in strips two inches longer than the width of the box. The side view is photographed to show the variation in the height of the cardboard strips, as well as the way they are inserted across the cut slits on the sides of the box. *Note* — As the cards go back they are higher to enable the viewer to see one part behind another.

A subject is chosen which either has related ideas with some objects in front and some farther back, or a subject concerned with different elevations such as a valley and a mountain.

The subject for this construction is "Where The Train Goes." The cut-outs from children's drawings are taped to the cardboard strips which separate different distances back.

In front are houses along the street with people in front of them. The back of the man's legs are fastened to the front of the box, and the front of the girl's legs are fastened to the opposite side of the same strip. The third figure is drawn on the house.

The back of the folded houses are fastened to the first cardboard strip, the train is fastened to the second strip, and the tree to the third strip. The landscape showing planted hills is fastened to a cardboard projecting up from the back of the box.

This type of construction is meant to be viewed from the front.

It is very important to have light colors against dark colors, and plain areas of color against patterned areas in order to separate one object from another.

LIVE WILD ANIMALS may be observed in a zoo or in a circus. If this is not possible films, slides, or book illustrations are substitutes.

Guided observation of animals gives children information they need for grouping different kinds of animals, learning what they do, and their characteristics. This information helps children form visual images of animals which they use as subjects for art experiences. The following suggestions will help children observe animals:

Different kinds of animals are separated from each other in cages or by fences.

Animals differ in sizes; some are large, small, very tall, or very fat.

Some animals need to live where it is warm; others where it is cold.

Some animals like to hide in caves.

Some animals live in water.

Some animals climb trees; some climb over large rocks or up mountains.

Some animals fly.

Monkeys do tricks.

Animals have different coverings; some have feathers, others have fur, others have hide.

Different kinds of animals eat different kinds of food.

Children can ride on ponies, horses, elephants, and camels.

A kangaroo carries its baby in its pouch.

CHIEF CHARACTERISTICS TO POINT OUT ABOUT A FEW ANIMALS

Elephants are the biggest land animals. Their bodies are heavy, thick, and gray. Their legs are quite short but wide enough to support their heavy bodies. Their broad feet are rounded in shape with five toes on each foot. The elephant bends his knee as he walks, and his knee is low on his leg. African elephants have very large ears, like rhubarb leaves, small eyes, and short tails.

Children notice first the elephant's long trunk, which is its nose and upper lip, and is a little longer than the distance from its head to the ground. Point out that the trunk is what makes an elephant different from any other animal. Children can see a few of the important things elephants do with their trunks: they reach high into trees to get food; they reach down into water, without bending over; fill their trunks with water; raise their trunks overhead and spray water on their bodies. Elephants use their trunks like hands and arms, for carrying things, even some things as heavy as lumber. An elephant lifts a boy or girl up on its back by curving the end of its trunk like a swing on which the girl or boy sits or stands. Elephants guide their babies with their trunks. They can stand on their hind legs and lift their front legs up in the air with their trunks curved above their heads.

Children's pictures can show the things elephants do with their trunks.

Lions belong to the cat family, as children may know. The male lion has long thick fur, called a mane around his face like a frame. It makes his head very important. The fur on the rest of his body is short and sandy colored. A changing curve continues down a lion's back to the end of its long tail, which has a tuft of fur. The beauty of this graceful curve is easily seen because of the short fur on the lion's body.

Children like to make a front view of a lion's head, showing its beautiful mane. See

"Lion,"

By Bill, Grade Three.

"The King,"

By Bobby, Grade One.

"Two Giraffes,"

By Jimmy, Grade One.

color illustration, following page 98.

Giraffes are the tallest animals. They have long front legs and very long necks for reaching high up into trees for their dinner of leaves. When a giraffe wishes to drink water from a pool or eat grass he spreads his feet far apart to reach the ground. Giraffes run very fast with their long, slender legs.

Point out the sloping line down the neck, along the back to the short tail, and that the front legs are longer than the hind legs. This is one way the giraffe differs from other animals. Their light brown hides with brown spots look like sunlight in the trees. This is the way nature protects them.

Children can show the giraffe's long slender body, with its pattern of brown spots.

Camels are very useful animals. They live in places where the sun is very hot, the ground is covered with sand, and there is practically no water. A camel is made to live in a desert — the hump on the camel's back is filled with fat which it uses for food, long eyelashes keep the sand out of the camel's eyes, and its body is covered with hair which protects it from heat and sand storms. Long slender legs help it walk long distances.

"Ways the camel helps people" are good subjects for children's pictures.

Camels carry people and loads as far as one hundred miles a day.

Camels give milk people drink.

Camels' hair is woven into cloth.

Boys and girls may ride on a camel's back. Some camels have two humps with a nice place to sit in between.

Monkeys perform acrobatic stunts on hoops, which children love to watch, hang from limbs of trees, and jump from one place to another. Their long slim bodies with long arms, legs, and tails help them move about quickly and easily. Monkeys use their arms and feet very much the way boys and girls use theirs. The mother monkey sits up and holds her baby in her arms. Monkeys hold peanuts in their hands to eat. They can wrap their long tails around a pole and swing from one place to another. They can also pick up things that they cannot reach with their feet or hands with their long tails.

"Monkeys Doing Tricks" would be a good title for a picture.

A SAMPLE PROJECT: RESULTING FROM A TRIP TO THE ZOO

Animals in cages.

a. Boxes are used for the animal cages.

b. Vegetation to represent the environment can be cardboard construction, papier-mâché, cut paper, sponges, or real materials such as trees, made from twigs or dried plants. Or the environment may be painted on paper the correct size to fit the back and sides of the box.

c. Model the animals in clay, plasticine, papier-mâché, or a sawdust mixture and place them in their environment.

(See Animals in Clay, page 267, Papier-Mâché, page 226.)

A moving picture. A subject is chosen extensive enough to give each child an opportunity to contribute a picture to it. Examples: Animals with different coverings, animals that fly, animals that live in water, or a combination of a number of subjects.

a. Each child paints or draws in crayon on drawing paper a picture of one animal showing what that animal likes to do. The picture must fit the opening of the movie

"Other Animals Seen in the Zoo"
(Merry-go-round paper construction)
Grade Two. Class project.

"Circus Parade,"
By a Second Grade, cut-paper mural. Clas
projec

box — for example, a 15½″ by 20½″ picture will fit an opening 15″ by 20″. The frame around the front of the movie box must overlap the edge of the picture slightly.

b. The pictures are fastened to a long strip of heavy paper to be rolled through a movie box (see Movie Box, page 145).

A booklet about wild animals. A division page is used to separate each different kind of animal. Drawings or paintings are made by children for each different animal that would be classified under one of the groups below.

Grouping of animals to accentuate the different kinds.

Animals that fly.
Animals that swim.
Animals that climb trees.
Animals that are very large.

"Zoo Animals,"
By a First Grade, painted mural. Class project.

Animals that live where it is very cold or hot.

Clay modeling. Children begin with a cylindrical lump of plastic clay. Parts, such as for the head and ears, are pushed out from the mass. Parts are dug out, like be- tween the legs. The child keeps the form compact so it will be solid and feel good to hold.

Bulky animals such as the bear, lion, seal, and elephant are the best subjects for children to model in clay.

A SAMPLE PROJECT: "MAKING A 'DISCOVERY' PICTURE"
(Grade Two and Three)

The teacher might say to the children: "Think of some animal."

"Does it have a long neck?"

"If so, what can it do? Eat leaves from a tree? Stretch out and come back like a spring?"

"Does it have a long tail?"

"Can it push itself around with its tail?"

"Can it brush flies off its nose, with its tail?"

"Does it have long legs?"

"Does it jump, with its legs?"

"Does it fold its legs up, when it sits down?"

"Does it have a big mouth?"

"Does it have long, sharp teeth?"

"Does its mouth look like a broad smile?"

"What animals have wings for flying in

in the sky? What others have feet for paddling in the water?"

"What animal has a long trunk to lift boys and girls on to its back for a ride?"

"*Close your eyes.* Think about one animal. Do not tell anyone the animal you have chosen."

"*First, have a picture in your mind of your animal's head* with eyes for seeing, ears for hearing, and a mouth for eating. Is its body long or short? Does it have long claws or feet like paddles, or another kind of feet? Does it have a long swishy tail?"

Give each child a sheet of white paper 14″ by 17″ or 12″ by 20″ and a black, shiny crayon for drawing. Tell them that the sheet of paper is where "your animal lives," and have them make an animal, in the center, as large as they can, and tell us, in the picture, all they know about the animal they chose.

This is called a "Discovery" picture, because everyone can have fun guessing the animal you have chosen to make. It can be a new kind of animal with a new name.

"A Small Bear Climbing a Tree,"
By Harry, Grade Two.

"Tiger,"

By Dennie, Grade Two.

SOME ANIMALS DONE IN CLAY

By Second-Graders.

CHAPTER XIV

Related Subjects for Group Projects

BOOKLETS CHILDREN CAN MAKE

A BOOK IS MADE BY BINDING sheets of paper together. A child's first booklet may be one or two sheets of folded paper fastened together. The name or title belongs on the cover. The booklet should have one subject.

MATERIALS FOR BOOKLETS

The cover may be of brown wrapping paper, wallpaper scraps, butcher paper, discarded window shades, colored construction paper, option bristle, or cloth.

Inside sheets may be typing paper, lined paper, mimeograph newspaper, wrapping paper, shelf paper, or drawing paper.

For fastening sheets together you need a needle and a thread — such as heavy cord, yarn, raffia, leather thongs, or strips of cloth that will not ravel — or staples. Punched pages may be held together with rings.

CONSTRUCTING BOOKLETS

1. *Single-section booklet.* Cover paper, 12″ by 18″, is folded in half. One sheet of inside paper, 12″ by 17″, is folded in half.

Place folded inside sheet inside the cover. Punch holes 2 inches from top and bottom. Punch one hole in center. Thread, yarn, or raffia is drawn through the punched holes, the end of the thread passed under the first top loop, and the two ends then are tied.

2. *Double-fold booklet.* Fold single-section booklet in half. This makes a quarter fold. Fold and fit cover paper. Allow about ½ inch on all sides of quarter fold. Sew in center the same as for a single fold. Cut folded ends of inside quarter fold.

3. *Accordion booklet.* A strip of paper

27″ by 8½″ makes five pages in an accordion booklet that measures 5½″ by 8½″.

The first fold is 5½ inches from one end. The children match the top of the fold-over end with the top of the paper underneath and hold the two pieces together, then crease the fold from top to bottom. Turn the paper over. The width of the folded sheet is a guide for the second fold which comes opposite the cut end of the first sheet. The child continues folding back and forth.

Covers. Two pieces of cardboard **6** inches by 9 inches are pasted to the front and back sheets for covers *a* and *b*. An accordion book is suitable for a class project. A single sheet may easily measure 18 inches by 24 inches. An accordion book made of heavy paper may stand on a table or shelf.

PLANNING THE BOOKLET'S CONTENTS

THE FIRST OUTSIDE PAGE is the cover. A cover tells what the booklet is about. Each page should tell something new about the subject.

First have each child choose a subject he knows about. Then he letters the subject on the cover, using words about one inch high. A border design, all-over stamped pattern, finger paint, or a symbol to represent the subject may be used with the words on the cover.

The child picks different things he can tell about his subject, and uses one picture to describe one idea on each page. On the page opposite he may tell in writing about his idea, or his picture may express all he has to say.

The color the child uses may be purely for enjoyment or he may use the colors he has seen in the objects he is drawing. The important consideration is that he uses colors that make him feel good and that clearly define his idea such as colors easily seen on the background color he has chosen.

Colored crayon or colored pencils are good for illustrations. If the paper the child uses does not have a pressed shiny surface, watercolors may be used over parts of the crayon drawing.

The following are a few subjects children have chosen for booklets coupled with means the teacher used to make the child sensitive to the subject as experience.

Jimmy chose, *"Animals That Live in Different Places."*

Teacher: "Jimmy, have you seen an animal's home, the home that the animal has made?" "Tell us about it."

Answers might be — A beaver's home in the water made of branches.

A bird's nest in a tree made of mud or other material.

Teacher: "Does an animal's covering help us to know where the animal lives?"

Answer — Fish with scales and birds with oily feathers live in water.

Animals with warm fur live where it is cold.

A visit to a wooded area, a sea shore, a farm, a park or a desert country give children the opportunity to see different animals in their natural habitat.

Jimmy made three sections in his book.

1. Animals in the woods.
2. Animals on the farm.
3. Animals in the water.

Mary chose, *"People Who Help Us."*

Teacher: "In cities there are people who help boys and girls and families. We help each other at school and families help each other. Mary, what do we call some of the people who help us? How do they help us?"

Mary made the following illustrations for her booklet, each one on a new page.

The policeman stopping traffic.

A policeman helping a child find his mother.

A fireman on a tall ladder, helping people to climb out of a window.

A gardener planting flowers in the park.

The mailman giving a letter to my mother.

John chose *Boats* because he likes them. John lived near the water.

Teacher: "John, you can show us in your pictures how each different kind of boat is made so that it has what it needs."

The following pictures were made by John for his booklet:

Cars going on the ferry boat.

The big hoses on the fire boat shooting water on a burning boat.

The wind pushing out the sails of the sail boat.

Fishing with my dad in our row boat.

ACCORDION BOOK.

Cardboard sheets 18″ by 24″ are taped together. The subject is "Machines Man Uses to Help Him With His Work." This is a class project, painted in powder paint. Second grade.

MAKING A MOVING PICTURE BOX

Appropriate subjects for moving pictures are subjects with chronological order such as: the manufacture of a product, like cotton from the plant to cloth; subjects that are related such as: people who serve the community, farm animals, or the functions of various railroad cars; a story children have imagined or read such as: *"Little Black Sambo," "The Wizard of Oz," "Little Frisky Goat," "The Elves and the Shoemaker," "What I Would Like to Be."*

Preparing the lesson. The teacher plans with the children the illustrations needed to tell the story the group has chosen. Each child chooses the specific subject he would like to paint or draw.

The pictures need to have simple, large areas of color that can be easily seen in all parts of the room. The most important part of each child's subject should be large and in colors that will stand out.

The subject matter and people in every picture must have the same scale.

Making the pictures. Paper for individual pictures is one inch larger on all sides than the stage opening. Each picture must be the same size as the stage opening. The child makes the important part first. Every detail of the picture must be fully explained — for example, a box of fruit should show every apple.

Placing the pictures on the long strip of paper. A long strip of wrapping paper,

the correct width, is placed on the floor. The boys and girls decide on the best order for placing their finished pictures to explain the subject. The first picture is on the left, eight inches from the end. Pictures are pasted or taped securely to the strip of wrapping paper, at least an inch apart. The ends of the paper strip are fastened to the rollers of the movie box.

Giving the moving picture show. One child turns the roller, as each child tells about his own picture or one child narrates the whole show.

Children need to practice rolling the picture at the correct speed, and the length of time to stop so that each picture can be seen and discussed by the group or described by the narrator. Direct light toward the pictures while they are being shown.

MAKING A MURAL

WALL SHAPES VARY in size and shape, and determine the size of any mural. Murals may be placed on a long horizontal wall on the side of a room or hallway; a vertical panel between windows; a square or rectangular space at the end of a hallway, by

MAKING A MOVING PICTURE BOX

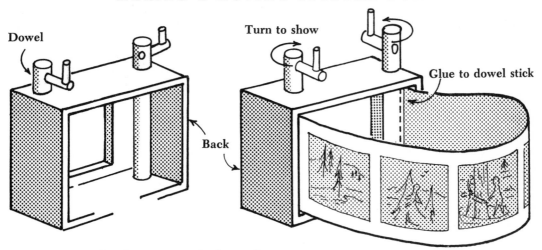

Wrapping or butcher paper strip fastened to dowels on both sides.

a stairway, or between rooms.

The mural should be made when the children have finished an area of study in which they are very interested. The subject matter needs to be varied and extensive enough in content to allow a group of children to work at once, each with an important part in the whole.

Related subject matter is grouped, with the guidance of the teacher, according to the children's own experience — from reading, discussion, and observation.

Group the children according to their subject, interest, and ability. Begin work on the mural when the children are enthused and ready. Preparation that lasts too long kills the interest of the children and results in dull, forced work.

PAINTING THE FIRST MURAL

Materials.

Mural paper 36″ wide, as long as the chosen wall space — butcher, screening, or wrapping paper.

Large, stiff bristle brush from 1″ to 3″ wide.

Tempera or powder paint, or for rough paper, chalk.

Color choice. Kindergarten and first-grade children should be given one color at a time. The darkest color to be used should be painted first wherever it will appear in the mural, and repeated at different levels and in varying amounts, to give a balanced look. Use a few well-chosen dark, middle and light value colors. Use several colors in the same family — as blue-green, yellow-green, and green in painting trees, foliage, or ground.

A Box used for a Moving Picture.

Adjusting to new size. Children in the habit of painting on 9″ by 12″ or 14″ by 17″ paper will probably paint the same size figures on 36 ″paper, just adding more detail to fill in the space. Give them an opportunity to paint people, trees, or other objects the size of a 30″ piece of paper before painting on the mural paper.

Planning the division of space on the mural paper. If the mural paper is placed on the floor, the children kneel to paint. The wall space determines the extent of the subject, as well as the number of children who can work at one time. Some subjects require big divisions of space with minor subdivisions (see *Child's Day*, page 105).

Position and working space of each child. The children should stand approxi-

mately thirty inches apart or an arm's length, in front of the mural paper, in the chronological order of the subject they are going to use. Each child needs to know approximately how much working space he has.

Suggested procedure. The children in kindergarten or first grade should paint at arm's length, directly on the mural paper. Second- and third-grade children may desire to draw main areas in with charcoal or black chalk before painting.

First the big subjects are painted for the entire mural, and the details are added as the mural develops. Children develop new ideas and discover better ways to make their ideas effective while they paint.

Each part of the mural is equally impor-

Related Subjects for Group Projects / 147

tant. Full-sized people, about two-thirds the height of mural paper, all must have the same scale. The subject is in flat pattern, with distance shown by placing far things higher up on the paper.

The forms on the left need to face in — to the right. The forms on the extreme right need to face in — to the left — to give a unified whole.

A strong horizontal line produced by a light-colored sky meeting a dark-colored earth, should be avoided, for it divides the mural. Sky may be omitted, and the entire background can be earth. If sky is used, color values should be close where it meets the earth, unless the color is distributed in well-balanced areas.

Children should stand away from the mural now and then to see if their work is strong enough to be easily seen, and to see how well all the different paintings go together. The finished mural ought to be a unified whole that leads the eye easily along. It is not an assemblage of separate pictures.

Good cooperative work habits should develop as children learn to share their ideas and paint with others. The same color is repeated and areas overlap.

Other Ways to Make Murals

1. Chalk may be used to draw on paper covered with buttermilk.

2. A background is painted, and objects made of cut and folded colored paper attached to it.

3. Texture in a background may be obtained by: finger painting, stamping with a sponge, or rolling a brayer charged with ink or opaque paint over the surface. Large, simple, boldly painted shapes of people, buildings, or large plant forms are placed over the textured surface.

4. Cut stencil shapes are transferred to a background by spraying with paint or by rubbing chalk over the stencil opening.

5. A mosaic can be made from linoleum, tile, rocks, or broken dishes. Cut or torn colored paper shapes are used alone and to overlap each other. Watercolor may be painted over part of the shapes and parts of the background. Black outlines may be used to emphasize parts.

6. Pieces of colored tissue paper may overlap each other to make new colors.

7. Patterned cloth and other materials may be used for areas of color or pattern in buildings, animals, people, or earth forms. Seeds, sawdust, or burlap make effective textures and patterns. Egg crates and corrugated paper make effective buildings.

Seasonal Experiences

PICTORIAL REPRESENTATIVE: of the different seasons should be made at the height of the season, when the child has first seen and felt its full intensity. With each season comes a change in plant colors, in animals' habits, and in the elements — sun, rain, wind. Plan walks to observe all these, and encourage the children to observe changes in weather on their way to and from school, and from the schoolroom windows, like the slant of the rain or snow and changes in the sky.

THE FALL

Color. Children gain a feeling for color from a romp in the fall leaves, finding many different kinds and colors among them.

A sample color lesson:

Let the children group different colors of leaves of the same kind.

 Green: yellow-green, dark green.
 Orange: yellow-orange, red-orange, orange.
 Brown: yellow-brown, red-brown, blue-brown.

Have the children find all the lightest colors of leaves and all the darkest colors, and arrange color groupings on the bulletin board, such as light colored leaves on a dark background like chocolate brown or dark green, and dark leaves on a very light background, like yellow. Straw mats, textured finger-paint paper, or colored paper make attractive backgrounds.

MIXING PAINT FOR FALL PICTURES

Prepare work areas to accommodate four to six children on the floor or on a table, and cover the work area with newspaper.

Provide for each child: one container for mixing paint, such as a baby food tin or a paper cup; one brush; one paper 14″ by 17″ or 12″ by 18″.

Place opaque paint in each area, each color in a separate container, about ½ full, and a wooden stick or spoon in each container to dip out the paint with.

Colors: Area 1: yellow and red. Area 2: yellow and turquoise blue. Area 3: yellow, red, and blue.

Mixing colors. Each child mixes together, in his containers, all the colors in their area, and paints the new color he has mixed all over a sheet of paper.

Children discover different quantities of each color will produce a variety of colors.

Area 1 (different kinds of orange)
   Yellow-orange, orange, red-orange.
Area 2 (different kinds of green)
   Yellow-green, blue-green, green.
Area 3 (different kinds of brown)
   Mustard yellow, terra-cotta, chocolate brown.

Some colors are light and some dark. Yellow is the lightest, blue and chocolate brown the darkest.

Using the colors to make a pattern of leaves. The children cut or tear leaves or trees out of the colored papers they have painted. They group them together to make a pleasing arrangement.

Dark colors with light colors.
Warm colors with cool colors.
Different greens together.
Different kinds of orange and brown together.

Each child chooses a color of paper to use as a background for the colors he has painted to make all the colors go beautifully together, and pastes his arrangement on the paper he has chosen.

Painting an all-over pattern of leaves with the colors children have mixed. Children derive an impression from looking at leaves covering the lawn, rolling in them, and tossing them into piles. Children transfer the sensation they receive to paper, using the many greens and browns they

"A Tree,"

By Yvonne, Grade One.

have mixed.

Encourage children to wash their brush between each color; to repeat the color they like best several times; to keep their colors clear and separate by allowing one color to dry before a second color is painted touching the first color, or suggest blending colors by adding new color areas while the paint is still wet.

Children may like to show the movement of leaves with their paint, such as leaves falling from trees or blown in the wind. If the wind is strong, leaves are swept along, then swirled in the air.

A Sample Project: Making a Mural of Trees

Preparing the lesson. Have children observe the differences in colors and shapes of various trees. Some trees grow tall, higher than houses. Some trees spread out, giving shade on warm days.

Choosing materials.

a. *To insure a variety in sizes of trees,* use paper ranging in size: 9″ by 12″; 9″ by 22″, 12″ by 18″, 12″ by 14″, and 24″ by 30″.

b. *To insure color variety* give a different combination of colors to each group of children, as described for fall pictures.

c. *To insure color balance* use the same color or kind of color for different tree shapes.

d. *To insure variety,* give children using the same paint colors a variety in sizes of paper.

e. *To insure a predominance of either warm or cool colors in the assembled mural* provide more papers of either warm or cool.

Have each child make one beautiful tree to fill his paper. Some children may

Tree,"

By Sharon, Kindergarten.

wish a long piece of paper for a tall tree. The paintings are placed flat to dry. The children cut out their trees or tear the outside edge carefully to make the whole a lovely shape. Light brown wrapping paper or butcher paper thirty-six inches wide is placed by the teacher, with the children's help, over the wall space or on the floor for the mural background. The children arrange their cut-out trees on the mural paper.

Things children think about in placing their trees on the mural. The whole mural is about trees. Since trees grow on the ground, sky is not necessary. Children can imagine they are walking through the trees. Some trees are placed high up, some low down. Group trees of different sizes, with variations in color, together. A very light tree, mostly yellow, touching a very dark brown tree will make this part of the group of trees important. Similar color differences must be distributed through the mural to help our eyes move across it.

Have the children view the finished arrangement from a distance, and re-arrange until they are satisfied. A small amount of paste is applied with a brush or stick, back from the edge of each tree to keep the trees in place. On mural paper that is over a cork board, use pins to fasten the trees to the paper.

The finished tree mural is most pleasing if interest is distributed throughout, allowing our eyes to move easily, without jumping from one group of trees to another.

Extending the experience. Children will enjoy re-arranging their tree mural, or adding to it animals, plants, and boys and girls.

PAINTING SUNFLOWERS
(First Grade)

LARGE SUNFLOWERS ARE SIMPLE shapes children can clearly see. Large yellow petals grow out from the center all the way around a pattern of dark brown seeds. It is easy for children to paint beautiful yellow sunflowers on dark brown paper.

THANKSGIVING DAY

AT THANKSGIVING, when gratitude is expressed for the bountiful harvest, give each child the opportunity to describe in words and in pictorial form things which provide the following:

Enjoyment because of their beauty, such as birds, flowers, clouds, water, land, rain, and sunshine.

Food such as golden grain, fruits, and vegetables.

Clothing such as animal and plant fibers.

Places to live such as houses and apartments.

Workers who help us, such as carpenters, bricklayers, and painters.

Care and love such as mothers and fathers give their children.

These subjects may be used for individual pictures, for illustrations in a booklet, or combined for a mural.

"We Give Thanks" may be used as a topic for a chart, large scrapbook, or wall mural. Use one word or phrase — such as clothing, food, beauty, weather — to title each section. Cut-outs may be contributed by different children or a complete illustration made using related ideas.

THANKSGIVING DAY BULLETIN BOARD

WINTER

Things people do to get ready for winter. People wear warmer clothing. (Clothes may be made for paper dolls, or designs made with yarn on mittens.) Cover tender plants outdoors. Install storm windows and doors in houses. Store wood and coal for winter. (Crayon drawings.)

Things animals do to get ready for winter. Some animals store food for winter. Some animals sleep all winter in sheltered places. Some animals burrow under ground.

Things for children to do.

Paint or crayon a picture to represent the animals hibernating or animals under the ground. Make the sleeping animal fill the entire space, as if the ground were removed.

Use a box to represent an animal shelter. Remove the front of the box to give a third dimension.

Cut paper shapes or use boxes or real materials to represent rocks, plants, or other forms to give the illusion of a cave or other shelter. Model the sleeping animal from clay or a sawdust mixture or cut a form from paper.

Use a large open box or strips of cardboard to represent animals above and under the ground. A horizontal partition is placed across the opening of the box. The lower part of the box is for the roots of plants and for the animals that burrow under the ground. The upper part of the box is for the leaves of plants that grow above the ground. Animals that live above the ground are added.

"Hibernating,"

By Karen, Grade Three.

WINTER BEAUTY

Observing bare branches of trees. The bare branches in the winter tell us how the tree is formed. First the trunk grows from roots deep in the ground. Limbs grow out from the trunk with branches growing from the limbs. Each branch in turn is a little smaller than the branch it grew from. Bare branches make very graceful lines against the sky. The trunk must be strong to hold a big tree up against winds and storms.

Materials needed for pictures are colored construction paper 12″ by 18″ in light gray blue, light red, or light blue violet; dark colored crayon, opaque paint, or black ink; soft bristle brush.

SUBJECTS FOR PICTURES
(Third Grade)

Tree branches making graceful lines against the sky. Graceful lines are moving lines, thick in some places and thin in others. To make *graceful lines* the child moves his brush, full of dark colored paint, or crayon smoothly and easily over the paper using free arm movements with strokes for the branches starting on the trunk of the tree and going out, reaching to different parts of the paper.

Evergreen trees with needles combined with trees having bare branches. Winter pictures may combine trees with bare branches with evergreen trees. Branches of pine and fir, brought into the classroom, let children see how the needles grow from the branches and the total shape of the branch. Observe the shape of the evergreen trees outdoors.

If children wish to make a dark, cold, stormy day they use colors that suggest a storm — like gray blue and purple. The background or stormy sky is painted first, giving movement by using lighter color tones with darker tones. After the background is dry the evergreen trees are painted in masses of green. After the green trees are dry the trees with bare branches are painted, using some colors lighter and some darker than the green used for the evergreens. Use opaque paint, to allow painting one color over another, or crayon or chalk. Greater beauty will result if some of the bare branches are seen against the green of trees and others are silhouetted against the sky.

For an experiment give the children fingerpaint in a middle value grayed tone to make movements for the sky. When this is dry the children paint the trees using opaque color over the finger paint.

"Bare Branches with Snow,"
By Freddy, Kindergarten.

A SAMPLE LESSON: THE SNOW
(Grade Two and Three)

The teacher might say to the children:
"Have you seen the soft, white snow fall

lightly from the clouds? It covers the roofs on every house and church steeple. It covers the roofs on every store and animal shelter, and every tree, plant, and tiny blade of grass."

"*A gray-blue, green, or violet color paper will help you make a beautiful snow picture. Choose a dark color of wax crayon.* See if it is darker than your paper. With your dark crayon make the things you want, in your snow picture."

"White chalk will make fluffy white snow. You can sprinkle chalk where you want it to be snowing. Use the side of the white chalk as well as the end."

"The paper will show through the strokes when crayon is used on its side. Dark crayon strokes are effective to use over the white for accents or outlines, such as the lines of tree branches or to outline a shape that is white against white."

Crayon with white tempera paint. Have the children draw with colored crayon on a middle value of colored paper for subjects such as houses along a street, trees, or children playing outdoors. Over the completed crayon picture, the child paints white tempera paint sparingly for the snow. The snow might be lightly falling or sprinkled over the houses, trees, and people.
Ideas for snow pictures.
   Winter Fun.
      Children building a snowman together.
      Children sliding down a hill on sleds and pulling their sleds up the hill.
      Children building a fort and throwing snowballs.
      Children skating on the ice pond in rhythmic movements.
      Children building animals and people of snow.

SPRING

THE EARTH SEEMS TO COME to life, clothed in a new and wonderful beauty with the first green of spring, the flowering trees and the varicolored wild flowers. Some of the small springtime blooms belong to our gar- den in the woods, others to meadows, others to city walks. Children's faces beam as they clutch the first flowers they have found for their teacher. See color illustration, Going For a Walk in the Park, Grade 3, page 100.

"Mural,"

By a Second Grade.

A lesson in seeing and learning about wild flowers: Ask the children to separate the different kinds of flowers to see how many they have found.

Flowers belong to different families, each with a different name. Small glass tubes may be taped to the bulletin board, and filled with water to contain one kind of wild flower arranged in a lovely spray. Have the name of the flower lettered under the tubes. As children bring in new wild flowers they can compare them with the

A wrapping-paper design, "Snowmen,"
By a Third Grader.

kinds on the bulletin board to learn the names. Give children the opportunity to see the beauty of shape, color, and pattern in tiny flowers by seeing them through a magnifying glass.

A springtime arrangement for a beauty corner. Violets, tiger lilies, clover, or buttercups with blades of grass, moss, or small ferns make a lovely, intimate arrangement in a piece of bark, shell, or low dish. Place the arrangement close to the children so they can see into the faces of the flowers.

Children observe flowers that grow in the garden, and see that different kinds of flowers have different shapes. A *bell shape* is seen in a lily, morning glory, foxglove, canterbury bell, and daffodil. A *round shape* with petals going out from a center is seen in a daisy, sunflower, and dahlia. A *cup shape* is observed in flowers with broad, rounded petals — an open tulip, water lily, lotus, single rose, and magnolia.

Flowers with petals of more than one shape:

Bleeding Hearts — are like little hearts strung along a gracefully curved stem. Compare parted petals at the top with the jewel-like drop hanging down in the center.

Fuchsias — have four pointed petals that hang like an open bell over wider petals

Seasonal Experiences / 157

that close around long hanging stamens. They are lovely lanterns for fairies.

Pansies — are many different colors. In the center is a small shape that looks like the pansy's eye. On both sides are two rounded petals with a broad petal at the bottom. Look carefully to see the patterns of stripes and dots on the pansy petals.

Lady's Slippers — are wild orchids. The hanging pouch-like shape with its pattern of dots seems to hold a secret of beauty.

Variety in centers of flowers:
The lotus with its large bulbous center with round holes.
The sunflower with its large brown center of many seeds.
The tulip with long black stamens.
The larkspur with tiny flowers forming a rosette.
Other flowers have centers like darts, crosses, or seeds like parachutes or wings.

A SAMPLE PROJECT: MAKE-BELIEVE FLOWERS WITH CHALK OR PAINT
(Kindergarten and First Grade)

Use large paper 18″ by 24″ or 24″ by 36″. Flowers may easily be 9″ to 12″ across.

Use chalk or paint. Pretend flowers are combinations of any colors that are lovely together. The colors of real flowers are the best guides for color combination.

The children paint beautiful flowers to enjoy. Encourage children to make flowers open wide as they look up to the sun. The children swing the brush strokes from the center out or round and round, then add pattern.

Children are attracted by the bright colors of flowers. They see big simple shapes like those in a sunflower. Their flower picture is likely to be spots of bright colors that resemble the faces of a mass of flowers with no discernible shapes. Children do not notice details of shape or size. Their paintings are two-dimensional patterns. The centers may be very large with small petals. The petals may be the most important part. Some centers may have small flowers inside with big petals all around. Some petals go round and round, with one row in back of another, all beautiful colors. Other petals overlap each other with a lighter color over a darker color.

SAMPLE PROJECTS: MAKING A FLOWER PICTURE
(Second and Third Grade)

CHILDREN THINK ABOUT all of the delightful parts of flowers such as their patterned centers, their petals, their colors, and their whole shape surrounded by green leaves. Children can tell with paint what they know about flowers. Good arrangements result when small flowers are grouped with large ones, the colors and shapes are balanced and we can see and enjoy every part of the beautiful flowers. Remind the children that green leaves help glorify the flowers.

"BEAUTIFUL FLOWERS WITH SEED PATTERNS"

The teacher could say:
"You have to look very close, to see the flower seeds. Seeds are in a round shape, like a cup, in the center of flowers. Some are close, in even rows. Some are piled up like a small mound. Some are tiny flowers.

Some are like shooting stars."

"All around the seeds, petals grow. Think how many shapes and colors you have seen in flowers. Petals may be striped or have dots. You can invent beautiful flowers, all your own. Remember all flowers have seeds."

"Choose cheerful, happy colors. Some flowers may be large with others smaller. Use a big brush to paint beautiful, big flowers all over your paper. You can imagine you are looking into the faces of flowers, in a flower bed."

"When your first colors are dry, use a different color for the pattern of your seeds in the centers. This will make your flowers still more beautiful. Remember light colors go with dark colors and dark colors with light colors. Look and choose just the right color for the centers of your flowers. If your flowers need leaves, add them."

A Sample Lesson: "A Growing Tree"

The teacher might say to the children:

"How does a tree grow?"

"Close your eyes and think about it. Think of all the different parts and how they are joined together."

"The roots, under the ground, are like long fingers reaching out to hold the tree in place. The big, strong trunk held to the ground by the roots, keeps the tree from falling over when a wind is blowing."

"Branches grow from the trunk. Twigs grow from the branches. Branches on some trees grow high, others spread out, farther than you can reach."

"Each different kind of tree has a different shape and a different kind of leaf. Some trees, like a pine, have needles."

"When you see a big, strong tree in your mind, then quickly put it on your paper, while you still see it clearly."

"Flowers,"

By Barbara, Grade One.

"Flowers,"

By Second-Graders.

Seasonal Experiences / 159

CRAYON ON CLOTH WALL-HANGING, 8 FT. BY 6 FT.
(A Third-Grade Project)

The tree was drawn first in crayon. The children made crayon flowers and birds in flat pattern. These were cut out and arranged on the tree shape. After a suitable arrangement was decided upon by the group, the wax crayon drawings were turned face down on the cloth and pinned in place. A warm iron was used to press the design on to the cloth. The hanging was placed on a table. At different times during the day the children added crayon to their design. When it was finished it was pressed to set and soften the colors.

"Use the side of a piece of chalk or crayon to make a growing tree. The branches grow out from the trunk, reaching into all parts of your paper."

"How many different greens can you make?"

"How many different browns can you make?"

"When you have finished your picture fasten it to the wall. Look at it from across the room. Are all the parts of your picture filled with a color or shape you enjoy? If you have big empty spaces near the center of your picture, think of things that go with trees. When all parts of your growing tree picture belong together, your picture is finished."

"Now you can enjoy your lovely tree picture."

ANIMALS OF THE WOODS

Baby rabbits may be seen in the spring and summer among bushes, in gardens, on the prairie, or in the woods. A rabbit's two long, pointed ears are the first things a child will notice. Their long hind legs are very strong. They can hop very fast and leap a long distance. See how their hind legs are when they sit down. The rabbit uses his short front legs like hands to hold carrots, lettuce, or tender leaves he is eating.

"KITES" — A Springtime Mural

The First-Grade boys and girls painted the way they fly kites on a windy day. The colorful cut-out figures and kites were placed on a bulletin board in the school hall. Note the direct crossing of the strings which add movement but not confusion.

Have the children watch the rabbit turn his ears in different directions, and find the places where he bends his legs, as he hops and sits up. Rabbits have two large eyes shaped like an oval. They slant in the same direction, as the profile of their face. Children may feel the soft fur and shape of the rabbit as they stroke his back. Children playing sometimes hop like rabbits.

Squirrels, gray and fluffy-tailed, are among the most graceful animals in the woods. Squirrels sit on their long hind legs and hold nuts in their short front legs. The squirrel's fluffy tail curves over its back to its head. The mother squirrel covers her babies with her big bushy tail to keep them warm. They also use their tails to dig holes to bury nuts.

Squirrels have sharp, big eyes to help them to see quickly. Their cheeks are fat, with pockets for nuts.

The beautiful curves of the body and tail of the squirrel are easiest to make if the child swings them in with soft chalk or paint.

Bears. The children have seen bears in national parks, a zoo, or circus. They know the story of the three bears, and toy teddy bears.

The bulky, simple body form of the bear with its long shaggy bristly fur is easy for children to remember. Its broad, short legs, which support its bulky body, make it a good animal for beginners both to draw and model in clay.

Bears can do many things. Baby bears, called cubs, are very playful. They can roll over, push each other with their paws, and climb from limb to limb in trees.

Their long claws help them scoop up honey from tree trunks, ants from rotted stumps, and fish from streams. Bears sit up and can stand up on their hind legs. When they are in these positions the pads on the

"Rabbit,"

By Linda, Grade Two.

"Bird,"

By Karen, Grade Two.

bottom of their broad feet can be seen, with the long sharp claws on the end of their feet.

Strokes made for the fur going from the body down with wax crayon or a dry brush, give the feeling of bristly long fur.

Birds are loved for their cheerful songs and many colors. Children may watch birds eating in a feeding place outside school or a home window. They can build bird houses to provide nesting places. Observing birds carrying materials in their bills for nest building, and carrying food later for their young, fascinates children.

The home of each kind of bird is where it builds its nest and raises its young. They use materials close at hand for their nests. A cliff swallow uses mud and sticks. Marsh birds use grass-like plants and cattails.

A bird uses its bill to help make a living. Birds with short bills, like a canary, use their beaks to crush and eat seeds. Ducks have flat bills for grubbing under water. The long bill of a humming bird reaches down into flowers for nectar. Robins pull worms out of the ground. Birds carry straw, string, moss, sticks, and other materials for their nests. They also build nests with their bills. Birds use their bills like combs or brushes to straighten their feathers.

Birds have two wings for flying. Their tails have long quill feathers, which support the birds in the air. Notice the shape of an outspread wing, tapering to a point on the ends with the widest part near the body. Wings have rows of feathers overlapping each other.

Birds' wings curve very gracefully as they fly. Young children pretend they are flying by moving their arms up and down like wings. When a bird sits with its wings close to its sides, it has one small curve for the head growing to a wider curve over the breast. Its back is almost straight from the

"Squirrel,"

By Clark, Grade two;
He used the side of a crayon to make soft fur.

"Squirrel,"

By Marcia, Grade One.

back of the head to the end of the tail. See illustrations in color, Birds Singing, grade 3, page 100 and Mother Bird with Baby Birds in a Nest, grade 3, page 100.

Turtles may be kept in low open dishes. Children enjoy feeding them, and can watch them easily because of their slow movements.

A turtle carries his house around with him. His shell consists of an arched upper, hard shield and a flat lower shield. Point out the place the two are joined together on both sides.

In front there is space for two legs and a long neck and head. In back a short pointed tail extends out in the center with a leg on both sides.

The children can see the following movements of the turtle:

It can stretch its neck out and turn its head around.

It can draw its head and legs in under its shell.

The turtle uses its long neck to flip its body over on its back.

The wide, webbed feet help the turtle to paddle in the water.

Its head and neck are covored with scales.

The shell of the turtle's back is its prettiest part.

One turtle could easily fill the paper, giving the child an opportunity to make a colorful pattern on its back, to show the scales on the neck, and the legs with their webbed claw-like feet.

Tadpoles and frogs. Tadpoles are all head and tail, in a round bulbous shape that extends on one end to a long tapering tail. They wiggle their tails to swim through the water. Wiggling tadpoles can make a nice border. Tadpoles grow into frogs. Frogs swim in water like boys and girls using the breast stroke. On land frogs hop. They bend their legs, like open scissors, before they jump. Look for the design on the frog's back. The face of a frog with its bulging eyes, and broad mouth, with its long tongue extended to catch insects, makes a very good subject for Halloween masks or for Indian totem-poles.

Birds come back and fly from branch to branch. They hunt materials for their nests. Soon young birds are stretching their heads out from the nest, for food. On sunny days, holding their heads high, the birds sing to the sun. *The animals of the woods* play together. The young rabbits jump about. The cub bears roll over, climb trees and run after each other.

The animals on the farm may be seen with their mothers. Children love to see the lamb, calf, pig, colt, puppy, and kitten as they enjoy the sun of spring.

A SAMPLE PROJECT:
"THINGS THAT LIVE AND GROW UNDER THE GROUND"
(Grade Two and Three)

The teacher might ask the children:

"Have you thought of the things that live and grow under the ground?"

"The rabbits burrow in holes."

"Have you wondered how long the road stretches from one rabbit's house to another? Do you suppose you would find baby rabbits, in the spring, asleep in a nest of down?"

"Other animals live under the ground also. Do you know how they fix their storehouse of food?"

"Roots of trees and plants spread out under the ground. Perhaps rabbits have to go up and down hill, in their roadway."

"Some of the vegetables you eat are bulbs (like onions), tubers (like potatoes),

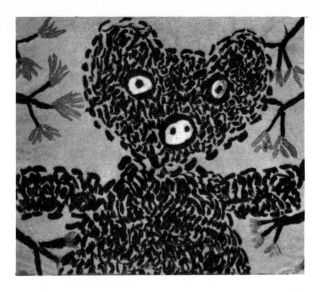

"A 'Fuzzy' Animal,"

By Carole, Grade Two.

DIORAMA

The inside of a box has been used to show the bears and their environment. The bears were modeled from clay and glazed. A child's crayon drawing is used for a background with cut-out trees standing on the sides. A rock and moss complete the environment.

Seasonal Experiences / 165

or roots (like beets). All of these grow under the ground."

"Making an 'under the ground' picture is something very few children have tried. All you need is to know what you want to do and let your imagination help you along.

"Let the top of your paper be the top of the ground."

"Let the bottom of your paper be down deep in the ground."

"Your imagination will help you, if you try to imagine what you would see if you could take an enormous knife and cut a big slice, down deep, right off the earth? Show us in your picture the things that live and grow under the ground."

THE FARM

MOTIVATION FOR A VISIT TO A FARM

FARM ANIMALS MOST children love are characters in many stories, such as, *"The Three Little Pigs," "The Three Little Kittens," "Ferdinand the Bull," "The Little Red Hen," "Mary Had a Little Lamb," "Billy Goat Gruff,"* and others.

Country children are familiar with the farm animals. They have a feeling of pride in telling their classmates how they help to care for the animals and growing plants. A few city children have a garden in which vegetables are grown. Many children have seen vegetables only without their leaves or stems in the market. Relatively few children in large industrial cities have visited a farm.

Children learn in school that much of their food comes from farms. The source of milk is the logical beginning for the study of the farm, since it is all children's staple. A visit to a farm in the spring gives children the added delight of seeing baby animals with their mothers.

A visit to a farm stimulates discussion, offers ideas for painting by providing real experiences, and permits observing animals from all sides for clay modeling.

Observations to make on the visit to a farm (to help children form visual images of farm animals).

Baby animals resemble their mothers and fathers. Children see the fluffy baby chicks or ducks. They see young lambs with their long legs and plump woolly bodies jump about in a frisky manner. Children see young calves and colts unsteady on their long thin legs. See color illustration, Mother Hen with Baby Chicks, grade one, page 99.

Some animals are small enough for children to hold in their arms, such as baby chicks, rabbits, kittens, or puppies. Children love to feel the softness of fur and the smoothness of skin. Children need guidance in the handling of animals both to learn to take good care of the animals and as a protection to themselves.

A child holding a baby animal is a charming subject for a picture. The child watches with affection the snuggled form.

VISUAL DESCRIPTION OF A FEW FARM ANIMALS

Cows. Children have learned that the milk they drink comes from cows, and they are intrigued by the idea of the milk coming from the teats in the udder of the cow.

Cows are white, black and various tones of brown; either all one color or spotted. A cow's body is broad, with prominent hips wide apart. Its long tail extends out from its straight backbone, with long hair on the end that helps it to brush the flies off its body. Its long neck extends down to a deep chest. A cow's sloping shoulders are close together. A pair of curved horns for protection are on top of the cow's head between its ears. A cow has two large eyes with long lashes, large nostrils, and a broad mouth. Cows use their lower teeth with their long tongue to pull up grass rather than to bite it off.

Subjects that interest children for pictures are:

The farmer sitting on a low stool milking his cow.

The cows standing in their stalls in a row, eating hay from the trough in front of them.

The mother cow with her calf in the pasture.

An animal portrait with the head filling the paper.

One single animal with something it would like.

Encourage the children to stress one pronounced characteristic which makes a cow different from another animal, such as the udder and horns.

Pigs. The stories of *"The Three Little Pigs"* and *"This Little Pig Went To Market"* are familiar to most children. They like the roly-poly shape of the baby pink pigs, whose low, long, heavy, broad, rounded bodies are covered by a smooth skin with fine hair. They are white, spotted black on white, or black. Pigs have a slight curve in their backs, with a tiny curly tail behind. The underline of the pig is approximately straight.

The pig's neck is wide, deep, and short

"A Jumping Frog,"

By Richard, Grade One.

and blends smoothly with its shoulders. Its broad head ends in a short snout, which terminates in a disk shape having two nostrils. The children can watch the pig dig with its snout in the ground for roots. Close to the pig's nose, on both sides, are two small eyes with eyelids. Their fat rounded cheeks add to the pudgy appearance. The pig's ears are wide at the bottom tapering to a point, and face forward.

The pig's legs are short and strong with hoofs divided in the center forming two toes.

The mother pig, lying on her side with all her little pigs standing in a row getting their dinner, is a delightful subject for a picture.

A pig's head with its round snout and pointed ears facing forward makes a good animal portrait.

Cats. Children love to hold kittens to feel their soft fur and to watch them play as they roll over, push a ball with their paws, or run after a moving string. Most children have watched a mother cat clean her kitten's fur and her own fur several times a day by licking with her rough tongue. They also lap up milk with their tongues, and clean meat from bones. The mother cat grips the loose skin on the nape of her kitten's neck with her mouth to carry it.

A cat's body is strong and muscular, bending and moving quickly and easily. Notice the changing curve — from the smaller curve at the top of the head, to a sloping line to the low part of the back, then a large curve over the hips or jumping legs. The rear of a cat's body is thin, making it light so it can jump easily through space. Its nimble body moves in very lovely, gracefully curved lines when it is curled up resting, washing its fur, poised for jumping, or sitting up. Its long tail adds beauty, especially when it is curled around the cat's front paws. As a cat springs, its tail helps

"Our Cow, Molly,"

By Joy, Grade One.

"Cat,"

By Margaret, Grade One.
She discovered that a dry brush made nice fur.

it to balance.

Cats have long, sharp claws, which help them climb trees. They draw their claws back into their toes when they walk noiselessly on the soft pads of their feet. Their heads are broad and rounded with bright circular eyes that are wide open when they are in dark places, and narrow and small in the sunshine. Their large, erect, pointed ears catch every sound. A cat's long, stiff whiskers are feelers that help it find its way at night.

Cats and kittens are of various colors — gray, white, brown, black, or any combination of these colors. Lions, tigers, panthers, and leopards all belong to the cat family and are similar in build.

Good subjects for children's pictures are things they know about cats — such as a mother cat carrying her kittens, kittens playing, a child holding a soft furry cat, a cat lying down resting, or feeding the cat and kittens. Cats are well-shaped animals to be modeled in clay.

Horses. Children at play ride a hobby horse, a cock horse, or an ornamental horse with plumes on a merry-go-round. City children may see ponies in parks, racing or polo horses and bucking horses with cowboys at country fairs, and circus horses gayly decorated with colorful trappings. On the street, children may see draft horses pulling wagons of vegetables or milk.

Many country boys and girls have horses of their own to ride. They have seen their fathers on horseback round up cattle or hunt. Some farmers still have teams of horses they harness to work in the field. Children love to hold the reins or sit on top of the hay for a ride.

The flowing mane along the edge of the horse's long neck changes with every movement of the horse's head. Children who have seen horses running, have probably

"My Cat,"
By Linda, Grade Two.
She has painted directly and clearly a well-defined form, fine in design.

"My Cat Likes to Lie on Her Rug by the Fire,"
By Susan, Grade Three.
She painted a simple and direct cat placed in front of a pattern of lines and dots.

noticed their manes and tails flying out behind them. Horses' long necks enable them to eat in the pasture without bending their legs. Horses have large nostrils, and eyes with eyelids and long lashes. Their pointed ears stand straight up from a long head when they are alert and listening. Horses can turn their ears in several directions.

Children enjoy drawing and painting animals they love. The five- and six-year-old child does not hesitate to draw a horse and rider. They often draw the rider beside the horse. The eight-year-old child who has seen a horse and rider, or has ridden himself, will show the figure straddling the horse and holding the reins.

To paint in one stroke the graceful line of the changing curve from the top of the horse's head down to its tail gives a lovely rhythmic feeling.

A SAMPLE LESSON:
STIMULATING THE CHILDREN BEFORE A PAINTING LESSON
(For Third Grade)

The teacher might say to the children:
"You need to know these things about the animal you are going to make: What kind of covering does the animal have to keep it warm and dry and to protect it? Does it have fur, hair, wool, hide or scales? What color is it going to be? What do you see first when you look at the animal you are going to make? How is the animal you have chosen different from any other animal?"

Each horse is made the way an individual child pictured it to be.

Examples of how children picture the ways mother animals care for their young: baby pigs, calves, colts, puppies, kittens, and lambs nursing their mothers; a mother hen covering her chicks with her spreading wings to protect them and keep them warm. The baby chicks' heads peek out between their mother's feathers; a mother rabbit thumping her long feet to call her babies; birds building nests for their young and teaching them to fly; a cat cleaning her kitten's fur by licking with her rough tongue; a puppy snuggled beside its mother.

CHILDREN USE THE WAYS THE FARMER CARES FOR HIS
ANIMALS AS A SUBJECT FOR A DIORAMA

They observe the farm buildings made of different materials that shelter different kinds of animals, to fit the size and habits of the animal, and to provide an eating place for the animal.

The chicken coop has bars of wood above the floor which provide a perch for chickens to roost. Grain is scattered on the floor or placed in containers for food. Narrow slats in front of the house for the nesting mother hen provide a place for baby chickens to run through into a fenced yard.

The barn has stalls for the cows and horses. Cows are milked and fed in their stalls. A trough in front of the stall provides a place for the cows to eat.

A pen for the pigs is enclosed by a fence. Food is usually placed in a trough.

Hutches are small pens where rabbits are kept. Usually there is one rabbit to a small wired-in compartment, except a mother who has her babies with her.

"Spotted Horse,"

By a Second-Grader.

The essential character is painted with one continuous brush stroke.

By Margaret, Grade One.

She has painted the background to make her white colt important.

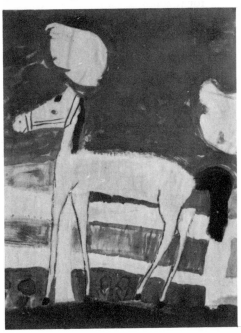

"A Big Fat Pig,"

By Jack, Grade Two.

"Horses with Their Colts,"

By Jerry, Grade One.

Every part of the picture is important, Jerry has drawn what he knows about a horse.

Each child chooses the animal or bird he likes best to model from clay, plasticine, or papier-mâché. The child builds a shelter for the animal he has made from cardboard, a box, or pieces of wood. He adds what he needs to complete his idea, such as baby animals or food (see cardboard construction, pages 216, 223; papier-mâché, pages 225, 226; and clay animals, page 165).

A picture of the animal in its shelter.

Teacher:

> "Make your picture large to show the inside of your animal's house. Remember your animal needs room to move about, a place to eat, and a place to sleep. Most important of all is the animal inside of its house. Choose a color for your animal that will make it important. When you have finished we will look at your pictures and see how many different animals have been made by all of you."

GROWING THINGS

Observing growing things. The child sees the way the farmer plants his flowers, vegetables, trees, and grain. The color, shape, size, and pattern of growing things, as well as the way they grow, give the child a visual experience to recall when he uses art materials.

Flower gardens are full of bright colors. Planted in rows each different kind of flower makes a new kind of striped color pattern. Planted in groups flowers make a patchwork of varied shapes of colors.

A color pattern of flowers for children to make with crayon, chalk, or paint. Looking into the faces of a bed of brightly

"Rabbits in Their Burrow,"
By Jefferson, Grade Two.

colored flowers is a subject for an all-over design of gay colors.

A vertical panel design for children to make. The tall vines of peas, beans or red tomatoes growing up and up make a lovely panel design for the side of a bulletin board or a wall between the windows.

First, have the child make the main stalk, then the leaves going out from the stems. The pods showing the pattern of beans or peas inside adds interest. Graceful tendrils curled here and there add variety in direction and kinds of lines.

A painted decorative horizontal panel to show the vegetables that grow above the ground and under the ground. A strip of mural paper 36″ wide and the same length as the wall space is divided horizontally with one color to represent the area above the ground, such as light green or light brown, and another color to represent the area under the ground, such as dark green or dark brown.

When the background colors are dry each child paints a vegetable that grows above or below the ground. Under the ground will be cone-shaped orange carrots, round red beets, white bulbous onions, and various shapes of potato tubers. Above the ground will be lacy leaves of carrots and the red leaves of beets.

Children see vegetables with many different kinds of beautiful leaves — lettuce with its frilly leaves, cauliflower with its snowy white clusters of bud-like forms surrounded by dark green leaves, and the green asparagus standing up straight like a small spire, and the vegetables that climb on tall poles. The farmer plants his vegetables in straight rows, with all of one kind together.

Each painted or drawn leaf and vegetable form must be large enough for its beautiful shape and color to be completely visible. The plants should be healthy and strong, going to the top and bottom of the paper.

Trees. Tall trees are often planted as windbreaks near the farmhouse. Fruit trees grow in rows with space all around them. In spring they are covered with blossoms, like a huge bouquet. The bees are busy gathering nectar from the flowers for honey. In fall the trees are covered with fruit. Descriptive words which help give a visual image are italicized below:

Apple trees are *low*, with branches *spreading out all around* them. They are *rounded* on the top like a *dome* or *big* umbrella. The *bright red, round* apples have *green* leaves around them. The *red apples* hanging from *each branch* make an *all-over-pattern* of *round red shapes* on the trees. The *trees* planted in *rows* make a *striped design.*

Animals. The children see the cows with their calves and the horses with their colts in the pasture. The children tell us in their pictures about the green pasture with the animals enjoying themselves.

Children can show in their pictures how they pick red apples from a big spreading tree.

MACHINES THAT HELP THE FARMER

Have the children make pictures showing how machines are used by the farmer. These may be used in a single picture or placed in a row for a movie (see Movie Box, page 145).

A *tractor* with two big wheels in back does the work of many horses.

A *truck* with sides that resemble a board

fence is used to carry pigs, cows, sheep, or sacks of grain. The truck with built-up sides is used to carry produce to cities.

A *wheelbarrow* is like a box with one big wheel in front. It is used to carry small loads, as of dirt or plants. The farmer holds the two handles attached to the back of the wheelbarrow and pushes it. Some children have small wheelbarrows they use to help

their father or mother.

A dairy farmer uses a *milking machine* to milk his cows and a *separator* to take the cream from the milk.

A grain farmer uses *machines to cut and separate* the grain from the stalk.

A fruit farmer uses a *spraying machine* to kill insects.

Small planes fly low to spray the fields.

A SAMPLE PROJECT:
MAKING A "FARM MURAL" TO COVER THE STUDY OF THE FARM
(Second Grade)

(See Murals, page 146.) The farm as a subject is varied, extensive in scope, and of special interest to children.

Suggestions for grouping children according to subject.

   a. Farmer's house and family.
   b. Farm buildings for animals and storage of produce.
   c. Farmer's work: caring for the animals — such as feeding them and providing shelter; planting the garden; cutting and stacking the hay; gathering the produce — vegetables, fruit and grain.

Background for mural. Butcher, wrapping, or screening paper 36″ wide, as long as the wall on which the mural is to be. Fasten the paper to the wall or place it on the floor or on a long table for working.

Steps to follow.

1. Divide the paper into large areas, suitable for the various group divisions of the subject. Sky can be omitted. If opaque color such as tempera or powder paint is

used, paint the ground colors first, repeating colors in areas all over the paper. When this is dry, paint darker or lighter objects on top of the ground color.

   a. ***Areas for the building.***

   Place the buildings first because of their block form and size. By leaving the front wall off the building, the child can show the activity inside the house or shelter. If the buildings are distributed throughout the mural — some higher, some lower — they will help unify the whole.

   b. ***The area for the garden.***
   c. ***The area for the pasture.***

The greens of the pasture and gardens placed in different parts of the mural repeat the green color as well as to balance the whole mural.

Following the divisions of space for subjects, have a few children work on each different area at one time. Animals, people, and machines are added as needed for interest, shape, and color.

A SAMPLE PROJECT: A SANDTABLE FARM
(A large waterproof box may be used on a table top. Second Grade)

1. ***Divide the space into areas for the following*** (space available will determine

the number of different things): buildings — the farm house, and the barns and shel-

"In the Country,"

By Gail, Grade Three.

"The Bulldozer,"

By John, Grade One.

"Working on a Combine,"

By Bobby, Grade Three.

"Tractor,"

By a First-Grader.

"A Turkey with Bright Feathers,"

By Mary, Grade One.

"The Farmer,"

By a First-Grader.

"A Hen Family,"

By a First-Grader.

"The Farm,"

By a Second-Grader.

ters; and planted areas — garden (vegetable and flower), orchard, grain or pasture, pond for ducks.

2. *Materials to use for construction.* For buildings — wooden or cardboard boxes, double-faced corrugated paper, scraps of plywood, shingles, or wall board.

For plants — fruit and other trees, vegetables, and flowers — artificial plants made from colored paper, felt, buckrum, muslin, or sponges; twigs or dried plant material;

real growing plants from seeds (a wooden or cardboard box lid filled with dirt may be planted with seeds such as barley, wheat, or grass).

For animals and people — ones modeled from clay, plasticine, salt and flour dough, sawdust mixed with wheat paste or papier-mâché. (Recipe for papier-mâché, page 226; recipe for salt and flour dough, page 283; paper construction, page 207; modeling people, page 266; modeling animals, page 265.)

Taking Care of an Animal in the Classroom

This develops a feeling of responsibility, of unselfishness, and offers children the opportunity for close observation.

Animals that interest children and that may be kept in the classroom for a short period of time are: rabbits, squirrels, hen with chickens, birds, ducks, white mice.

Taking care of the animal. The plan for the cage must include: sufficient space for the animal to move about as well as for sufficient air of the correct temperature. Provision must be made for feeding the animal, for a sleeping place, and for keeping the cage clean.

Studying and discussing the animal's needs. Plan a definite routine, for a certain feeding time each day and for daily cleaning the cage. Have the children use this opportunity to observe the characteristics of each animal and its habits.

The child can tell in his picture about:

How the animal eats.

How the animal looks when it is asleep.

The kind of covering the animal has to keep it warm or dry.

The most important thing about the animal.

CHAPTER XVI

Prints

A PRINT IS AN INDENTATION or mark made by the pressure of stamping on a soft material such as clay or by pressing on cloth or paper.

Prints children can observe. Words in books are printed with ink from raised type. Children have seen their footprints in sand or snow as well as those of animals. Borders and all-over repeated designs are used on shelf paper, wallpaper, gift wrapping papers, textiles, and floor coverings.

Observation of a simple design with one or two repeated motifs will help children notice the organization of various all-over patterns. Ask the child to find one motif, then point to the same motif each time it is repeated. Is it repeated in rows that are straight, up and down, across, or is it like a checkerboard?

The print process is used to make several copies of the same design. Children may combine their prints or each child print several.

KINDS OF PRINTS CHILDREN CAN MAKE BY STAMPING
(Kindergarten, Grades One, Two, Three)

Materials for stamps. Blocks must be small enough (for children to grasp firmly), flat on one surface, and must absorb liquid color. They are best long or thick enough to keep children's fingers from touching the inked pad.

Wood blocks — scraps from furniture factory, wood or carpenter's shop.

Spools of various sizes, some cut in half or in quarters.

Buttons, dowels, burnt matchsticks, or *meat skewers.*

Stick printing sets composed of geometric shapes of wood (may be purchased commercially).

Corrugated paper (about 2″ wide) firmly rolled and tied with a string. The end is used for the stamp, making a circular textured pattern.

Rubber stoppers, erasers, hose ends, or

shower sprays.

Cork of all sizes.

Sponge of various sizes and shapes.

Materials for printing.

1. **Stamp pad.** Absorbent cloth such as flannel or felt or a piece of blotter is placed inside a coffee-can lid, a saucer, or similar waterproof container.

2. **Liquid color.** This is poured over the pad until it is saturated but does not ooze out of the pad when the stamp is pressed on the surface of the pad. Any of the following may be used: vegetable coloring, water-color paint, colored ink, tempera paint, or bluing.

3. **Paper.** An absorbent paper with a smooth surface is used, such as newsprint, white or colored construction paper, tissue, manila, paper towel, or fiber tint.

4. **Cloth.** Absorbent unsized cloth without wrinkles, such as bleached muslin, large man's handkerchief, or scraps of cloth from torn sheets, pillow cases, or tea towels.

Prints made on striped cloth must be made with carefully selected colors. Prints also may be made on paper over designs made with a batik dye process or paper that has been crumpled, dipped in dye, and then pressed flat.

Suggestions for colors of paper or cloth to use with color of paint, dye, or inks. Transparent colors should be used in a dark color printed over a light color of paper or cloth.

Cloth or paper:	Liquid color:
yellow	brown
	blue
	green
orange	brown
red-orange	black
pink	terra-cotta
	violet
	blue
yellow-green	turquoise
	brown
light blue	dark blue
golden brown	dark brown
peach	brown

Colors close in value are used to produce a color tone. Light colors are suitable for wallpaper to be used in small areas, such as a playhouse.

Color of wall or paper:	Liquid color:
yellow	peach
	yellow-green
	apple green
white	light blue
	pink or peach
	yellow

COLOR COMBINATIONS

Pleasing color combinations for the use of *transparent* color or ink, dye, or watercolor on colored cloth or paper are:

Cloth or paper:	Dye, ink, or paint:	Result in color:
green	yellow	yellow-green tone
blue	red	purple tone
yellow-green	blue	green tone
red-orange	blue	brown tone

Variations possible in using transparent liquid color. The color of the paper or cloth shows through the color of the stamp making a new color. Stamps may overlap, making very pleasing gradations of color.

Using opaque color for stamping. Opaque color used for printing has coverage. Thick tempera paint and oil paint are opaque. A light color of paint may be printed on a dark paper or cloth, or a dark color printed on a light or middle value color paper or cloth. One color paint printed over another color paint does not show through or intermix unless the color is thin.

Other variations in color. Paper which children have dipped into dye, or painted large plain areas of color all over, may be used effectively as backgrounds for stamping. The colors must relate — for example areas painted in yellow, orange, and golden brown on paper with dark blue stamped in a design on the surface, would be very striking. Base color choices on the printed paper or cloth selected, and on the surroundings.

THE PROCESS

THE CHILD DISCOVERS a new kind of design. The child first presses one end of the stamp on the pad saturated with a color, then presses the stamp directly down on the paper or cloth prepared for printing so that the entire face of the stamp touches the paper. The child lifts the stamp straight up. He sees the print he has made. The teacher needs to watch the beginners and help them print correctly.

The child presses the stamp on to the pad *each time* before he makes a print, using the same side of the stamp each time. Young children enjoy the manipulation of stamping. Every shape and size of block makes a different design when repeated.

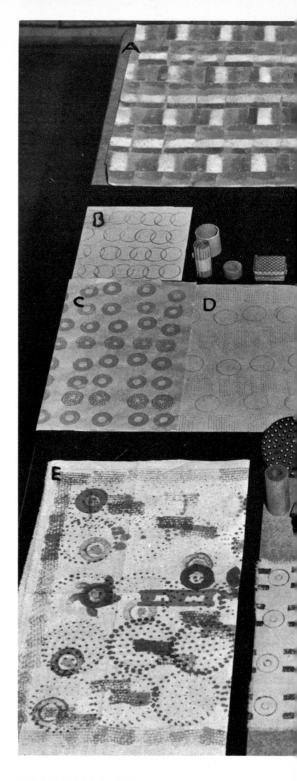

PRINTING WITH STAMPS

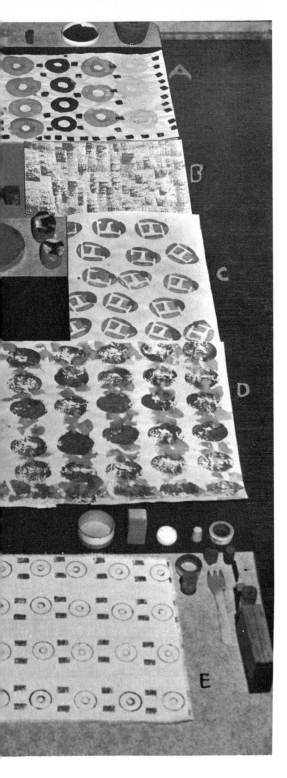

Right side top to bottom.

A. Two sizes of wooden circles and a square piece of wood used for stamps. A dark color and a middle value color with a white paper background. Note the rows of circles separated by rows of small squares. A dark row is in between two middle value rows.

B. Two sizes of square sponges have been stamped. The large sponge was stamped first. The small sponge was stamped second with a dark color. Note — All stamps are in the same direction forming stripes.

C. A potato has been cut in half — part has been cut away to result in a raised design. The potato was pressed on a color pad and stamped to make the design on the right.

D. A sponge has been stamped in a dark color, then a potato print added in a middle value color.

E. A stamped design on cloth. Two sizes of rings have been used and a rectangular shaped wooden stamp. The circles were stamped first. Thread was stretched between pins to keep the rows straight. Note other materials that may be used for stamps.

Left side top to bottom.

A. The end of the sponge has been used for the narrow rectangles. The top side of the sponge has been used for a square shape. Three color values were used. The hazy appearance is due to a texture made with a light color.

B. A piece cut from a cardboard mailing tube has made a circular line pattern. Note the overlapping which results in a second shape.

C. Two circles approximately the same size are repeated in rows. One circle is made by stamping with round wood and the other by a rolled corrugated cardboard fastened securely with a tape which makes a texture.

D. A paper used for padding with a raised bumpy surface has been used with the line circle for this design. Each is repeated in a row going across.

E. The child has been inventive, using the stamps to the right overlapping some prints, repeating different shapes and amount of color as he stamped on stretched cloth. The rubber shower nozzle has made the circle of dots.

AMPLES OF REPEAT DESIGNS

Children love to experiment and discover the many patterns they can make.

The child organizes a design with stamps, making a border design. A border design is a unit repeated along the edge or boundary of some material.

Helpful suggestions for printing (to avoid fingermarks). Strips of paper are fastened to the paper or cloth to guide the rows of prints and to keep the unprinted area clean. For each new row the strip of paper is moved to the right the desired distance. Instead of a strip of paper a sheet of paper may be used to cover the entire area below the space for the printed row, or a thread may be stretched between two pins to use as a guide on cloth.

Organized border designs. One block is used for a stamp. The child gains variety by grouping in a regular repeated manner, as below:

O OO O OO O OO
One, two, one, two.

OO OOO OO OOO OO OOO
Two, three, two, three.

One shape, two sizes (alternating in a row). Stamp large circles, first, far enough apart to allow room for the small circle.

O oo O oo O oo
One large, two small.

O °o O °o O °o O
One large, two small
(one above the other).

OO ooo OO ooo OO
Two large, three small.

Two shapes that vary in size and shape.
One large shape made of three straight
    lines such as a triangle. (The letter V.)
A smaller shape made of a curved line
    such as a circle. (The letter o.)
Stamp *triangles first*, stamp *circle second*.
V o V o V o V
V oo V oo V oo V
    Triangles in a row.

Circles in a row below the triangle.
(One, two or three rows.)

VVVVVVVVVVVVVVVVVVVV
oooooooooooooooooooo
VVVVVVVVVVVVVVVVVVVV
oooooooooooooooooooo
VVVVVVVVVVVVVVVVVVVV

VV VVV VV VVV VV VVV
o   o   o   o   o   o
VV VVV VV VVV VV VVV
o   o   o   o   o   o
VV VVV VV VVV VV VVV

Two shapes that vary in size and shape (both with straight sides are squares and rectangles).

Making an all-over repeated design by repeating borders, one below another. Each shape or group of shapes is repeated a minimum of three times across and up and down to make an all-over pattern. Different blocks used together make a group. The entire group is a unit, repeated a minimum of three times. One shape is repeated all over with one color. Following this a second block is repeated all over, using the same or a contrasting color.

The space between shapes and rows is important. Background shapes are formed. These are seen after the shapes are stamped as part of the design.

Placement of shapes may make stripes.

Keep one shape most important if several are used together.

Primary children should keep the block in one position while stamping.

Children mature enough to understand composition and grouping should experiment to produce pleasing original designs.

Making a print with a vegetable (Grades two and three). Choose good, firm, textured vegetables: potato (used for cutting away design); carrot (used for shape); parsnip (used for shape); okra (used for shape).

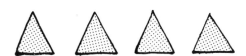

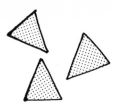

One group.

One variation.

REPEATING SHAPES FOR ALL-OVER DESIGN

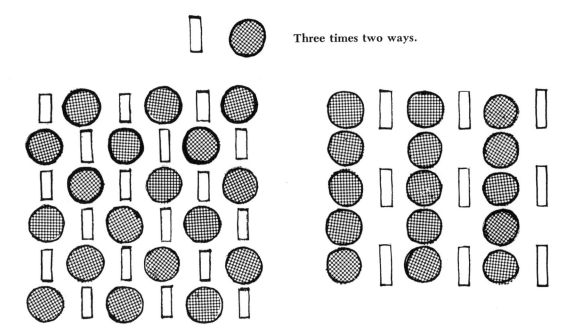

Three times two ways.

Cutting tools: a nail (the head is used to scrape parts out); a pen nib — insert the point of the pen into a pen holder, so that the curved half-circle serves as a gouge; a meat skewer, orange stick, or nut pick; pad (see page 179); paper (see page 179); color material (see page 179).

Process for potato print. Cut the potato crosswise or lengthwise, not smaller than 1¾" in diameter by approximately 1" thick, a size that a small hand can grasp and hold firmly. The outside edge may be left as is or cut. Give each child a piece of potato.

By painting the cut surface of the potato a dark color the child can see the part he cuts away easily. Each child uses a cutting tool to scoop out a design in relief from the flat surface of the potato. The dark raised part makes the print design.

The first time children cut away a portion of the surface, they tend to cut too much. After printing, the child realizes that the part he has cut away does not print. He must understand this before a second experience in cutting.

Printing the potato design. Potatoes

contain water; hence water-soluble paint or dye should be used on the stamp pad. The same methods are used for vegetable prints as for stick prints. A potato print must be started and finished in one day. A cut potato dries and shrinks when it is left out of water, and spoils if left either in or out of water too long.

Used cut pieces may be left for one night in water, if all the color is removed and the potato pieces are covered with clear water.

Carrots, parsnips, okra, and other vegetables also make good prints. Make a cross cut to remove the end. Stamp on the flat side. Follow same process for printing as for a potato.

Making prints with felt or heavy flannel (Second and Third Grade).

Materials needed are paper for cutting a pattern; scissors; felt from discarded hats, pennants, or new (any color); a wooden block the size of the felt shape; glue.

Cutting shapes from paper. Give children squares of paper two and three inches in diameter or rectangles two and one-half by three inches.

It is important to cut many shapes freely, and as large as possible from each paper square or rectangle. Shapes may be geometric or symbolic — of people, animals, birds, flowers, leaves, houses, trains, or toys. Encourage the children to make very simple contours with wide areas.

Choose the best shapes, place the paper pattern on a piece of felt and cut the same shape out of the felt.

Making the felt block for stamping. The felt shape is glued to a flat wooden block, the same length and width as the pattern so that children can see the exact place they are printing.

The small hand of a child has to grasp the block for stamping; hand size governs the size of the design mounted on the block.

Printing with the felt block. Dye or colored ink is printed on cloth (for directions for printing, see pages 181, 182).

Drying the finished printed paper or cloth. Place it carefully to dry flat on a clothes dryer, a table, pinned to a board or hung on a line stretched under the chalkboard, in a closet, or other place where air circulates. Allow twelve hours for drying printed cloth. Roll the printed textile on a cardboard tube or over a roll of paper.

Printed paper dries quickly. Leave it flat on the printing surface while children have recess, rest, or lunch.

Clean the block or stamp each time a different color is used, as well as following the completion of printing. To clean the block, wipe the end across a wet paper towel, rag, or sponge. Place the clean stamps in their containers.

Clean the pad that is filled with water-soluble color, by soaking it in cold water, draining off the colored water. Then wash it in warm soap suds. By using a rubber plunger the pads are quickly and easily cleaned, and can be used many more times.

Pads that are to be used soon again must be kept moist with water or coloring to avoid hard, caked paint.

Articles children can make from printed paper include:

Covers for books — scrap, telephone, spelling, social studies, stories, number, or note pad.

Cover for large cans used as wastebaskets.

Borders for writing paper, shelf paper, napkins, tablecloth, or notices to be sent home.

Decorated paper for gift wrapping or backgrounds for a plant, modeled clay, behind glass cupboard doors or with bulletin board arrangement.

Articles children can make from printed cloth include: handkerchiefs, head bands, pot holders, borders for towels, borders for an apron, curtains, place mats, table or chair covers for the playhouse. Repeated patterns as background for plants.

MONOPRINTS

Mono means one. No two monoprints are the same. Different patterns, textures, and forms can be printed on paper by using different methods.

Materials needed: A hard, smooth nonabsorbent surface such as a sheet of glass, aluminum, formica, glazed masonite, or enamel pan.

A tacky paint with a creamy consistency that ranges from thin to thick, such as opaque tempera, finger paint, or water-soluble printer's ink.

Brayer, large brush, or stiff cardboard 2″ x 3″ to apply the paint or ink to a hard surface.

Glazed nonabsorbent paper such as butcher, shelf paper, or finger paint paper.

Making a texture pattern. An even coat of paint the consistency of cream is spread with a brayer over a smooth hard surface like glass. A piece of glazed paper is placed face down over the ink. Use both hands to hold two corners of the paper. Touch the opposite end on the glass, then gradually lay the paper down. Carefully rub the back of the paper with the palm of the hands until all parts contact the paint.

Several ways to make monoprints involve:

Various ways of lifting up the paper, such as moving it quickly back and forth or up and down, jerking to one side, or lift rapidly then pause.

Varying thickness of the paint.

Using different related colors in areas on the glass or extreme difference in value such as very light blue and very

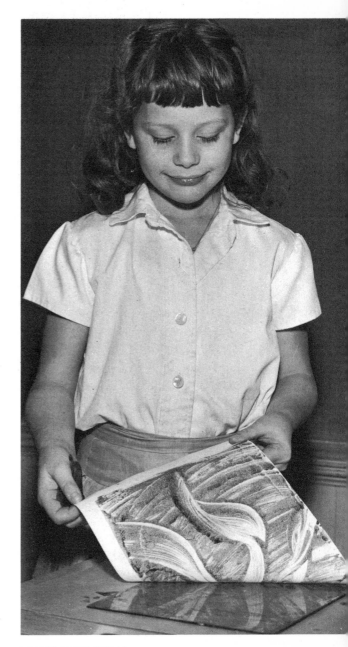

MONOPRINT

By Ann, Grade Two.

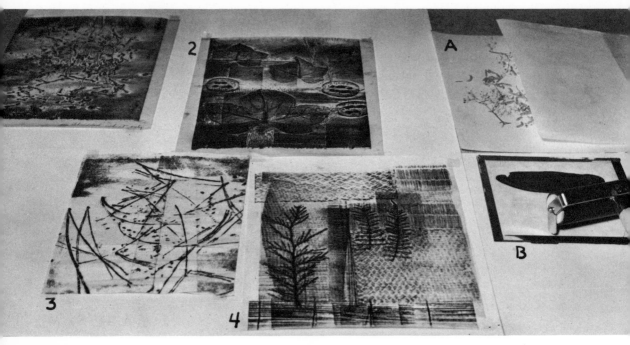

BRAYER PRINTS

A. Flat material such as maple seeds, fern, rice kernels, and leaves are placed on a sheet of paper over a hard, flat surface. A sheet of thin pressed paper such as typing paper or white tissue is placed over the texture material.

B. Water-soluble printer's ink is placed across a glass in a very small amount. The brayer is rolled over the ink, then over an absorbent piece of scrap paper, then rolled over the tissue which covers the texture material.

The prints above have all been made this way. The material used for each follows:

1. Bran Cereal.
2. Leaves and dollar-plant seeds (the dark strips result from strokes made by the brayer).
3. Pine needles and small seeds.
4. The background was brayed first. The texture resulted from different straw mats. The printed paper was placed over a small branch of cedar on the left and the fern to the right of the center.

CAUTION: Do not overlap objects. Remove a few leaves from a branch.

Paint that is too thick covers up the pattern.

Paper must be thin or the impression will not show.

Water-soluble ink does not adhere to oily paper.

Oil ink may be used but is not advised for primary school children.

Cover material completely with the printing paper to prevent textured materials from sticking to the brayer.

The photograph shows the brayer very close to the subject. The ink, glass, and brayer should be placed on a separate table close to the material.

This process is full of surprises.

dark blue or light gray and black.

Introducing flat materials such as ferns, string, sand, seeds, leaves, or grass on the color which covers the glass. Place the glazed paper over this and press down. Lift up the paper.

Drawing on the back of the paper which is pressed over the color on the glass. Lift up the paper.

Creating expressive forms. A smooth coat of printer's ink or finger paint is spread over glass or a pressed smooth paper. The child uses his hands to make forms in the ink by pushing ink away as he moves his fingers through the paint as in finger painting. When the whole page is composed, a clean sheet of absorbent paper is laid over the design and pressed directly down to contact the ink at all points. Lift the paper up and dry the print. Pieces of cardboard may be used to scrape away ink to make designs in place of the hands.

A monoprint may combine the above methods or be made a new way a child discovers. The results are appropriate to use as decorative paper for gift wrapping or to cover boxes. Single prints may be mounted as pictures.

STENCILS

A STENCIL IS A PROCESS used to make a single design suitable for a greeting card or a repeated design for a mural, a panel, a textile, or decorated paper.

Materials.

Paper for the cut stencil should be firm and nonabsorbent paper, such as: wrapping paper, heavy wax paper, backs of mimeograph stencil paper, tag board, butcher paper, or stencil paper. The minimum size is 4″ square; or 6″ square, 4″ by 6″, 6″ by 9″ or 9″ by 12″.

Paper for the stencil print should be absorbent with a slightly rough surface — such as cream manila, mimeo-news, white drawing, oatmeal or screening, colored construction paper, fibertint, or paper towel.

Sizes of paper or cloth should be the same size as the negative stencil, or larger for a single print if a margin is desired. Increase the size for all-over patterns.

Allow ½″ for finishing cloth.

Cloth for the stencil. See page 179, number 4 cloth.

Color combinations. See pages 98, 179.

Use water-soluble paint or chalk on paper, textile paint, or colored ink on cloth.

Tool for printing: sponge or dauber with a pad of color, large stiff bristle brush.

Scissors — Primary or embroidery.

(Other materials needed for a specific kind of stencil will be listed in the description of that process.)

Cutting the design for the stencil from nonabsorbent paper. The children first cut many designs from scrap paper, such as from magazine sheets.

Method 1. The child cuts out a design on the center fold of a piece of paper. The child then has two pieces, one fitting exactly into the cut-out portion of the other. This design is always symmetrical.

Open paper. Uncut paper must be all around the cut-out portion, at least 1″.

Method 2. The stencil paper is left flat (unfolded). The child cut a slit straight up from the center of the bottom edge at least 1″ long. From this point the child cuts out a continuous shape that ends at the opposite side of the starting point. The slit opening from the bottom is closed with tape. The cut-out portions must be one complete shape. This type of cutting gives the child the opportunity to see the shape grow as he cuts, and is best for free cutting. This is the best way to cut irregular shapes.

It is something he fully understands. Children need to practice cutting with scrap paper first.

As in Method 1, the child has two pieces of paper when he has cut a shape out of the paper.

Points to stress in cutting stencil designs. The paper for the cut stencil must be nonabsorbent. The slit cut in from the edge is closed by the use of tape. Shapes should have simple contours, without narrow projecting parts.

A plain area of paper must be left around the cut-out shape at least 1″ wide at all points. This space helps the child to keep smudges of paint from his finished stencil.

Both the negative and positive parts of the cut stencil may be used; they must be one complete shape made by continuous cutting.

Place the cut stencil over a piece of absorbent paper to make the print. Tape the negative stencil to the paper in the center of each side to hold the paper in place. (The child holds the positive stencil in place with his left hand.) The child presses a sponge or dauber on the pad of color then pats the open area of the negative stencil or the area around the positive stencil on the printing paper. The cut stencil paper is lifted up when the paint is dry. The process is repeated for as many prints as desired.

When the positive stencil is used for a design, the design will be the color of the paper or cloth. When the negative stencil is used the design is the color of the paint.

The second time give each child a piece of paper an over-all size to fit the shape to be stenciled, for example:

Place mat. The paper used for the cut stencil is the same size as the paper used for the place mat.

1. **Fold.**
2. **Cut-out portion.**

3. **Positive shape: the middle, cut-out portion makes the positive stencil design.**

4. **Negative shape: the remaining, surrounding portion makes the negative stencil design.**

A wall hanging or cover for a screen. Several children combine their stencils. Paper in the shape of squares and rectangles is given, the size needed for each individual design.

Border design. A shape cut out on an accordion fold may be used for a repeat design (see page 205), and cut-paper designs suitable for stencils, page 205).

Suitable subjects for stencil designs are people, animals, trees, insects, flowers, abstract shapes, buildings, large capital letters.

Subjects suitable for combining the stencils made by individual children are a large tree with stenciled leaves, flowers, fruit, and birds; a community with stenciled buildings, trees, cars, trucks and people.

As a background for puppet plays or dioramas, irregular edges may be used for land forms, clouds, and water.

Stencil designs may be used as repeated designs for borders or all-over patterns on shelf paper, place mats, curtains, box covers, pillows, book covers, gift wrapping papers, wastebaskets; as a single design complete in one unit: greeting card, announcement, matted for picture print, cover for booklet, place mat, cover for box; or as wall hangings. Variety in pattern is gained by grouping and by overlapping stencils.

CHALK STENCILS

Materials.

Chalk. Use dark chalk on light printing paper, use light chalk on dark printing paper, use dark, light, or middle-value color on white or cream-color paper.

Use a slightly rough absorbent paper like construction or manila.

Materials needed to apply the chalk to the stencil are: a dauber (made by stretching soft cloth around a cotton ball and tying the loose ends); folded piece of paper towel; piece of blotter; a soft brush.

Method 1. The repeated tree stencils were made as follows:

Chalk Stencil Process.

1. Cut-out the tree shape allowing margin all the way around.
2. Place negative cut-out over print paper. Hold cut-out in place with tape or paper clips.
3. Draw a heavy chalk line around the tree opening as indicated above.
4. Use a cotton dauber to rub the chalk over the edge of the opening, with a circular motion, on to the paper as indi-

cated by arrows in *B*.
5. Cut leaves in positive stencil, pattern *C*, then draw chalk line around cut-out shapes, see *C*.
6. Place stencil pattern *C* over the stenciled tree *B* [1] on the print paper and rub the chalk with a dauber as indicated by arrows in *C*. See finished stencil of tree with leaf pattern *D*.

Stencil patterns *E*, *F*, *G*, are placed between the trees for variety and interest. People, houses or flowers are also appropriate to use.

Method 2. The child daubs a cotton pad on powder paint or chalk dust, then pats the open area of the stencil with the pad.

The design is the color of the chalk. The background is the color of the paper.

Using the negative stencil keeps the child's finger marks from soiling the finished stencil, since the printing paper is covered; this is the most satisfactory method for five-, six- and seven-year-old children.

The positive shape stencil is placed over

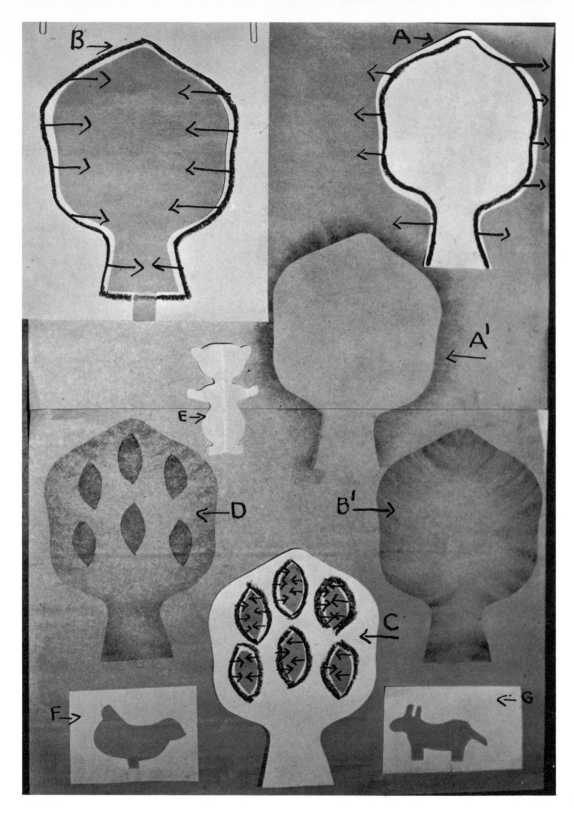

PAPER CUT-OUTS
FOR CHALK STENCIL

A Positive tree stencil pattern with chalk outline.

B Negative tree stencil pattern with chalk outline.

A[1] Positive tree pattern stenciled on paper with black chalk.

B[1] Negative tree pattern stenciled on paper with black chalk.

C Positive tree stencil with cut-out leaves outlined in black chalk.

D Finished stenciled tree with pattern of leaves.

E Positive pattern, bear.

F Negative pattern, bird.

G Negative pattern, animal.

the center of the printing paper, and a chalk line drawn all the way around the positive stencil about ¼″ from the outside edge. The chalk is rubbed with the dauber, from the chalk line over the edge of the positive shape onto the printing paper.

The design is the color of the paper. The background is the color of the chalk.

Variations for chalk stencils.

Use large sheets of paper for stencil designs: 20″ by 24″, 12″ by 18″, or 15″ by 20″.

1. Use both the negative and positive shapes.

2. Use a negative shape repeated in one row. Use positive shape repeated in a second row.

3. The positive shape may overlap the negative shape. Use one color for the negative shape and a second color for the positive shape. A third color is made in the area the two colors overlap.

4. Use strips of paper no smaller than 1″ by 6″. Place the strip of paper on the printing paper away from the edge, and draw a chalk line in from the edge of the strip of paper. Using a dauber the child rubs the chalk over the edge of the strip onto the paper beneath. The strip is moved to overlap the first stencil or to a different place on the paper. Each time the child draws a fresh chalk line he rubs the chalk over the edge of the strip of paper. The effect is similar to that of searchlights. A second or third color may be added. As one color crosses over another, a new color is made.

Encourage children to make very simple shapes at least 1½″ wide at all places.

Building a design by combining chalk stencils. For individual designs, use paper 15″ by 20″ or 24″ by 30″.

For a group project, use mural paper 36″ by 72″.

Stencils combined and added to a large stenciled tree form. The children may make an individual tree or work as a group on a large tree. The stencil for the tree trunk with bare branches is cut first. It may be made to fit a vertical panel approximately five feet high.

The children cut stencils to represent leaves, flowers, fruit, birds, and animals, and place their cut stencils directly on the tree mural. The stencils may be grouped, with some overlapping and others used as a single stencil, but the whole must balance. Use extreme contrast in value when light is used over dark, such as, white on dark green.

SPONGE STENCILS
(For Kindergarten, Grades One, Two, Three)

Materials needed are sponge, negative stencil, absorbent paper, pad saturated with liquid paint.

Method. Place the negative stencil over the absorbent paper. Pour liquid paint over a large pad placed in a pie pan or large lid. Press the sponge on the pad. Pat the sponge on a paper towel to remove excess paint.

Pat the entire opening of the negative stencil, going over the edge of the opening, with the sponge (pressing straight down). Dry the negative stencil thoroughly before lifting it.

Spatter stencils.

Materials. Cover the top of a wooden chalk box or other wooden box, about 4″ by 6″, with a fine mesh screen; remove the bottom of the box.

Water-soluble paint, tempera or powder paint, dye, colored ink.

Stiff bristle brush such as a toothbrush or piece of scrub brush.

Absorbent printing paper, 4″ by 6″. Cut a negative stencil, with the outside measure-

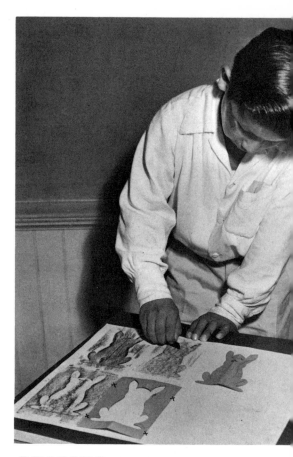

RUBBING

Billie has placed a cut-out paper rabbit under the paper he is rubbing with the broad side of a wax crayon. He moves the rabbit to rub another form. The rectangular paper with the cut-out rabbit may also be used.

Children may rub over many different shapes of paper. Flat materials such as leaves, screens, string, pine needles, woven straw, and seeds are a few good materials for rubbing designs.

ment of the paper the same as the inside measurement of the box — 4" by 6".

Procedure. Place the absorbent paper on a flat surface, and the negative stencil over the absorbent paper.

Place the open or bottom of the wooden box over the negative stencil. The wire screen is over the top of the box.

Dip a stiff bristle brush into liquid paint. Pat it on an absorbent cloth or paper towel to remove the drips of paint from the brush.

Draw the paint-filled brush over the wire screen. The exposed paper in the opening of the negative stencil will be spattered with paint. For deeper colors, spatter twice.

Dry the spattered stencil thoroughly. Lift up box; then lift negative stencil directly up. Place the finished print in a clean place.

As many prints as are desired may be made with this method.

Cleaning materials. Use a brush to scrub the paint from the wire screen. Wash the paint from the stiff bristle brush. Use a damp paper towel or rag to wipe the paint from the negative stencil.

Other materials for a spatter paint design (materials must be flat) are: pressed materials such as leaves, grasses, flowers, cedar, fern, seed pods, or grain; shells, like clam shells; discarded materials such as buttons, pieces of wood, rick-rack.

Procedure. Fasten the printing paper to a cork board; pin the material flat to the printing paper so that no part overlaps another part and the complete contour of every part is distinct. Remove any leaves that overlap a branch, or petals that overlap each other. Slant pins so they are not over the area to be printed.

Place the chosen materials on printing paper under a screen-covered box for a spatter print. Dry thoroughly before removing the materials.

STENCILING

SPATTER STENCILS
(For Third Grade)

Materials needed are: atomizer or spray gun, negative stencil, natural or discarded materials, dye or ink, absorbent paper, newspaper.

Procedure. Fasten printing paper to a board. Pin stencil onto the paper, and place the board in an upright position, with newspaper around the outside. Hold the spray gun at least twelve inches from the stencil and spray the opening of the negative stencil with color. Dry thoroughly before removing the negative stencil.

SAMPLE GROUP PROJECT — THE COMMUNITY
(A chalk or sponge method is suggested.)

Combining stencils to make a "Community" mural. Divide the children into four groups, one group to cut stencils for one type of subject: Group 1. Stencils to represent building. Group 2. Stencils to represent trees. Group 3. Stencils to represent people. Group 4. Stencils to represent cars, trucks and trains.

The buildings should be stenciled first; then the trees in groups all through the mural; then the people near homes and by trees; then the cars, trucks and trains.

VARIATIONS IN COMBINING STENCIL PROCESSES

A SPATTER, SPRAYED, or sponge stencil may be combined with stick prints.

Procedure. Stencil the negative shape. Stamp the background, using a round dowel or other shape for an all-over pattern, or leave the background the color of the paper, and stamp a pattern in a darker color than the stencil paint over the stencil design.

Print the positive stencil and stamp an all-over stick print pattern on the paper surrounding the positive stencil.

Experiment with various combinations.

Stencil combined with watercolor. Paint areas of watercolor over absorbent paper. Try using stencils with varying edges to make rhythmic movement. Third graders who have had some experience with stencils may combine several different stencils. When several are used, transparent paper is best for the cut-out stencil pattern, because the child is able to see the two stencil shapes together.

SCREEN PRINTS

Materials.

Screen. Cloth such as cheesecloth, scrim, mosquito netting, voil, organdy, or silk screen cloth is tightly stretched over a wooden frame. Tape solidly all around the inside edge. (A heavy cardboard frame with cloth stretched over the opening, stapled to the frame can be substituted for the wooden frame.)

Squeegee (one of the following): A strip of rubber fastened to a handle (the rubber is narrower than the inside measurement of the screen frame), such as: window squeegee, rubber dish scraper, wedged-shape piece of wood, stiff piece of cardboard.

Finger paint.

Absorbent printing paper, as unprinted news, fibertint, construction paper.

Stencil paper should be thin, for example typing or tracing paper.

Procedure (for Second and Third Grade). (Children enjoy helping to make a screen print. Each of the following represents a duty for a single child.)

Cover the working surface with wrapping paper or flat, unwrinkled, want-ad sheets from the news paper. One sheet of printing paper is placed on a flat surface for each child.

The negative stencil design has been cut out of light-weight paper the size of the screen frame. Place this on top of the printing paper; place the screen frame face down on the cut negative stencil.

One tablespoon of screen paint is placed across the top of the inside edge of the screen frame. Place the squeegee on top of the paint. The child grasps the squeegee handle firmly with both hands and pulls it to the lower inside edge of the screen, spreading the screen paint over the entire surface of the screen. The ink adheres the cut negative stencil to the cloth on the frame.

The paint is forced through the mesh of the cloth over the open areas of the design, making a print on the paper beneath. The uncut areas of paper serve to block out the screen paint.

The squeegee may be left in the frame with the top resting on the lower edge of the frame, or be lifted out and placed on a large lid or plate until the next print is made.

The screen should be lifted directly up by one child. Another child picks up the

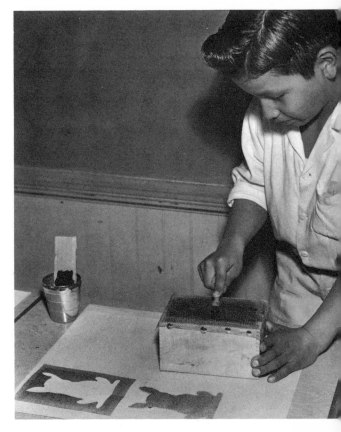

SPATTER-PRINT

print and places it to dry on a flat surface (some paints dry almost instantly). A number of screen prints can be made from the same design while the paint on the screen is wet. Dry paint clogs the screen.

Cleaning the screen after printing. Allow cold water to run through the screen, using a brush if necessary to clean all the paint out of the weave of the cloth, leaving the clean screen ready for a new design.

Paper stencils may be washed off with water. Place clean negative and positive cut stencil designs between a folded paper with the child's name on the otuside.

Screen print combined with cut paper shapes (Third Grade). Cut colored paper shapes are pasted on a background of absorbent paper. For beginners large, simple rectangles and squares are suggested.

The negative cut paper stencil design is adhered to the screen and printed over the cut paper shapes. It is advisable to keep the cut paper shapes close in value or in related colors. The stencil design may be a darker related color. For example, yellow, orange, and golden brown paper shapes are pasted to a manila background. The stencil is in dark brown. The stencil may overlap the cut paper shape and be printed partly on the manila paper. A gay print with a circus theme might be in red-orange, yellow, turquoise blue, and black.

WAX CRAYON SCREEN PRINTS

Materials needed are: wax crayon (one dark color) used for block-out in place of cut stencil, and the same other items as for screen print.

Procedure: cut paper the size of the screen opening. The child draws a design with one color crayon. Parts may be lines with some areas filled in solid and others

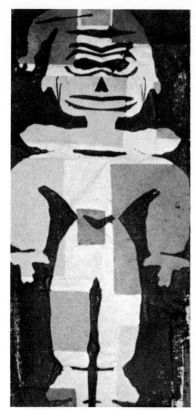

TWO SCREEN PRINTS OVER COLORED PAPERS

left as texture. The subject may be imaginary or something the child knows about — a self-portrait, an animal, a house, a train, a plant, a boat, a character from a story. The space must be well filled with clearly defined shapes and lines. Self-confident children may draw directly on the screen. Rubbings also may be made over materials such as bark, woven straw mats or seeds, for texture.

The screen frame is placed face down over the crayon drawing. The child can see the crayon design he has made through the thin cloth. The child draws the design on the cloth with crayon, following his crayon design on paper. A firm, even pressure is needed to fill the weave of the cloth. The crayon acts as a resist or block-out for the water-soluble screen paint.

Place the crayon design on the screen frame, face down on the printing paper. Apply the paint with a squeegee as for other screen prints.

After several printings, if the crayon becomes thin, more may be added on top of the original crayon areas.

SCREEN STENCIL PRINT

A. Positive cut-out shape.
B. Negative shape.
C. Wooden frame with stretched cheesecloth is placed over the negative paper stencil.
D. Wooden frame with stretched cheesecloth placed over positive paper stencil. Finger-paint solution has been poured along the top edge inside the frame. The right hand holds a wedge-shaped block of wood called a squeegee.

A. Arthur, a third-grader, is pulling a finger-paint mixture with a piece of cardboard over a crayon drawing he has made on a piece of scrim stretched across an embroidery hoop. In front of him is the original crayon drawing of a cow and the first print he has made.

B. A rectangular opening has been cut in a box lid for a frame. Organdie has been taped across the opening. Above the frame is the print.

C. Jean, a third-grader, is pulling a piece of cardboard she is using for a squeegee from top to bottom of her screen design to force the paint through the open mesh of the cloth. Cloth was stretched across an opening cut in a cardboard frame, then stapled in place. Note that the cardboard has buckled because it was too light in weight. Use double-faced corrugated cardboard for this. Jean's print is in the lower corner.

A POSITIVE AND
NEGATIVE PRINT

Materials.

1. Shapes which make design: shapes cut from adhesive paper with variety in edges; shapes cut from Kraft tape folded in half with details cut out along the fold; round holes cut with a punch; miscellaneous stickers, such as stars and circles to add variety.

2. Screen supplies (see page 194).

Procedure. The stickers and adhesive paper shapes are arranged and stuck to the cloth on the outside of the screen frame. The screen is placed face down on the printing paper, and printed like other screen prints (pages 195, 196, 198). Make these clear, sharp prints.

MAKING A BLUEPRINT

CHILDREN ENJOY THE surprise element of seeing a print emerge, as well as the clarity and beauty of a finished print.

Materials.

Pieces of cardboard, window glass and (slow-burning) blueprint paper, all the same size — 4″ by 6″, 6″ by 8″, or 9″ by 12″.

Eight clip clothespins or clamps. (A photograph frame may be used instead of the cardboard and clothespins.)

Two blotters equal in size to the blueprint paper.

Two pans of water slightly larger than the blueprint paper.

Newspapers, stencil material, and sunlight (choose a sunny day for printing). Hydrogen peroxide.

Preparation of stencil material for pattern of print. Choose materials that are flat, such as grass, leaves, small thin branches with leaves, cedar, ferns, seed pods, feathers, moss, small vines, butterfly wings, and single-petaled flowers; or cut shapes from paper — plants, animals, or beautiful imaginary shapes.

Press the material between magazine sheets and place under a weight. All moisture must be removed from pressed mate-rial before it is used for the print.

Prepare printing materials and print in a shady or darkened room. Place blueprint paper, with blue side up, over a sheet of cardboard. Arrange the dry stencil material or cut paper shapes on the blueprint paper, without any parts overlapping. (The teacher needs to examine each arrangement to help the child find overlapping parts and to remove them.)

Place the glass over the arrangement, and clamp firmly to the cardboard on the bottom or fasten with tape. Expose the arrangement to sunlight; the paper will whiten — the blueprint paper and the intensity of the sun will determine the length of exposure needed. Children enjoy experimenting with different lengths of time to determine that required to make the clearest print. When the paper turns gray remove the blueprint from the sunlight.

Place the blueprint paper in clear water only until the print emerges.

Add a few drops of hydrogen peroxide to the second pan of water, and place the print in this solution. This sets the print.

Rinse the print thoroughly in running water, holding two corners at the top to avoid wrinkles.

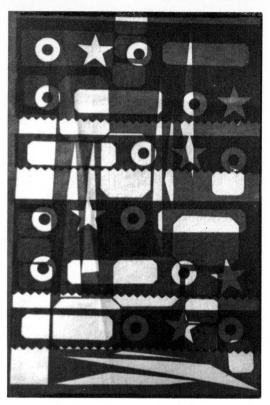

**TWO EXAMPLES OF PRINTS FROM
ADHESIVE PAPER STENCILS**

Place the print on a flat surface until it is nearly dry.

Then place the print between sheets of absorbent unprinted paper, such as towels or blotters, under a weight until completely dry. A warm iron may be used to press a wrinkled print. The finished blueprint mounted with a white mat makes a delightful picture or greeting card. Blueprints are also suitable for program covers.

CHAPTER XVII

Cut Paper

GUIDANCE FOR LEARNING TO USE SCISSORS

(Second term of Kindergarten or when child has sufficient coordination.)

PAPER IS AN inexpensive basic material children are familiar with in different colors as well as in varying weights. Bright colored papers delight children, as they cut, fold and join parts together to invent new forms. The examples chosen suggest ways for creating other forms.

Explain that the scissors are designed for cutting: 1) The loops in the scissors are made to fit around the thumb and second finger. The loops in left-handed scissors are reversed from the ones on right-handed scissors, the blades are the same. 2) Two sharp blades are fastened together to enable them to move toward each other, making it possible to cut paper, cloth, and string.

Discarded sheets from magazines are advised for the first cutting. The child should cut in a continuous straight line, holding the paper near the center of the left side with the left hand, and keeping the paper between the blades close to the center of the scissors.

The eyes should focus on the point toward which the scissors are to cut.

The blades should slant slightly as they are moved up and down in cutting, without completely closing.

The right hand holding the scissors moves slowly ahead, and at the same time the left hand holding the paper, moves it gradually toward the scissors.

Kindergarten or beginning first-graders may easily need several experiences with scissors before they have developed the coordination necessary to cut with an easy, smooth movement.

Suggested steps for first cutting. Have the children cut from colored sheets in magazines, cutting from the bottom up, out or around.

1. *Straight strips of paper.* These could be woven or made into chains.
2. *Houses,* one from a sheet. (These are straight edges but have different directions.)
3. *Big circles,* one from a sheet. Children need guidance in gradually turning their paper around.
4. *Large simple shapes* children have

drawn in pencil or crayon.

5. *Edges* such as scallops along a straight strip of paper, or a zig-zag like the letter "V".

If the child is confused or his finger muscles tighten up, he is cutting something that is too small or intricate, or he is too immature for the process.

Habits for children to develop.

1. To cut shapes from paper with as little waste as possible.

2. To choose paper suitable for the size and shape of the object to be cut.

3. To cut paper over a table, and place discarded *small* scraps in the waste-basket.

4. To use scissors *only* for cutting, and to keep them in a supply box when not in use.

THINGS TO MAKE BY CUTTING PAPER

Shelf paper, designed with a cut edge, for the playhouse or cupboard shelves in the classroom. Choose colored paper to harmonize with the color scheme of the room.

A. Cut the paper to fit the dimensions of the shelf (plus one inch if the edge is to extend down over the front edge).

B. The end which is to be at the front of the shelf should be folded back about one inch. This fold will mark the depth to which the edge is cut.

Suggested edges to cut from scrap paper are: arcs in groups; reversed arcs in groups; pointed edges of different heights and widths; straight edges grouped in different heights and widths of rectangles and squares.

Encourage children to cut a broad repeated shape to insure a stronger edge.

Portrait is drawn in crayon and mounted on light green construction paper. A cut-paper border (made from folded paper) was added on both sides.

By a First-Grader.

Repetition of one shape at equal intervals is important to produce a rhythmic movement with variety in widths and heights.

Let each child choose one edge he has cut and cut this edge on his shelf paper. *Crayon designs add color to the finished cut edge.*

Encourage children to try their own ideas. Border designs are things in a row. Children see trains, one after another, trees and houses along a street, flowers in a row, as well as toys in a game such as nine pins.

Use cut edges for place mats, for doll table in the playhouse, as place mats for the lunch period, for a beauty spot, such as under a plant, a clay figure, or a book, or for presents.

Materials. Choose contrasting colors of construction or wallpaper 12″ by 18″ (one color lighter than the other, such as yellow and green or pink and violet); scissors, paste, wax crayon.

Since something is usually placed on the center of a mat, the outside edge is the important part. Discuss with the group the different possibilities for varying and decorating the edge.

A SAMPLE PROJECT: MAKING A DESIGN OF PAPER SHAPES
(First, Second and Third Grade)

Materials. A supply table accessible to the children should contain separate piles of colored poster paper, with one pile of gray papers 12″ by 18″ or 18″ by 24″ to be used for backgrounds. Have children select sizes of paper large enough to place

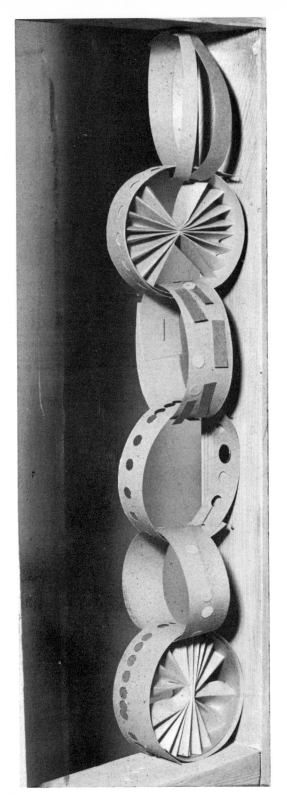

Paper Chain Hanging in a Frame.

MELODIE AND JOHN WEAVING PAPER STRIPS
Grade Three

A PLACE MAT

Weaving strips of paper through slits cut in a rectangular shaped paper. The fold determines the center of the pattern and places the vertical stripe. The length of the cut determines the width of the stripe. *Note:* Two cuts are made to give each horizontal line width. These may vary.

FOLDING AND CUTTING

1. Fold a rectangular piece of construction paper 9″ by 12″ in half, making a strip 6″ by 9″.

2. Fold the right edge toward the left folded edge. Fold the left edge toward the right folded edge. The distance the edge overlaps determines the position of the stripes.

3. Cut in from the right-hand fold toward the left; and from the left-hand fold toward the right.

4. *Note:* The stripe is *not* cut to the edge of the paper. It is advisable to have children make a trial cut from a magazine sheet.

Delightful patterns are made this way. The spacing of cuts offers design possibilities not found in just squares (so often used).

smaller shapes upon, and colors of paper that contrast.

Suggested sizes of poster paper. (Colorful wrapping papers may also be used to add sparkle).

Squares	Rectangles
9″ by 9″	9″ by 12″
4″ by 4″	2″ by 7″
1″ by 1″	4″ by 9″
3″ by 3″	1″ by 6″

Colors

Blue	Pink
Green	Red
Yellow	Black
Violet	Light blue

Procedure. Encourage children to cut some free-form shapes and some shapes cut from folds.

Let outside edge of the paper be the outside edge of the design. Circles and triangles may be cut from squares and rectangles.

A ROW OF FIGURES CUT ON A FOLD TO HOLD HANDS

Second and Third Grade

A. Accordion fold of paper.
The center of the figure and the hand are on the fold. The folded paper is held together and the figure cut out around the contour on the right side. *Do not* cut around the hand. The hand must remain on the fold. Notice the large broad, straight feet to give support to the figures. Two strips may be cut and joined for a long strip.

B. Cut out figures with the hands on the end taped to make a complete circle with all hands joined.

C. Double row of figures joined at the top of the head and the hands. An accordion fold is used and then the folded paper is folded across the center, or a double fold is made. The top of the head, the center back, and the hands are cut on a fold.

See illustration D for cutting. — — represents fold. Cut out striped area.

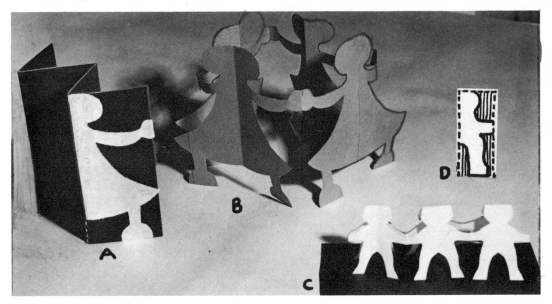

For Grades One, Two, Three

Details for cutting are given on the right.

A. Textured paper with a pattern of open triangles.

B. Primitive head and arms cut on the fold. The shape fits a rectangle. Variations may be used to make a cut-out totem pole with one above another.

C. Long narrow triangular slits cut on the fold. Compare with A.

D. A strip of paper 15″ by 12″ is folded in half. The horizontal strips joined in the center are ½″ wide by 7″ long. The end of each strip overlaps the beginning of the strip and is pasted, forming a ring. Note the way they alternate.

Try fastening the top to the bottom of the center strip to make a large circle with smaller circles around the big circle. This form also might make an imaginary tree, or be used along the back of an animal.

E. Paper is 6″ by 8″. Slits are cut on a vertical fold (see detail above). The slit portion may be bent forward or back, be used for an animal covering (as on page 223), or cover a cylinder.

F. A series of lanterns have been pasted to a cardboard mailing tube (see detail). This might hang from a mobile or be a tree form.

G and H are the same basic fold and cutting. G has more curved half circles. A vertical space of at least an inch is left down the center. Experiment with different folds such as the half of the circular shape on the left folded back with the corresponding one on the right folded front. Alternate; try different widths. The center might be painted a color to contrast the ouside. These are attractive hangings which move with air currents.

H. The outside contour is an oval shape with the square paper cut away.

I. A crown, top for a bird's head, mane for a horse or lion, or flower form. The length of the strip depends upon its use.

J. Paper 11″ by 11″ has been folded in half (see detail). This shape is suitable for an open flower. Fold back on dotted line.

K. The fold and cutting is the same as for J. The two straight uncut edges are overlapped and jointed to make circles (see detail). Center top is pasted to center bottom.

L. Method used to join two pieces together. Slits are cut in the two pieces to be joined the same length. Example: two cards measuring 8″ by 6″.

Card 1 — cut from *bottom* to center of card.

Card 2 — cut from *top* to center of card. Combine the two by sliding the cut in card 1 into the cut in card 2 the full length of the slit.

This method may be used for buildings, attaching a bird wing to a body, legs to the body of the animal, arms on a person, and abstract shapes such as circles.

M. Catsteps. This fold makes a spring. It is used as legs for a jumping jack or animal, as a neck, or as a hinge to fasten parts together — such as a lion's head to its body. A paper approximately ¾″ by 11″ makes a catstep 2″ long and can be pulled to a length of 3½″. Fasten *a* to *b* at right angles. Fold *b* over *a*, then *a* over *b* then *b* over *a* and continue until the end of the strips are reached. Keep the folded corners straight.

N. Fold paper 9″ by 12″ in half. Cut slits as indicated. Hang from smallest center triangle. Try varying the proportion.

O. Paper 12″ by 12″. Fold in half resulting in 6″ by 12″. Fold in half again, result is 6″ square. Fold diagonally as shown in detail above with folded side *2* against two folds *1* and cut as indicated by horizontal lines. Note the way the lines alternate, and that they are cut partway across. Open and stretch. Balls may hang in the center. This lacy shape may be stretched over a colorful cylinder or tree shape.

For a built-up design, openings are not cut in the paper, just shapes with varying edges, some — like circles or squares — with unbroken edges.

Have each child combine his cut-out shapes to make a design. The child chooses a background color, and places his largest shapes on the paper to balance the entire space. Some shapes may be darker and others lighter than the background color. He places smaller shapes on top of larger shapes in colors that go well together. Very small shapes may be grouped. Confetti may be used for an all-over pattern.

The child pastes his completed arrangement to the background paper by slipping a little paste under the edges of shapes with a toothpick. Built-up designs may also be made from pieces of cloth.

Making a design with cut-out openings in shapes. Grades one, two, three. The preparation for this lesson is the same as for the previous one, and the same size papers may be used. A few shapes should be left plain without cut openings. Place some of these shapes behind cut-outs so the color shows through the opening, and use other plain shapes by themselves to keep the design from being too busy.

It is easiest to cut openings inside an area by folding the paper and then snipping out small shapes. Cut parts may be folded back to make an opening, as well as a third dimension.

Cutting paper or cloth: strengthens the child's fingers; aids his coordination of eye and hand; emphasizes shapes, sizes, edges; teaches respect for paper as a material.

STANDING CUT-PAPER FORMS

The illustration below shows the paper folded over and over. The striped part is cut away. Note the parts of the animal on the fold which joins the nose and back of the body. This design is appropriate for a cut stencil, a rubbing, or for a border around a box.

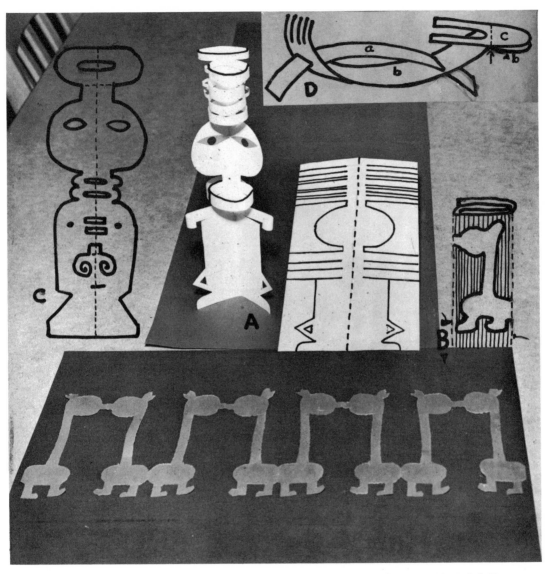

IMAGINARY ANIMALS CUT ON A VERTICAL FOLD
By a Second-Grader.

PAPER CUT-OUT BUILDINGS

A. Box shape with figure extended on one side. The box may be used as a container for candies, nuts, or flowers. The extended part may be an animal, person, house, bird, or plant form, either on the front or back (see detail below for cutting).

B. Seated animal cut on the fold. Slits cut in the arms hold the name plate. The same idea may be used for a person. A broad body with legs straight on the under side support the body. Color may be added with crayon or paint.

C. House shape with folded flap at the base for support. Note the variation in the contour of the top edge. The same fold and silhouette idea may be used for a plant form, fish, or bird. Construction-weight paper is needed.

D. The body of the lion is drawn in crayon. The round head of the lion is made from a white circle of paper pasted on to a larger gray circle with features added. Felt or cotton could be used instead. A folded paper hinge joins the head to the card, thus placing the head in front of the body. The name plate extends out from the background (see detail).

E. Paper is folded in the center with a paper cut-out figure on one side. Suitable subjects are: a tree, flower, leaf, animal, house, or abstract shape. Instead of cut paper, crayon may be used.

F. Fold a paper 2½" by 1½" in half. The "chick" fits the space 1¼" by 1½". The top of the head and tail are on the fold. The — — — separates the body from the feet. Fold along this line on both sides, turning the feet outward. The flat feet on each side support the "chick."

G. The extended animal head is in the center of the rectangular shape. This may be a person, a flower, or other object. The — — represents the flap. Place end *a* over *b* and paste, making a cylindrical shape. This shape can be placed around a paper cup, a salt or oatmeal box, or tin can.

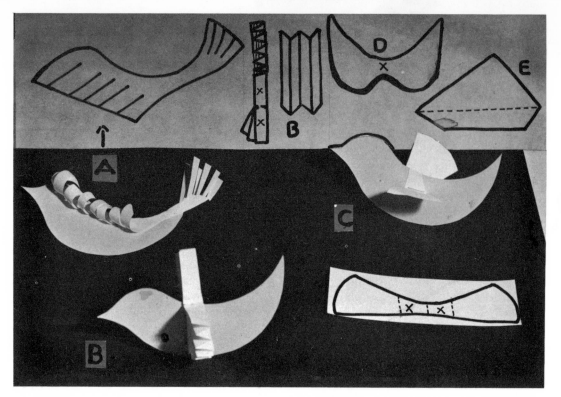

THE SAME BIRD SHAPE USED WITH VARYING WINGS

A. Curled feathers. The upper edge of A follows the contour of the top edge of the bird. Cut slits are represented by black lines. These are curled back to represent feathers. Paste the two top edges together.

B. Pleated fan-shaped wing. Paper 10″ by 2¾″ is folded in ½″ accordion pleats. The pleats are held together in the center with a staple. The left side of one end (X) is pasted to the body of the bird on the one side and the right side (X) pasted to the opposite side of the bird (see detail B above).

C. Single fan-shaped wing cut on the fold. Fold on dotted line. Fasten to both sides of the body of the bird at points X.

D. Cut on the fold a wing shape. Cut a slit down the center back of the bird about ½″. Insert the wing at point X into the slit. The wing is at right angles to the body of the bird.

E. Cut two wings. Fold back on the dotted line. Paste the flap to the side of the bird. Try different directions: the wing may be straight or slanted; the top may be curled or folded down.

ANIMAL FORMS
Grades Two and Three

These imaginary animal forms are based on a cylinder which is made from a rectangle. Note the cuts on either side of the rectangle for the legs given in pattern 1 for A and B. The tail may extend out from the rectangular shape as in B or be added as in A.

The pattern on the back and under side of

animal A is made by inserting a strip of a contrasting color of paper through slits cut into the cylinder. The same strip extends to make the tail and is looped for the head. See No. 2 pattern. See woven paper mats page 204.

C is made from two three-quarter circles, one slightly larger than the other. A strip with a pointed edge has been inserted between the two cone shapes. Tabs are used on the under side of the larger cone shape to fasten it to the cylindrical body, making the head as in B. *The rabbits D and F are made from cylinders.* Straight strips have been used for legs, ears and eyes. See pattern on lower right hand corner for joining legs to the cylinder. For the lower legs on D use one strip of paper across the bottom of the cylinder. Make loops for legs by pasting the center of the strip to the cylinder. Ears are one long strip looped and fastened on the side to the cylinder.

Animal E is cut on a fold. The legs are cut in silhouette on the side. The folds give support to the standing animal form. Parts of the head have been added. See pattern lower left.

Try other animals based on the basic shapes

KINGS AND QUEENS

Grades One, Two, Three

Roll straight pieces of paper to make a cylindrical body. Roll half circles to make cone shaped figures. A straight strip of paper with five vertical folds may be joined by overlapping the ends making a four sided figure. Vary the height of the figures by using different widths of paper. Wrap a straight rectangle or square shape around the figure to make a robe or cape. Cut an edge on a straight strip of paper and join the end to make a crown. Arms may be rolled cylinders or strips of paper going around the figure, fastened to the back. The bottom of the cylinder must be straight and wide enough to support the figure. Cut paper shapes added for hair, features of the face and pattern on garments add variety and interest.

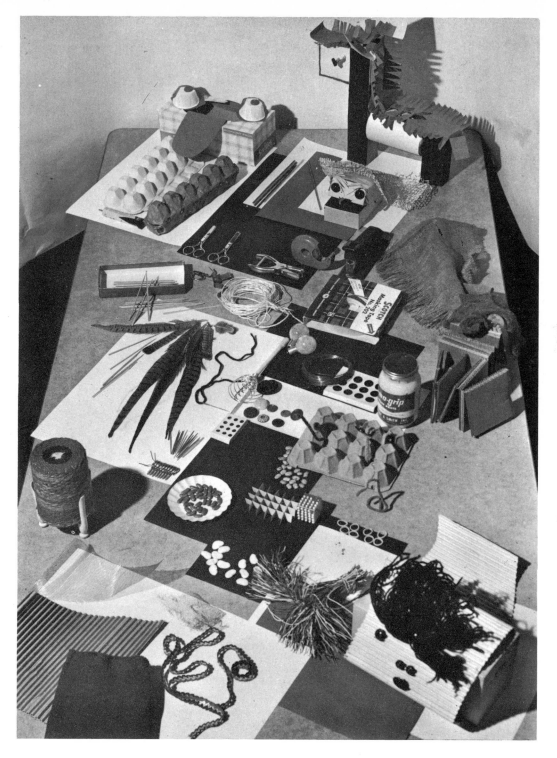

COMPOSITE VIEW OF MATERIALS NEEDED
FOR MAKING BOX ANIMALS

CHAPTER XVIII

Box Animals

Making box animals gives children the experience of joining parts together to make new forms as well as to change the form itself by cutting, adding discarded materials and by color. The finished animal must be balanced to stand. They are suitable for stage properties, puppets and projects for Social Studies and Science.

Before starting this project, draw the children's attention to the many different sizes and shapes of boxes used as containers for food, clothing, toys, and drugs. Have the children collect boxes to use in making imaginary box animals.

Appropriate boxes are: cylindrical ones of different sizes found in oatmeal and salt boxes; cardboard tubes used for mailing, paper towels, wax paper, toilet tissue, Christmas ribbon; long narrow boxes with lids that open, as in wax paper, foil, and cracker boxes; square boxes from cotton swabs, gelatin, jello, tea, paper napkins; large boxes with lids such as shoe or gift boxes; boxes with openings in the top like Kleenex boxes; boxes with uneven surfaces, like egg boxes.

Ask each child to choose two or three boxes of different sizes. By placing one box over another or at different angles, the child learns to visualize ways of combining the boxes to make an imaginary animal.

Tubes of cardboard, or smaller square or rectangular boxes, may be joined to a larger box to make a head or legs. Parts may be joined together by pasted overlapping tabs, by staples, or by lacing with string. The children should not expect animals made from boxes to be like real animals, except that they have legs, necks, heads, bodies, and ears. Imagination and ability to assemble material is developed.

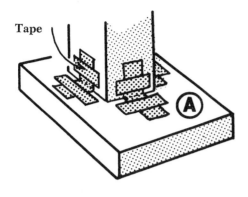

Tape

To attach one rectangular shape to another, paste tape between the two and reinforce with tape across, as fig. A.

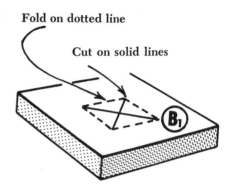

Fold on dotted line

Cut on solid lines

Some attachments are accessible from the under side and may be fastened without showing. Place the smaller form in position on large, trace around and cut across the traced shape (fig. B). Fold on outline and glue to smaller form (figs. B₂ and 4).

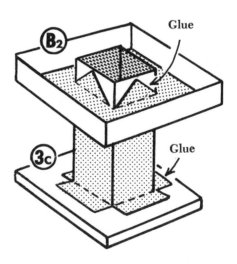

Glue

Glue

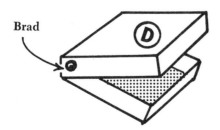

Brad

A lid is tipped up and fastened with a brad making an open-mouthed animal.

Note: Some cardboard contains short fiber and when folded will break easily. To prevent this, tape may be glued on the area to be folded, most effectively on the side being folded away, where fiber must stretch around bend.

The neck and head may be formed from one continuous tube or long box by reinforcing that portion to remain before cutting A "V" in the under edge. The same tape may decorate and attach the ears. (Wide gummed tape is handy.)

Heavy, flat cardboard can be a very graceful neck, and continue on as the head.

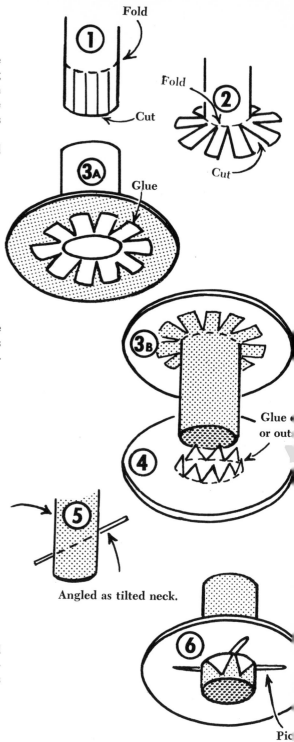

To attach cylinder to other forms — make equidistant cuts (fig. 1), fold back where cuts stop (fig. 2), glue to top (fig. 3a, 3b), or bottom if accessible (fig. 4).

Angled as tilted neck.

Picks each way against wall.

Some long attachments, like necks, may need added support to hold in slant or upright position. Toothpicks (fig. 5-6) and glue on tabs help.

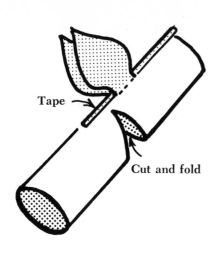

Tape

Cut and fold

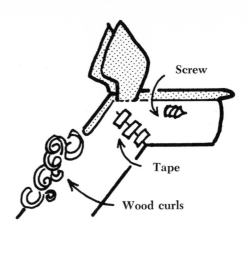

Screw

Tape

Wood curls

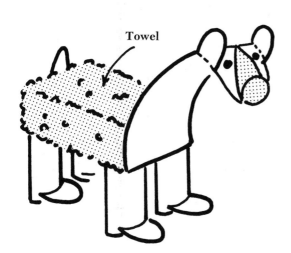

Towel

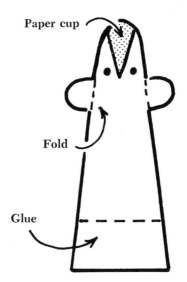

Paper cup

Fold

Glue

AN ANIMAL FROM CUT PAPER

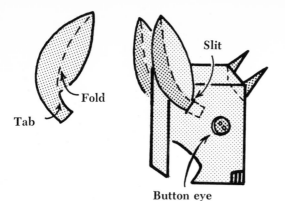

Tab

Fold

Slit

Button eye

MAKING EARS AND HORNS

Tabs on horns and ears may be glued into slits cut in boxes. Some ears and horns may be folded and bent to add form. Slits cut into the sides of the head may hold strips drawn through the head. Some cloth may be added for floppy ears.

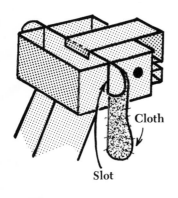

Cloth

Slot

Cut

Tube

MAKING NOSES AND EYES

Tube is cut and passed through cardboard for eyes. Beads may be placed inside and secured by passing pins into their holes.

Slash is cut across box and the strip of cardboard is passed into opening.

Interesting shapes with holes, tubes, or boxes may form eyes. Beads, buttons, seeds, and paper cups may be used.

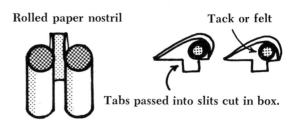

Rolled paper nostril

Tack or felt

Tabs passed into slits cut in box.

IMAGINATIVE ANIMALS MADE FROM DISCARDED MATERIALS

A FANTASTIC PAPER-CUP DRAGON'S HEAD

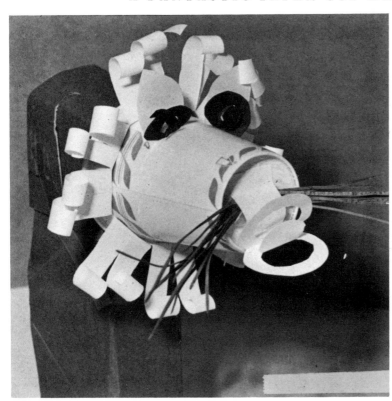

A paper cup is used for an animal head. A curled paper strip for a mane, a double-fold cut circle for the mouth, a spiral cut circle for the eyes, pine needles for whiskers. By changing the position of the eyes and ears the head becomes a cow, pig, horse, or other animal.

Third Grade.

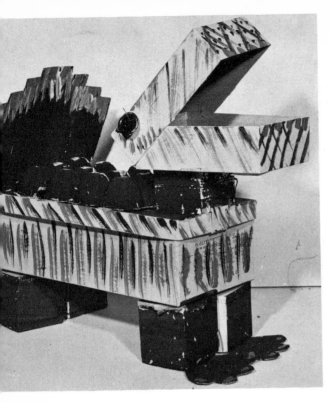

An egg crate fastened to the lid of a shoe box makes the bumps on the animal's back. Note the use of a box lid to represent an open mouth. Feet of cardboard have been glued to the box to help support the body.

Second Grade.

TWO DRAGON-TYPE ANIMALS IN PAPER

Four boxes are joined for this animal structure. A square Q-tip box for the head, a wax-paper box for the neck and front leg, a salt box for the body, and a small milk carton for the hind leg. The eyes are black buttons joined with wire. One strip of paper fringed on both sides continues from the tip of the nose down the backbone to the tail. Ears are made from paper cut in a triangular shape and folded back. Elmer's glue joins the parts.

Third Grade.

A GUINEA HEN MADE FROM DISCARDED MATERIAL

Packing paper used as a bird covering. Colored telephone wires make the tail. A ball of cork is the head. A hat pin forms the eye, walnut shells are used for feet.

Third Grade.

CHAPTER XIX

Papier-Mâché

PAPIER-MÂCHÉ IS A substance made of paper pulp mixed with glue and other materials. It is molded when moist and becomes hard and strong and light in weight when it is dry. It is suitable for shaping puppet heads, animals, birds and people. Since there are no set rules papier-mâché allows for full use of the imagination and resourcefulness of the child.

To make papier-mâché, tear newspaper into small pieces and soak them in water for a week. Scoop up the pulp with a sieve and run clear water through it until the ink is removed. Squeeze the water out of the pulp. Mix liquid paste with the pulp until it is like mush. If desired, color is added to the liquid.

Modeling birds from papier-mâché. Birds children see and read about in the spring and fall are good subjects.

First press the general shape into form, something like an egg shape; the tail, neck, head, beak, and wings are pushed out from this form; the neck is pressed in, as are the narrower parts of the body. The form should remain compact. Insert a wire for legs if the bird must stand on a branch, or insert wire in the back to provide for hanging.

When the pulp is dry have the children use opaque water paint to make their modeled birds like the ones they know about or any color they would like a bird to be. Remind them that birds have feathers of many different colors.

Ornaments for a Christmas tree — balls, bells, angels, Santa Clauses, snow people, birds, animals or pretty shapes may all be made from papier-mâché.

To hang modeled objects from a tree, insert one of the following below the surface while the object is wet: a large drapery hook, paper clip, bent wire or pipe cleaner; or pierce the object while it is wet with a large needle. Pull a cord or ribbon through the hole after the object is dry.

Since the ornaments do not stand up they can be modeled in the round, or they may be flat like gingerbread boys or girls.

To make ornaments, have a child cut a shape from heavy cardboard, and cover it with the pulp. (If the children cannot cut their own shapes, leave this method to use only with older children.)

Adding color or other materials to the ornaments. Paint is added after the shapes are dry. Sequins, beads, and sparkle may be pasted to the outside. Pleated, folded, and curled colored papers may be joined to the surface. (See page 237 for modeling puppet heads from papier-mâché.) People, animals, and various properties used for dioramas may be modeled from paper pulp.

Good work habits in using papier-mâché. Hands of a child modeling with paper pulp are sticky and should be kept on the working surface. It it is necessary for a child to leave his modeling, the first thing he should do is wash his hands. Cover unfinished pieces with a damp cloth. (Work must be completed in one day.)

Objects may be painted any time after they are dry. If they are painted when damp, the paint may run and be dull in color. Finished pieces should be taken to a designated place to dry, newspaper put in the wastebasket, and the tables washed if necessary.

PAPIER-MÂCHÉ ANIMALS

Materials needed are: newspaper, pan, string, powder or tempera paint, wallpaper paste or other liquid paste.

Building the structure (for an imaginary animal or real animal). The basic animal structure, started under supervision, can be finished during an independent work period.

Firmly roll newspaper into a cylinder approximately two and one-half inches in diameter, the length needed to reach from the nose to the end of the tail of the animal to be made. A wire may be in the center of the roll. Turn the edge of the paper in toward the roll.

Wind string around the cylinder the full length of the newspaper as many times as needed to hold it together firmly, and also to have it pliable enough to bend.

The next step is to bend the roll to form the head, neck, body, and tail. The basis for determining the exact places to bend the paper are governed by the kind of animal being made — does it have short legs? How long is its face? Is its tail long or short? How long is its neck?

The tail may be bent in any direction desired. The head may be bent to look ahead, to the side, or back.

Legs. Make two rolls of newspaper twice as long as the leg desired plus about five inches. The edge of the paper at the end of the roll is turned under and the cylinder is wound with string. The center of one roll is placed across the first roll, or body, to make the hips. The center of the second roll is placed across the first roll to make the shoulders. Both rolls are bent downward to make the legs. Hold the legs firmly in place and criss-cross the string over the legs, reaching around the body to hold them in place (see *B X*). The end of the legs may be turned up at right angles to make a foot. The legs help to balance the animal, and must be wide enough to support him. The more the neck extends outward, the wider the legs must be. One leg may be ahead of another leg (see example *C*).

Building the animal form. Consider the size and shape of the ears desired: are they to be long, wide, standing, drooping? Ears may be of rolls going around the head (see illustration). Cross the string fastening the ear to the head. Ears may be made of cardboard. The center is fastened to the center, back of the head. See page 220.

ANIMALS MADE FROM ROLLED NEWSPAPERS

Grades Two and Three

A. Newspaper the length of the body is rolled to show the edge turned back.

B. The rolls of newspaper assembled. Note where the paper is bent for the legs, ears, and tail. This represents just one way. Experiment with different lengths of rolls for legs, body, and ears.

C. The basic structure B where parts bulge is covered with crumpled newspaper, and tied. Paper cups make bulging eyes and feet. Papier-mâché is added on top of the shaped form.

D. Finished papier-mâché painted animal. Heavy yarn has been added for the mane

and tail. A center fold was used to cut out the cardboard ears which go around the back of the head. Note the difference in the basic shape from structure B.

E. Raveled burlap for animal covering.

F. From left to right — shavings for animal covering; pine needles for whiskers or eyebrows; straw and yarn for shaggy hair or mane; perforated paper used for animal cover (see Bird, page 223).

G. Buttons for eyes. Cotton for wool, accordion-pleated paper for tail or ears. Heavy crochet cotton to tie parts together.

Have the children find the widest parts of the animal, and crumple and tie newspaper to the basic structure in places where bulges are desired, such as for the stomach and cheeks.

After the underlying shape is finished, papier-mâché is used to give the final form to the animal.

In one method, the work surface is covered with newspaper, and paper pulp covers the structure (see page 226).

In another method, strips of newspaper or paper toweling about ½″ by 4″ are torn and placed in a container. (Torn paper sticks more smoothly.) A pan half-full of wallpaper paste is placed on the worktable. The child holds one end of the strip in his fingers, then dips the strip into the liquid paste. The pasted strip is placed on the animal structure and pressed down. The children add one strip at a time to cover the form, criss-crossing the strips to make the form stronger. Many layers are added on top of each other, all over the form. To make it easier to see each layer, alternate strips from the want-ad section of the newspaper with torn funny papers, or paint each layer a different color of thin paint. Each time the paper completely covers the color. If a place needs to be rounded out, add more strips. Paste all pieces down evenly with no parts protruding, unless a rough surface is desired to suggest shaggy fur. Several children may work together building the form.

Set the animals aside to dry slowly.

Variations. Discarded materials add interest. Colored paper, raveled burlap, rope, or straw for the tail and mane; straw, reeds, or pine needles for whiskers; buttons or beads for eyes; fur, feathers, straw, or bristles from brushes for body covering or details.

Paint the animals with opaque tempera when they are dry.

Encourage observation of pattern on animals, such as stripes of zebras, chipmunks, or tigers; spots on giraffe, fawn, or frog; design on turtles or fish.

Allow the children's imagination, plus their love of color and pattern, to produce animals that belong to their world of make-believe, such as: a purple animal with yellow-green spots; a bright green animal with yellow and violet stripes; a black animal with red circles around its body.

Where to put the pattern. The structure of the animal helps determine the places suitable for decoration, as well as the kind. Divisions of space made by color changes should unify the animal form, hence, color ought not be used to separate parts like the head, legs and body, with each being a different color. The head should be one color, since the face has features.

A few examples of variations are: stripes following the line of the backbone; stripes around or up and down the neck; dots over the full part of the body with the same color repeated in wavy lines down the neck; contrast the lower part of the animal and the top side of the head or neck to the color of the back.

Keep part of the animal undecorated.

A coat of varnish or shellac added after the paint is dry makes a washable surface.

LAMINATED PAPER

(Grades Two and Three)

To LAMINATE means to construct by pasting layer upon layer of paper or other material. The paste or glue becomes hard when dry. For this reason the laminated paper is shaped when it is wet over a mold and retains the shape when dry and is reasonably strong. This material may also be shaped while it is wet by pushing up forms and by covering bunched paper or boxes to hold it in shape until it dries. Boys and girls feel pride in the results they attain from this simple and inexpensive material.

Materials needed are: sheets of newspaper, wrapping papers, shelf paper, or transparent papers; wheat or flour paste the consistency of cream; forms to use for molds such as fruit juice cans, cardboard boxes, or mixing bowls; opaque paint; shellac.

To make laminated paper, more sheets of light-weight paper are needed than of heavy paper. The use of the article determines the weight of paper needed. Since a quantity of paste, which adds stiffening, is used newspaper is satisfactory for making most objects.

Cut six pieces of newspaper the same size; to determine the size, wrap a piece of paper around the object to be used as a mold — for example, a two-pound coffee can requires one-half sheet of newspaper.

The child places one sheet of paper on a flat, dry surface, and covers the entire back surface of the paper, going over the edges with paste. A cardboard or brush is used to spread the layer of paste perfectly smooth. A second sheet of paper is placed on top of the pasted paper. The entire surface should be covered evenly with liquid paste, and this is repeated as each sheet of paper except the last is added.

Process for shaping a bowl or box. The mold — a box, bowl, or can — is placed upside down on the table in front of the child. The child places the unpasted side of the damp laminated paper over the mold and presses it carefully over the form. Pleats

PREPARING NEWSPAPER FOR LAMINATION

Glenn is spreading liquid wheat paste over layers of newspaper ready to place over a mold.

A. Bottom of square baking dish used for a mold for B and C.

B. A tray with a design inside. A stamped design was placed face down on the bottom of the mold with layers of paper on top. When this dried the stiff tray shape was flipped over, revealing the design inside.

C. A scratched crayon design to be applied to the base of a mold.

D. A large juice can is used as a mold for a circular shape appropriate for a mask or a May basket.

E. Laminated paper shaped over a large light globe. This piece will be glued to a second piece of the same size, filled with beans, and used for a rattle in musical rhythms. Puppet heads and fruit may be shaped the same way.

must be made around a circular bowl and on corners.

The paper shell is left to dry on the mold until thoroughly dry, when it is removed from the mold and painted.

Let the children plan designs for their laminated boxes or bowls, for the inside or the outside. Water-soluble opaque paint is best to use for the design — stripes, an all-over pattern, a border design or one central motif. Paint shellac over the dry object to make it waterproof.

Uses for laminated paper containers.

Boxes for art materials, puzzles or seat work materials . . . Boxes for May Day flowers . . . Tall fruit juice cans make containers for knitting . . . Bowls for yarns or sewing materials . . . Laminated paper shaped over one side of a large fruit juice can makes a foundation for a mask . . . Ornaments for Christmas or a party.

Other uses for laminated paper.

1. The damp laminated paper may be pushed into shapes to make hills, mountains and valleys. To hold points in place until the paper is dry, bunched newspaper may be placed under the wet, limp paper until it is dry and stiff.

2. *Stage properties.*

   Rocks, plant forms, clouds, Indian oven and others.

3. *Buildings, people and animals* also may be made simply by pushing the laminated paper into the shape desired. Other materials such as burlap, feathers, pieces of cloth, wood shavings or colored paper may be added to the structure for interest.

LAMINATED PAPER LAND FORMATIONS

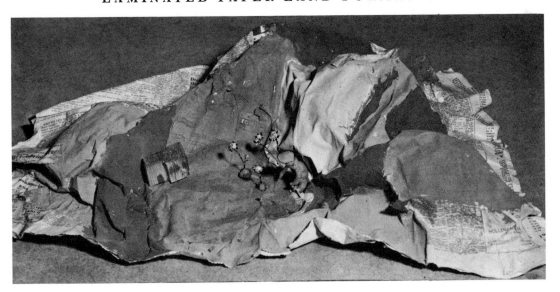

CHAPTER XX

Masks

CHILDREN WEAR MASKS because they love to pretend. Making masks offers many opportunities to develop imagination. Masks should differ from any face a child has ever seen.

Primitive peoples use masks for funeral rites, comic dances, and ritual dances to the sun, rain, and other gods. Masks made by children may be inspired by primitive masks, by animals, or by materials which arouse imagination and invention.

A mask's facial features may be grotesque, distorted, or exaggerated. Its facial expression may make us laugh, cry, or afraid. The following are some of the pronounced animal features which stimulate children's imagination: mouth and teeth of an alligator or crocodile; mouth and eyes of a frog, a fish, or a cow; ears of an elephant or a rabbit; beak of an eagle; antlers of a deer; horns of a mountain goat or cow; nose of a pig; bill of a duck; tusks, mouth, and whiskers of a walrus; goatee of a goat; the lion with its long mane around its face.

BASIC SHAPES FOR MASKS

Simple paper fold. Fold heavy paper in half, and cut animal head or imaginary head shape. Use sturdy paper or stiff cloth, like tarlatan or buckram. Devise a way to fasten the piece to the child's head.

A mask for the eyes. Encourage the children to observe the eyelids, eyelashes, and eyeballs of different animals and people to note the variations — as between a frog, a cow, a grasshopper, an eagle, an owl, a turtle, or a cat. The eye mask covers only the forehead and eyes, extending from ear to ear and to the top of the nose. An elastic band or tape fastened to each side goes around the back of the head.

A mask for the nose. Animals that suggest different kinds of noses are the pig, elephant, cow, horse, and camel, or beaks of such birds as pelicans. Tape fastened to flappers on the side of the nose may be adhered to the face with adhesive tape, be continued around the head and tied in back,

HEAD-SHAPED MASK

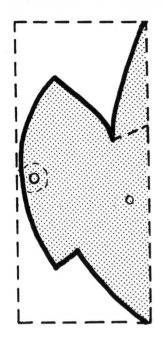

The mask is fitted to the child's head. Openings are cut to match the child's eyes. Large eyes may be painted around the openings.

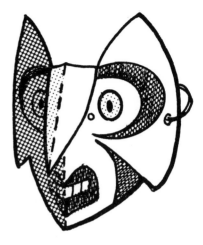

STRIP-PAPER MASK

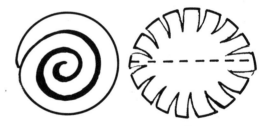

Suggested eyes.

Projected eye area, looped away from background.

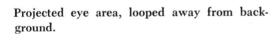

Strip-paper mask.

or be fastened to each ear.

The ears of rabbits, elephants, cocker spaniels or pigs suggest exaggeration in size and form. The back of the ear mask can be shaped like a hook to fit over the child's ear.

A headdress made with stiff cardboard or tag board frames the face and is fastened to a headband, skull cap or discarded hat crown. Children have seen crowns and headdresses on kings, queens, princesses, and other characters in stories and on television. Many primitive peoples wear headdresses for ceremonies.

A paper bag mask. A strong paper bag large enough to fit over a child's head is used for a foundation. A child slips the bag over his head, and another child marks with chalk the location of eyes, nose, and mouth.

The bag is removed and the child cuts out the openings for the eyes, nose and mouth, using his imagination to exaggerate one facial feature by color and size. Hair, cap, or hat is added to the top of the bag. Cut paper, paint, and discarded materials such as feathers, rubber rings, shavings, buttons, or rope add interest.

Laminated paper mask. Three to six sheets of newspaper (tabloid size) are pasted together and while damp are placed over a form, such as a large juice can, and allowed to dry. The openings for the eyes, nose, and mouth are cut in the curved shape. Features with protruding parts are added.

Paper plates may be curved and shaped to the child's face for a foundation; or stretchy cloth such as used in long underwear, may be pulled over the child's head, and openings cut for the eyes, nose, and mouth.

Discarded materials to use on masks. For hair: raveled rope, wood shavings, strips of nylon hose, gunny sack, excelsior, straw, dried grass, pine needles, corn silk, cornhusks, shredded newspaper. For headdress: jewelry and buttons, egg cartons, feathers, seeds from squash, pumpkin, watermelon, sunflowers, rick-rack, braid or ribbon, decorated papers, sequins, speckled beans, burrs and acorns. For ornaments to hang from ears: chains, bottle tops, rings from jars or curtains, fans, bent wire with rocks, chicken bones, or sticks. A stocking fit over a child's head makes a foundation for a mask.

DETAIL FOR NOSE AND MOUTH OF MASK

PAPER BAG BASE FOR MASK
Grades One, Two

Heavy paper box.

Paper bag is trimmed at the bottom to fit over each shoulder, allowing bag to rest on child's head. Small holes are cut for the eyes.

A BOX MASK MADE FROM CARDBOARD
Grade Three

Inside of box mask made from cardboard.
Tabs are left to fasten sides.
Strips may be extended from sides for ears or decoration.
Same procedure for eye holes fastener.
Mask may be painted or scraps of colored paper folded to form features.

EXAMPLES OF DIVISIONS OF SPACE
SUGGESTED BY PRIMITIVE MASKS

Forehead ending with line of eyebrow.
Fringe, rope, or burlap.
Oval head designed on fold.
Forehead, nose, mouth, form one area.
Ears joined to eyebrows and nose.

Half oval.
Division of space for areas of color.
Dividing the head into areas with counter-change of color.
Separating areas with pattern.

CHAPTER XXI

Puppets Children Can Make

PUPPETS PROVIDE THE imaginative child with the experience of creating a character, of manipulating it and speaking for it. The puppets described are within the scope of the abilities and interests of primary school boys and girls.

ONE-PIECE CARDBOARD PUPPETS
(Kindergarten and First Grade)

Cardboard puppet to fit over a child's hand. The child paints an animal or person approximately eighteen by twenty inches on light-weight cardboard; the contour should be simple with a straight front view. He cuts the finished painting out around the outside edge, then fastens bands to the center back (bands must be wide enough to go over the child's hand and arm.)

A stick puppet is made by fastening a long narrow stick instead of bands to the back of the cardboard puppet. The child holds the figure in front of him and speaks for the character he has made. Stick puppets also may be used as shadow puppets. These are the simplest form for puppets.

A JOINTED CARDBOARD STRING PUPPET
(Second Grade)

THE CARDBOARD BODY PARTS are joined together with paper fasteners so that they will move. The child may need to draw the entire form first, then cut away the body parts. When the final pattern is made the arms, legs, and neck are extended to allow for overlapping the body at the joints. The cardboard puppet is painted on both sides.

Holes are punched in the cardboard for the paper fasteners. When the parts are joined together holes are punched for the strings used to manipulate the puppet.

Attach strings where they will balance the animal.

Cut cardboard rings; place one between each body part and the part of the body to which it is joined. Punch a hole in the center of each washer, and tie strings through. The strings must be long enough to allow the legs of the animal to touch the floor, as the child who holds the strings is standing.

HAND PUPPET OR GUIGNOL
(Second or Third Grade)

PUNCH AND JUDY shows use hand puppets. Hand puppets are made to fit over the child's hand so that by moving his fingers and wrist he manipulates the puppet.

The teacher should discuss with the children characters for a specific puppet play. Let each child choose the character he will make and decide how the character looks and what part he will accentuate in his puppet. Since the head is the most important part, facial features should be exaggerated.

Different kinds of simple hand puppets. The basic structure of each hand puppet should be made to fit a specific child's hand. Since an eight-year-old's hand is larger than a five-year-old's, the pattern given here — for an average seven-year-old's hand — must be adjusted to fit.

One child helps another make three tubes of light-weight cardboard to fit over the child's fingers. One is for the index finger, one for the thumb, and one for the second finger. Instead, the child's own fingers may be used as the puppet's arms (see illustration, page 238 for details of tubes and puppet's dress).

Dress pattern for hand puppet. A man's shirt sleeve may be used, or two pieces cut on the fold of the cloth. The hands may be sewn with the dress. Tack the cloth neck opening to the neck tube, and the cloth sleeve opening to tube for the arms.

A stocking puppet. The heel of the stocking is used for the head. The toe of

Back of cardboard puppet showing position of the child's hand used to manipulate the puppet.

the stocking may be cut off and used for a cap, or as a base for a headdress or hair.

The head or heel is stuffed with cotton or rags. The child inserts his index finger, covered with a cardboard tube, into the stuffed head. A string is tied around the stocking under the head for the neck, while the child's finger is inserted in the head. Children may wish to add clothing to the outside of the stocking.

A paper or cloth bag puppet. The face may be painted on the bottom of the bag, or materials, such as buttons, seeds, or cut paper or cloth shapes, may be fastened to the bag for the features. The end of the bag is stuffed with paper, rags, or cotton. The bag is slipped over the child's hand with his index finger in the center, and tied with string (around the child's finger) to make the neck. Details of hair, cap, or a ruffle around the neck are added as desired.

A cloth puppet. Two pieces are cut the same size and sewn together, with the bottom of the dress shape left open for the child's arm. The hands and head are stuffed, and details sewn on.

Puppets with papier-mâché heads (Third Grade, see recipe for papier-mâché, page 224). The child presses wax paper or aluminum foil over the top of a small-necked bottle, and forms paper pulp into an oval shape over the covered top of the bottle. He then pushes in parts, adds more pulp for protruding parts, or takes pulp away to shape the head of the puppet. All parts must be kept firmly packed together. If the pulp has a tendency to fall apart a stronger adhesive such as glue is needed.

The neck should be about the length of the child's first finger. The addition of a slight shoulder or curve outward at the base of the neck provides a place to fasten a dress later.

Encourage children to make long noses,

ANIMAL PUPPET

protruding eyebrows, eyeballs extending from the eye sockets, thick extended lips, and large ears.

Suggest to children that they hold their puppet up to see the profile view. Use a shadow for this observation.

Children too young to model facial expressions can paint them after the papier-mâché is dry.

The neck of the garment is sewed around the puppet's neck. Yarn, frayed burlap, ravelled stockings, or sweaters may be fastened on to the head with glue to make hair, and hands may be cut from cardboard or made of stuffed glove fingers. The hands are fastened to the end of the puppet's sleeves, or the end of the carboard tube.

When puppets are not in use they may be kept upright over the bottle, or hung from a line with a clothespin fastened to the bottom of the dress. The child can shake the puppet's head and clap its hands.

COMPONENTS OF HAND PUPPET

Button eyes, yarn hair, felt or cloth glued for mouth.

Light-weight cardboard 4″ long, 4″ wide is wound around child's index finger, and tied or taped together to form a tube extending into the puppet's head. The head is then shaped over this tube.

Head, ⅔ actual size.

Ring for hanging

Tie two bunches of yarn, cross and fasten to head, trim.

Crush newspaper, tissue, or cotton around the top of tube. Cut toe of stocking or cloth and cover padding; gathering and stitching stocking to the side of the 4″ long tube at neck area.

A Puppet Stage

A TABLE CAN BE MADE into a stage by covering the front with a cloth or paper to hide the puppeteers behind the table. A screen of cardboard or wood may stand on the floor or on the top of a table, high and wide enough to conceal the puppeteers. An opening, approximately two, three, or four feet wide and fifteen to twenty inches high, is cut in the center panel for the stage.

Children may stand, kneel, or sit to manipulate the puppets. If they sit their elbows may rest on the tabletop. The height of the stage should equal the height the child can reach above his head. Scenery is made to hang from above the opening of the stage, or to extend up from the bottom.

Shadow Puppets

SHADOW PUPPETS may be stick or hand puppets or the children themselves. A sheet is stretched on a frame or on ropes and placed across the room about five feet from the front wall. The room must be dark. The performers act behind the sheet, and a light is behind them.

The silhouette is very important. Cardboard figures may be used in combination with children's figures. Children learn from experience how they can use their arms and legs effectively for a silhouette, as well as other properties that can help explain their story, such as a horn, a broom, or a toy.

String Puppets

A STRING PUPPET can be made from rolls of paper or cylindrical boxes.

Cylindrical boxes of different sizes are used with mailing tubes for body parts, such as: a large oatmeal box for the body; a salt box cut down one-third for the head; mailing tubes cut into sections for legs and arms.

The parts are fastened together at the joints by punching holes in the ends of the tubes to match holes punched in the body, and running string through the holes to connect the parts.

To attach the strings to the puppet, lay the puppet down on a table with the arms touching the side of the body. Fasten a strong, black thread to each wrist and to each side of the head at the ears (see illustration for length of strings and control).

The strings from the puppet's wrist to the control must be long enough for the puppet's arms to hang to its sides and for the child to hold the controls about at his waistline.

A simpler control is the use of two sticks, one for each hand. Strings from the head are tied to one stick, and a string from each hand is tied to the second stick.

Other ways to make string puppets. Newspaper is rolled in different lengths for body parts, tied or taped securely, and joined with cords.

The center of a piece of rope is looped for the head and the two ends are knotted for joints in the legs. A second piece of rope is tied under the head for the arms.

A cloth or stocking doll can be made by stitching back and forth for each joint.

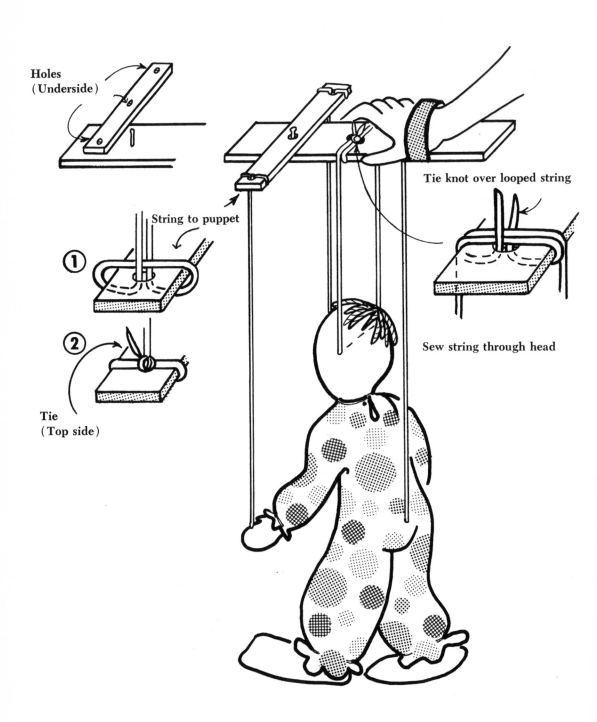

Holes
(Underside)

String to puppet

①

②

Tie
(Top side)

Tie knot over looped string

Sew string through head

Man's heavy cotton stocking

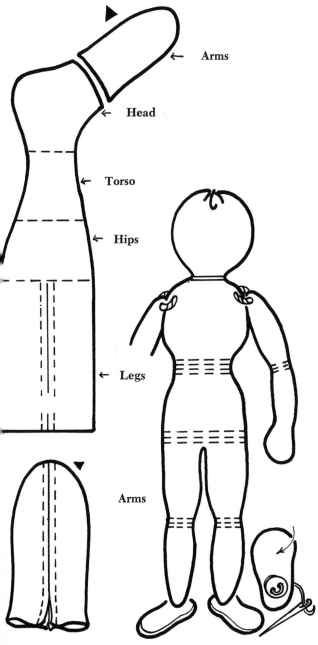

Arms

Head

Torso

Hips

Legs

Arms

Arms

Steps:

1. Knot or sew top.
2. Stuff head.
3. Gather and tie a string around neck.
4. Stuff torso.
5. Stitch ¾″ (slightly gathering in waist).
6. Stuff hip area.
7. Sew, then cut split between legs; stuff from hip to knee, stitch; stuff from knee to ankle, sew end.
8. Add weights to ankles (pebbles — fish sinkers). Sew bottom together.
9. Sew foot-shaped cardboard to ankle, using a button at heel to keep thread from pulling through.
10. Sew each side of center line drawn with chalk on toe of stocking.
11. Cut up center line, separating arms.
12. Stuff arms to elbow, stitch, stuff to end of hand and sew ends together.
13. Attach loosely to shoulder of torso with string loop.

CHAPTER XXII

Weaving

CHILDREN IN THE primary grades associate fabrics with their uses and with seasons of the year. They may observe woven materials in rugs, draperies, upholstery, in linens, clothing, and bedding. Experience in weaving materials for specific uses gives children a feeling of accomplishment. As a result of weaving, boys and girls learn to notice the variations in color and kinds of fibers in various materials.

Children enjoy the repeated motion in weaving, and it is a craft they can start and stop at any time, as well as a quiet one they can do independent of help.

A study of threads from various sources is a subject suggested for a third-grade Science lesson. It might include: animal fibers, such as wool from sheep and silk from the silkworm; plant fibers, such as cotton from the boll of the cotton plant, linen from flax, and jute from the jute plant; mineral fibers such as synthetics made from cellulose pulp, carbon, air and water — for example rayon, nylon, Dacron, Cellanese, and Orlon.

Weaving materials children in some areas can find outdoors are appropriate for

SIMPLE LOOMS

Top row, left to right.
  Threads pulled from burlap.
  Loom made from tongue depressors.
  Yarn woven in and out of onion skin bag.
  Bag woven on cardboard loom below.

Second row, left to right.
  Holes are punched in the sides of a box. Yarn is laced through the holes from one side to the other. Colored paper shapes are in the background.
  Cardboard loom for a place mat.
  Yarn woven in onion-bag netting.
  Wooden frame loom for rags or yarn.

On the counter from left to right.
  Flat wooden sticks held together with string to make a mat.
  Threads laced through holes in cardboard to make a design.
  Rag rug.
  Center, cattail leaves woven together with yarn.

Bottom row from left to right.
  A wooden frame loom with a raised center pole used to form a shed (see detail, page 247).
  Woven mat.
  Chipboard loom.

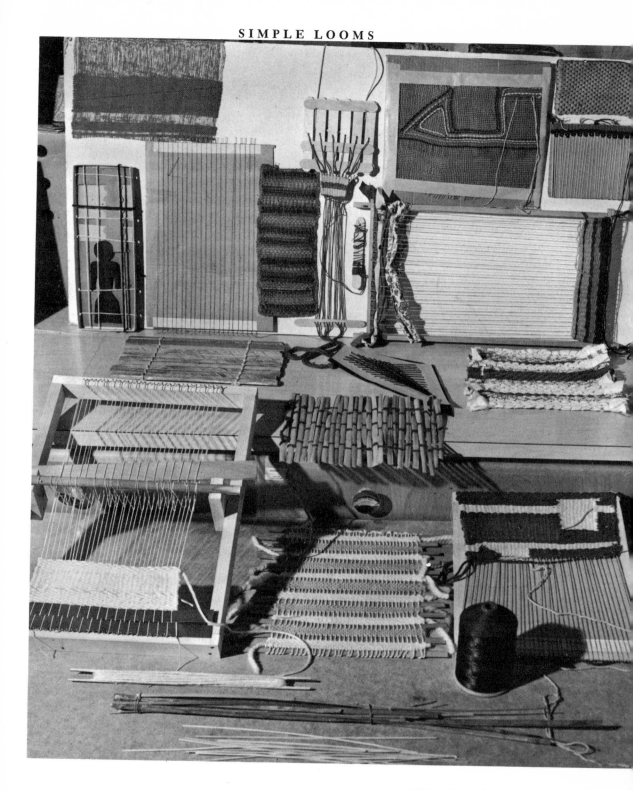

purses, mats and baskets; for example: raffia, made from palm leaves that grow in Madagascar; pine needles from evergreen trees; straw — the stalk or stem of grains, wheat, rye, oats, and barley; cornhusk — the dry external covering of an ear of corn; slough grass — spear-like blades of grass that grow in muddy ground; common rush — grass-like herbs with hollow stems found in marshy places; cattail leaves grow on a tall reed-like marsh plant; wedge grass is rush-like or grass-like with sawtooth edges, and grows in wet places; bamboo from discarded matchstick curtains.

THE PROCESS OF WEAVING

A LOOSELY WOVEN fabric with coarse threads like burlap is a good example to illustrate the warp and weft (or woof) threads. By pulling out the first thread that runs crosswise, the children can see the weft thread as well as the warp thread, which runs lengthwise.

The warp threads run from top to bottom across a frame called a loom and form the framework for weaving. Warp threads must be strong and elastic.

Carpet warp — coarse crochet cotton or twist cord.

The weft thread is woven at right angles to the warp threads, binding them together.

Weft materials are: raffia, non-ravel rag strips, jute, grass, yarn, reed, cotton roving, string, raveled knit-wear, raveled burlap sacks, stocking cut round and round the leg, in one or two-inch widths.

A cardboard loom is made from heavy chipboard. The cardboard should be cut the size of the object to be made. An odd number of pins are placed an equal distance apart along the top of the cardboard.

Warp the cardboard loom with string or carpet warp. Two colors make a plaid design. For place mats, belts, or scarfs, one side of the cardboard is warped; both sides are warped for bags or purses.

Using both sides to make a purse. Wind warp thread around first pin (*a*) top left — continue warp thread down the back and

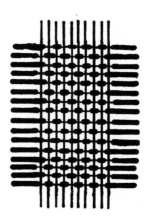

CARDBOARD LOOM

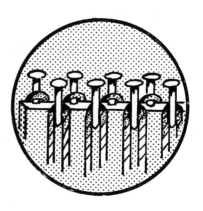

NAVAJO LOOM

up over the front to second pin at the top. Put thread around second pin, come down the front, up the back and wind around third pin. Go down the back to front and continue until the last pin is reached. Tie the warp to this pin and cut about one inch from the end.

Weaving the weft through the warp. The weft thread may be all one color or different colors grouped to form stripes. A bobbin, bent wire, large safety pin, or bobby pin is useful in drawing the weft thread under and over the warp threads. Start the weft by weaving under and over about six warp threads from left to right at the top, then start weaving from right to left, going on both sides of the cardboard. It is best for a young child to achieve variation by using a second color to form stripes, or by a very simple change in weaving, such as under two threads and over one for several rows.

A comb can be used like a beater, to push each row of weft thread tightly together to make firmly woven cloth.

Before the weaving is taken from the loom, overcast the top edge of the bag with a thread to avoid raveling. Then remove the pins and the cardboard.

A lining may be added to the inside, and the bag closed by a drawstring, a zipper, or a flap.

Wooden box loom (for place mats). Finishing nails are driven in every quarter inch across both ends of the box. A strip of ¼″ graph paper may be pasted along the ends of the box as a guide for the nails.

To warp the loom jute is a good weight to combine with heavy weft cotton yarn,

reed, or rags. Use double thread for first two rows and last two rows to make a stronger selvage. Go from top to bottom around each opposite nail. Tie securely at the end. A strong wire may be used on each side to keep weaving straight. The weft thread is woven over and under the wire on the sides. The wire is pulled out when the mat is finished.

Materials such as reeds are cut the width of the warped loom. These are woven over and under the warp threads from right to left.

A Navajo loom has a frame made from limbs of trees. Leather thongs or clothes line rope are crisscrossed over the corners, joining the crossbars or yarn beams to the vertical beams. The base must be fastened securely to the ground or to a table top with clamps. The warp is strung over the beams in a figure eight. A heddle stick about 1½ inches wide is inserted between alternate threads to separate them so it passes over those threads in front and under those in back. The tension of the warp thread holds the heddle stick in place.

To weave, thread the shuttle with two or three yards of wool yarn or rags. Pull the heddle rod toward you. Pass the threaded shuttle from right to left through the shed. Push yarn to the front with a comb. Turn heddle rod the opposite way to form a shed with alternate warp threads. Pass thread through the alternate shed from left to right. Push down with comb. Continue weaving. *Caution:* Loop at each end of row should be loose. Do not *pull* wool thread across. Tie a new thread so the knot does not come at the end of the row.

WEAVING WITH RAGS

For SMALL UTILITY rugs to be used in a kitchen, bathroom, or bedroom, which need

frequent washing, use cotton. Use the same kind of cloth for one rug, for example, all

THIRD-GRADERS WEAVING ON SIMPLE LOOMS

A. Box loom.

Roger is inserting a shuttle filled with cotton yarn in and out of the warp. Note the warp thread going around two nails on the ends. Laying across the shuttle stick is every other warp thread.

B. Cardboard loom.

Colleen is weaving a small rug, making a pattern with her weft threads. Note the ruler inserted to make the heddle stick, which separates alternate warp threads. The weft thread is tied to a long dowel. Pins are used on the end to hold the warp in place.

C. Christine is winding warp thread around a heavy piece of cardboard, preparing to weave a bag.

D. A cardboard loom warped to make a bag with a flap. John has discovered he can lap the second thread over the first to make a variation in his weaving. Note the top of the front of the bag (see arrow). The bag is woven first across the front, then the cardboard is turned over and the back is woven to the end, which is the bottom edge of the flap when the flap is turned down.

cotton or all wool rags.

Discarded cloth for rags:

Linen-like weaves — towels, draperies, slipcovers, ticking, overalls, jeans.

Knitted weaves — underwear, T-shirts, cotton socks, dress materials.

Resilient wool rags — flannel, light blankets, crepe, tweed, or gabardine. (Avoid materials that ravel badly.)

To prepare rags for weaving, rip all linings from garments, open all seams, wash material in soap and water.

Warp. Cut or tear strips of fabric one inch wide lengthwise on the material. Cut end of each strip on the bias, and sew strips together to make a continuous strip. The one-inch strip is folded in the center, then rolled into a ball, criss-crossing the strands.

Weft. Cut or tear strips of cloth two or three inches wide. Cut the ends of the strips on the bias and sew together.

Fold each side of the strip to the center, overlapping one side. Turn under the raw edge. This may be pressed in place with an iron or sewn together with an overcast stitch. Roll into a ball.

Frame for weaving rugs. Make a wooden frame the size of the rug desired. Reinforce the corners with metal braces. Drive box nails about 1½″ long with a flat head in a row ½″ apart across the top and bottom to a depth of ½″. A line drawn across the center of the top and bottom board serves as a guide for placing the nails.

Weaving the warp. Make a loop on one end of the warp (either knot or sew) and fasten to the top nail on the left side.

Bring strand of cloth down and under the first and second nail on the lower left side. Bring strand up and over the second and third nail at the top. Continue winding warp from top to bottom to top, going over two nails each time. When last nail is reached tie the end of the warp to this nail. Do not have warp stretched too tight. It must be even and firm.

Weaving the weft. Begin with the end of the strand facing toward the center on the right side. Weave over and under the warp strands going from right to left. When the left end is reached, weave from left to right *under* the beginning strand. When the right end is reached, turn and weave from right to left. Continue weaving. Check to see that one row of weft starts over then under and that the following row starts under then over. After each row press firmly together with a beater or the fingers. When the weaving is completed lift it carefully off the nails, and overcast along the edge. Binding may be sewn across the end instead of using knots. Rubber rings sewn to the back side hold the rug in place.

WEAVING OR DARNING IN AN ONION-SKIN BAG
(Grade Two and Three)

AN ONION-SKIN bag is flimsy, with a loose weave in a wide mesh, usually red, brown or yellow, not smaller than 9″ by 12″. Simple geometric shapes may be woven into it, or shapes forming vertical and horizontal lines, such as buildings, animals, or people.

See examples, page 243.

1. ***Cut stiff cardboard*** to fit inside the bag, to hold it in place, and to keep the child from weaving through both sides of the bag.

2. ***Materials are*** very heavy yarn, raffia,

or jute, in earth colors such as deep blue and red orange, orange and brown, or green and yellow to harmonize with the bag color.

A safety pin, large darning needle, long paper clip, bobby pin, or bent wire to weave the thread in and out.

3. *Qualities of good weaving.* The weaving should be as loose as the mesh of the bag.

Yarn may be woven either up or down or across or both, but the width of stripes should vary.

One color should predominate.

The ends of the threads are woven back in opposite direction, in and out, for about an inch.

Lining makes the bag stronger.

SPOOL KNITTING
(Grade Two and Three)

THE LONG TUBULAR strip which results from spool knitting may be used as a cord for lacing, a draw string, drapery pull; it may be woven as weft thread in a loom into material suitable for a scarf, rug, or cap; or several strips may be joined together with stitches to make a place mat.

Materials needed are a large spool, firmly twisted yarn or string, crochet hook, 4 finishing nails ½″ long.

Casting on the yarn before knitting.

Top view of spool with nails

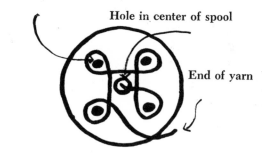

Hole in center of spool

End of yarn

The Teacher
1. Mark square on top of spool.
2. Drive one nail in each corner. Use ½″ finishing nails. Let ¼″ extend above the top of the spool.

Hole in center

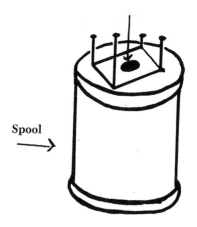

Spool

Loop around nail

End of yarn or knitted strip

SECOND-GRADERS SPOOL KNITTING

Knitting. Directions for the teacher to give to the child:

1. Push end of yarn down through the center hole of the spool to the bottom.
2. Hold the yarn and the spool in the left hand.
3. Loop the yarn once around each nail from left to right. See detail above.
4. When you return to first nail, wind the yarn around each nail above the first loop.
5. Lift the loop over the nail with a crochet hook or similar instrument and drop the loop inside the center hole of the spool.
6. Repeat.
7. Cast off, by lifting the loops off the nails, passing the end of the yarn through the loops, and pulling tight.

CHAPTER XXIII

Stitches

STITCHERY IS CREATING beautiful designs on cloth with threads. The teacher motivates the child's imagination and thinking by supplying bright colored yarns, loosely woven cloth and large needles for the child to use and discover stitches he can make. As the child's ingenuity develops he may add pieces of cloth, beads, braids or buttons for an accent or to express some idea.

Materials needed are durable and pliable fabrics, such as basket-weave material — monk's cloth or burlap; onion-skin bags or similar loosely woven material stretched over cardboard; heavy yarns such as carpet warp, rug cottons, wool, cord, jute, raffia, string, or twine (avoid yarns that split or stretch); and needles that go into the fabric easily — large-eyed tapestry or rug needles, or bodkins.

Designs using two-dimensional symbolic forms work best in stitches, and the design should be large and simple. The shapes should have large, well-defined outlines, instead of many little designs. Children will enjoy trying different stitches together and learn that patterns develop through creative stitchery.

Different ways of preparing designs.

1. The children place heavy yarn into the shapes of their design directly on the cloth and then sew the yarn down with another thread; this is called couching.

2. The children draw directly onto the cloth with chalk. For a dark color of cloth use white chalk or tailor's chalk.

3. The children make straight-line designs of the main shapes with crayon on paper the same size as the cloth. Then they transfer the crayon design by placing it face down on the cloth and pressing the back of the paper with a hot iron — the wax crayon melts onto the cloth, making a design in reverse. The child adds pattern or details, if desired, as he works.

Things to make by stitching include borders for aprons, tray covers, pockets, mittens, wall hangings, and mats.

Use of appliqué with stitches. The child cuts different shapes with simple contours from paper, and chooses from these the ones he will use as patterns for cutting

Weaving a second thread through a running stitch.

Several yarns may be grouped.
Heavy yarns make a wide stitch. Stitches may slant in any direction.
Chain stitch may be narrow, wide, or single.
Cross stitch may form lines, stripes, solid areas, or be interwoven — the slants made in one direction and then crossed.
Weaving threads under running stitches to form a background.
Buttonhole stitch.
Featherstitch may vary with the angle of the needle used in stitching.

SIMPLE WAYS TO VARY A RUNNING STITCH

shapes from cloth. The cloth shapes are arranged on the background cloth and fastened with a running or blanket stitch.

It is advisable to use assorted kinds and colors of cloth which do not ravel, such as corduroy, felt, and cottons.

Good stitching habits.

1. Before beginning to make stitches, the cloth must be well pressed by the teacher or parent.

2. Loosely woven cloth that stretches may need to be stretched in a frame such as an embroidery hoop or over cardboard.

3. Right-handed pupils should sew from right to left, *toward the body,* for running stitch.

4. The children should use medium length threads, for a thread that is too long will become tangled.

5. They should hold the material and insert the needle so that the needle point is always visible.

6. To fasten the thread when they begin to sew, children should take a few running stitches toward the starting point with a back or a loop stitch. To start a new thread, pass it under several preceding stitches to anchor the end. For blanket and buttonhole stitches, start at the left side of the fabric and stitch to the right. The thread will fall under the needle for loop stitches if the needle is inserted correctly.

7. To fasten thread at the end, weave it in and out on the wrong side of the cloth.

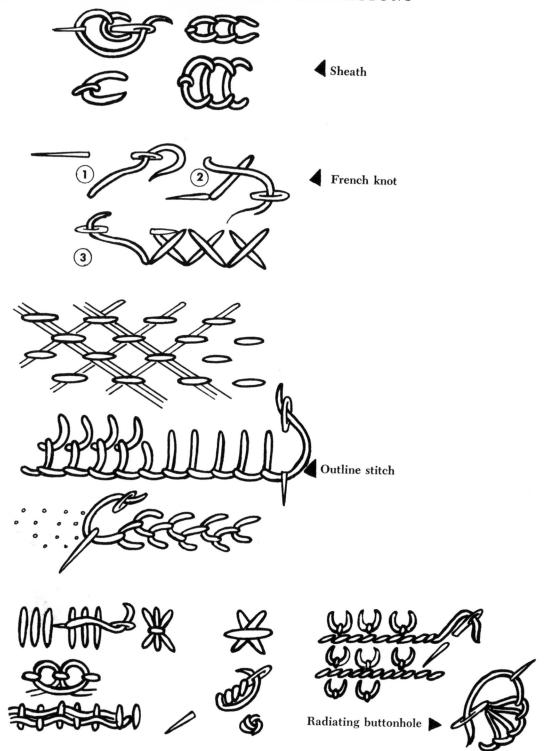

◀ Sheath

◀ French knot

① ② ③

◀ Outline stitch

Radiating buttonhole ▶

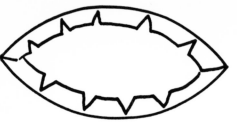

CHAPTER XXIV

Clay

CLAY TO THE YOUNG CHILD is a kind of "super-mud" he can shape with his hands and feel its cool, smooth, moist surface. The child has a similar experience when he feels sand and mud with his bare feet and hands. Before seeing his fingers make prints in moist clay he has seen animals' and birds' footprints in mud and snow.

Children have seen bricks; tiles; terra-cotta flower pots; dishes, vases, and figurines, made from clay.

Find out if there are deposits of clays in your community, for children enjoy digging their own clay. Clays vary: in different localities some are red, yellow, blue, white, gray, black, and buff. Some clays are also coarser than others.

MODELING MATERIALS

Materials used by the group:

1. *A one-pound ball of clay* per child of: natural clay (see preparation, pages 276, 277, 278); prepare clay in pug form ready to use; or powdered clay mixed with water, aged, and wedged ready for use (see mixing-powder clay, on page 276).

2. *Covered container for clay,* approximately ten-gallon size, waterproof, and airtight, for example one of the following: earthen crock, zinc-lined clay bin, wooden barrel, galvanized garbage pail, three-coated-enamel stock pot, polyethylene can.

3. *Oil cloth, plastic material, or rubber sheeting,* to keep mixed clay airtight and moist.

4. *Rolling pin* for rolling out clay for tiles.

5. *Pitcher or jar* to contain slip.

6. *Wedging table with a plaster bat and a stretched wire* for cutting the clay (see page 278).

Materials needed for each child.

1. *A working surface,* which may be:

A plaster bat which can be kept damp, or a dry plaster bat that will absorb excess moisture from clay.

A large unbreakable plate.

A receptacle with a low, raised rim around the edge, such as a tray, lid, or pie pan.

Wooden board coated with enamel, shellac, or varnish.

Heavy cardboard coated with shellac.

A heavy piece of butcher or kraft wrapping paper folded back on each side, making a tray to catch loose crumbs.

2. *A sponge* to use moist over finished pieces.

3. *A plastic or metal bowl* to contain water used to dampen a sponge and cloth.

4. *Absorbent cloth* such as turkish towelling about 12″ by 18″, used to keep the child's fingers moist.

5. *Containers with covers* for individual clay pieces to be kept overnight or several days — large coffee or juice cans, wax-coated cartons, plastic food containers such as used for cottage cheese, crockery bowls, terra-cotta flower pots turned upside down over a modeled clay piece placed on a damp plaster bat (the pot should be covered with plastic).

6. *Tools for modeling clay:* tongue depressors used whole or split in half, meat skewers, crochet hooks, large nail heads, large knitting needles, nut picks, small wooden spoons, commercial wooden modeling tools, popsickle sticks.

7. *Tools to make textures on the surface of the clay:* small graters or strainers, rippled edge of clam shells, wooden forks or spoons, rounded end of pen nibs, combs, piece of double-faced corrugated cardboard, paper clips, twigs, pieces of fire bricks, sponges, and stamps made from clay and biscuit fired.

Timothy is completely engrossed in rolling out the clay.

PREPARING OF THE CLASSROOM AND CHILDREN

COVER THE TABLES or desk tops with paper, the back of oilcloth, or any non-absorbent material. Give each child the following: a lump of wedged clay; a clayboard, tray or other suitable working surface; an apron or smock; a damp absorbent cloth to keep his hands moist and to wrap up clay he is not currently using.

Provide a place to dry finished pieces slowly and a place to keep unfinished work.

Be sure all long sleeves are rolled up and rings and bracelets removed.

DISCOVERING CLAY

THE CHILD BEGINS with a lump of clay which he models with both hands. To see the clay change form, in response to the touch of his fingers, is an exciting experience. Like magic to the child is the new form he has made, which he calls a ball, a worm, an animal or a person. He learns to control the form, and enjoys the activity of handling the soft clay rather than the beauty of the forms he creates. The child discovers that: 1) He can take clay apart and put it together again as his concept changes. 2) He can squeeze clay to change it into a new shape. 3) He can poke deep holes into clay with his fingers, or dig out an opening all the way through the clay with a stick, and then see through to the other side. 4) When he pounds or punches clay with his fist, the shape of his fist is left in the clay. 5) He can roll clay in the palm of his hands to make balls or long worms. 6) He can make a round ball and then pat it until it is flat and round like a plate or cake. 7) He learns that one clay piece will adhere to a second if he pushes them together. 8) He can make different designs on the surface by pressing shapes into the soft clay to

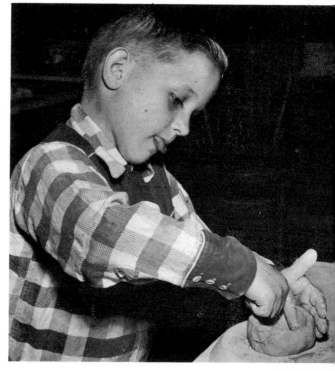

Gregor puts his all into shaping a clay bowl.

make parts lower and other parts higher such as: his fingertips, his knuckles, or seeds. He dents stripes in the clay by scraping the wavy edge of a shell, a notched cardboard, or comb up and down or around the clay.

Desirable habits in using clay. The children may either stand or sit, keeping their feet flat on the floor, and hands on the table until they are finished modeling. If they need to leave their seats, they should learn to close their hands making a fist and go to the sink to wash their hands.

Have each child pinch off enough clay from his lump to roll a small ball. As they work they use the small ball to pick up bits of clay that accumulate on the working surface. Repeated patting of the clay ball to pick up crumbs prevents dropping into laps and on the floor.

In modeling, the children should use their fingers, because the heat of the hand is in the palm, and would dry the clay, making it hard and unpliable. The children keep their fingers moist by rubbing them over the damp absorbent cloth beside the modeling boards. This helps keep the clay moist, and avoids dry crumbs from accumulating on the child's hands.

Taking care of clay work. Pieces made by children who are in the manipulative stage, weak pieces, and ones full of cracks, should be put back in the clay jar with a little water and covered with a damp cloth; they will soften into clay usable another time. Holes are poked in dry pieces and filled with water.

Finished work in good condition. Ask each child to select one piece he has made and place it to dry on a board which is in a cool place — too much heat causes cracking.

Cleaning up. Have children pick up every clay crumb by patting it with a clay

Karla, Kindergarten, is stimulated and intrigued by her discoveries with clay.

ball, and wash their oil cloth and rag. The clayboards are scrubbed with a brush and stood up to dry (preferably in a rack along one wall).

If hands are covered with clay, children should wash them first in a bucket of water, to avoid clogging up the sink drain. (Clay that is the right consistency does not stick to the hands.)

Demonstrations should not be given of how to model clay before the entire group. Kindergarteners and first-graders are individualists who want to use their own ideas in working out their plans. However, it may help the group to ask a child who has succeeded in any constructive step in modeling to tell the others how he achieved the result.

THINGS TO MAKE WITH CLAY

Making beads from balls and discs. To make balls, the children roll different amounts of clay in a circular motion between both palms. To make flat discs, the children press a ball between both palms. They may incise or indent repeated shapes such as melon seeds, into the edge of the disc.

Preparation for stringing balls and discs. A steel knitting needle, stiff wire, or toothpick is placed upright in a clay base. The center of each ball is pushed over the end of the needle. The balls are left on the needle or wire until the clay is dry. Each child paints his balls (with tempera or powder paint) while they are on the needle. When they are thoroughly dry they can be covered with shellac or varnish.

Suggested color combinations for beads are group one: light orange, light blue-brown, and yellow; group two: turquoise blue, yellow, and violet; group three: yellow, yellow-green, and brown; or group four: red, black, and white.

Grouping and stringing beads. Beads or ornaments are more attractive when different sizes are grouped together with a planned repetition. Colored yarns, jute, cotton string, or raffia are appropriate to use for stringing the beads. Each bead may be held in place with a knot.

Modeling fruit and vegetables. After children's first experience in rolling, patting, and punching clay, they become conscious of objects differing in shape. Modeling of fruits and vegetables — which can be used in the playhouse, store, or for a lovely arrangement — fulfills the desire to make something useful.

Have the children observe real objects on all sides to see the contours and surface patterns. Show them, for instance, the beauty of shape in a pear — its two bulbous shapes, one larger than the other, joined with a lovely flowing line. In modeling, the side of the thumb is a good tool for shaping this curve, pressing low parts and pushing to build others out.

Children enjoy choosing a fruit or vegetable to make out of clay.

Hollowed-out bowl. The child rolls a large clay ball the size of the bowl desired. He inserts his first finger or thumb in the center of the clay ball and pushes out the clay, using a circular motion which makes the center opening of the bowl larger and larger. It is important for the child to keep his fingers moist by rubbing them on a damp absorbent cloth while he works. To prevent cracks the clay ball must remain moist and soft. The child works to attain an even thickness in the walls of his bowl, and discovers that bowls tip unless they are flat on the bottom. Show them the best way to level the base of the bowl — revolving it over a small amount of water which has been placed on a board.

Suggested colors. A bowl used for plants should be a color which harmonizes with the green leaves — such as the following earth colors: golden brown, terra-cotta, sage or olive green.

A bowl for use on a desk should harmonize with the browns of the wood, such as gray-blue, black, wine, driftwood gray, golden brown, red brown, or dark green.

A candy or pin bowl should harmonize with the cloth used on tables or with the wood — such as rose, light gray-blue, golden yellow, or chartreuse. These containers should be fired and glazed.

A flower holder may be made from a ball or a single irregular shape of clay. The child punches holes with his finger deep enough to support the stems and wide enough to hold them. A flat rock or piece of lead or iron can be used on the bottom of the clay to make it heavy enough to hold the flowers and not tip.

Unfired clay holders can be used to support dried grasses, seed pods, or bare branches for winter bouquets.

Flower holders should be a color that blends with the plant or container, such as a green or brown.

Holders to be used in water must be made waterproof, by being fired in a kiln or coated with shellac or varnish. (Try submerging the dry clay holder in shellac or waterglass.) This experience offers the teacher a splendid opportunity to explain the difference between fired and unfired clay.

A candle holder must have an opening wide enough to hold a commercial candle (or one the child has made) and deep enough to support it. For example, a candle ⅞" in diameter needs a hole 1⅛" deep. The wall around the opening must be thick enough to guard against cracking or chipping away; for a ⅞" opening, a ½" rim is suggested.

A circular ball is used as the basic shape. The base must be wide enough to support the height of the candle. The child punches a hole down the center and tries the candle in the opening for size. The child attains variations in shape by pushing the clay out in places, or by adding texture to the surface by making depressions in it with a tool, such as the end of a wooden spoon, or by pressing materials such as seeds into the surface.

Another way is to flatten clay balls into discs, and pile them one on top of another, painting clay slip between each one. (Slip, for joining two pieces of clay, is made by mixing clay powder with water, and should have the consistency of thick cream; slip should be made of the same clay it is to join). After the discs are adhered the child makes a hole down the center.

A pencil holder for a desk or table should be just the right size and shape to hold a pencil without tipping. The child

Flower holder Grade One
(for dried materials)

Paperweight
Grade Three

Pencil holder
Grade Two

presses a pencil into the modeled clay in a slanting or vertical position to make a hole the correct size. Stamps pressed into the surface in an all-over pattern, or shapes of clay added to the surface with slip, are suggestions for decorations.

A file for a desk can be made by placing a long nail, wire, or knitting needle into a firm clay base. The clay base must be wide enough to keep the vertical needle from tipping. The child thinks of something tall like a cone, a building, or a standing animal such as a bear.

A paperweight might be made of flat forms like turtles or frogs or a coiled snake making a solid circular form.

MAKING A TILE OF CLAY

Steps in shaping a clay tile.

1. Cover a board with a damp cloth.
2. Place two sticks, ⅜″ thick, parallel to each other on the cloth, the same distance apart as the width the tile is to be.
3. Add dabs of clay between the sticks until the surface of the board between them is built up slightly above the sticks.
4. Use a third flat stick with a straight edge for a scraper. Use both hands, with one on each end of the scraper, to draw the scraper towards you across the clay.
5. Remove the sticks. Mark the size and shape for the tile on the surface of the clay, which may be a circle, a square or a rectangle.
6. Cut away the excess clay with a tongue depressor or meat skewer. Be careful to cut straight down through the clay.

When tiles will be used as wall plaques an opening for a wall hook should be made one inch from the top center, by pushing a blunt pencil point into the clay, slanting

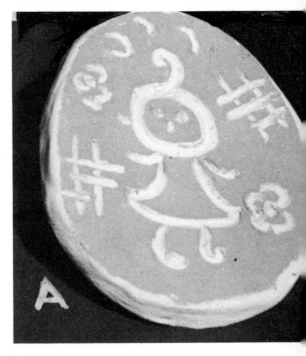

A. *Sgraffito tile design.* A white clay tile was covered with red clay slip. The design was formed by scraping away the red clay slip with a nail head, revealing the white clay underneath.

the point upward for ¼″. A paper clip may be inserted into the clay if it is *not* going to be fired.

Making a design for the clay tile. The child draws a design on a piece of thin paper the same size as the tile, of a subject he knows, such as himself, his house, an animal, a flower, a tree. He should fill the whole paper, then place it on top of the tile and slowly trace over his lines with a rounded pencil point or a meat skewer. When he lifts the paper up, he uncovers the line impression on the tile surface.

Variations of tile designs:

1. The line can be widened with a wooden tool or a large nail by pressing the tool along the line, resulting in a sunken line pattern.

2. Some areas can be covered with a texture or repeated pattern using a stamp, leaving other areas plain in contrast.

3. Clay may be added to the surface, a small amount at a time, to make some areas project in low relief from the background. Balls or coils must be joined to the clay body with slip.

4. Unfired clay tiles may be painted with poster paint, and when dry, shellac over that. Enamel paint may be used when the tile is completely dry.

PAINTING TILE TO BE FIRED IN A KILN

Underglazes consist of clay mixed with metal oxides such as chrome, iron, or cobalt. They are applied to the surface of leather-dry clay with a brush (leather-dry means the clay is hard and firm, still the color of wet clay and still feels moist but it is not thoroughly dry.)

A cut-paper stencil is placed on top of the clay tile. The underglaze is brushed over the entire surface, thus covering the exposed areas with underglaze. Then lift

B. *Low bowl.* The child painted red clay slip directly on the inside of his white clay bowl to make the bird design. An orange stick was used to scrape away the red clay slip to suggest feathers.

the paper stencil straight up, off the tile.

Sgraffito is a design scratched through a coat of slip to reveal the color of the clay body underneath. The entire surface of the *leather-hard* clay tile must be covered with slip of a darker or lighter color than the tile. Three coats of slip are applied with a brush, each in a different direction. When the slip is dry enough so that it does not stick to the fingers, a design is scratched through the surface coating of slip, with a nail, wooden tool, bobby pin, blunt pencil point, or broad pen nib for making lines, or a piece of stiff cardboard, end of wedge-shaped wood, tongue depressor, wooden spoon, or table knife to scrape away larger areas.

Stamping or stippling with slip is done on leather-hard clay. Pour slip, the consistency of thin cream, into a lid or small dish. A rubber stamp is coated with the slip, then pressed on to the tile surface. A sponge dipped into the slip makes a stippled design when applied to the tile.

Finished tiles should be placed across two sticks one-half inch wide or over a wire cake-cooler to allow the air to circulate around them.

GROWTH IN CLAY MODELING
(Past the manipulative stage)

MOST YOUNG CHILDREN think in terms of each part, rather than of the whole. In an animal or person, for example, the child shapes single parts one at a time, such as rolling a coil for each leg and arm and a ball for the head. Many five-year-old children are satisfied just to make the parts.

When children have developed to the extent of relating parts to each other they will join parts of the body together. At this stage they know the head joins the body at the neck, the arms at the shoulders, and the legs at the hips. Remind children to keep the parts they are making in a damp cloth, so they will stay pliable.

The teacher should help a child make the joints strong, so that he will not be discouraged by having the parts fall apart. Where an arm or leg is to be added, make a small depression in the body with the thumb. The limb is scratched on the end, painted with clay slip, and pushed into the depression. The clay of the body is pushed up over the coil. A thin coil wrapped around the joint strengthens it. The edges of the coil are worked into the clay beneath by pushing small amounts of the clay down, filling in the crack between the coil and the joined parts.

Another way a child models a figure is by bending a piece of clay to the desired position. If the clay is very plastic and moist enough, he is usually quite successful, with only a few cracks resulting in places with the greatest stress. These can be filled in by smoothing bits of clay into the mass. This is the simplest visual image for the child because the silhouette of the figure is formed more readily.

Beginners also push out parts from the lump of clay with the pads of their thumbs. A young child may or may not have an idea of his goal before he begins to model clay. As he squeezes and pushes parts out from the lump of clay his active imagination guides his shaping of a new form, which he may or may not give a name.

It is helpful for the teacher to find the boys and girls who are making parts strong, and let them explain to the others how they join parts or make new solid forms. Children must be careful not to pinch off parts by pressing in the clay at the joints. Children enjoy rolling tiny balls for eyes and small coils for rows of curls which they can press on to the head. You must remind children to add slip to parts they join together.

As children grow in understanding they also grow in powers of observation, and see different shapes and sizes in objects they see every day.

The block of clay to be used for modeling should be placed so it can be seen on the top and from back, front, and sides. The first step in modeling is to shape the clay into the same geometric form as the object to be produced. Figurines representing animals or people may be placed in a box for illustration. During the time the child shapes his form the clay remains in an upright position. Many children lay the clay down as they work, pressing and flattening the mass, and when their object is finished it is too thin to stand up — like a gingerbread-man cookie which is made to lay down.

Children discover that animals and people must have thickness to stand up. Parts need to be close together to be strong, such as a tail touching the body, and ears joined to the head. An animal in a resting position is the best position for children to model with the legs tucked in, seeming to be part of the body.

Note: Children still in the manipulative stage, or ones who are not trying to make an animal or person to stand up, should be given clay to manipulate; they should not be expected to model from the mass until they are more mature.

MODELING ANIMALS

THE CHILD BEGINS with a lump of clay the shape of a potato. Clay may be pulled out from the mass for the head with the ears pulled from the head. To place the legs the child presses a cross shape with the side of his hand on the under side of the lump of clay.

The projecting parts (*a, b, c, d,*) may be gently pulled and shaped to make the legs. The form can now be recognized by the child as a basic animal shape.

Clay is added to round out the stomach, for feet, or for any other projecting part.

The child pulls the clay away with his thumb from a place which is smaller, such as a neck, to a place which is thicker, such as the chest, or from the hollow of the back to the thighs. Using the discarded clay,

PREPARING CLAY
TO MAKE LEGS

parts may be added in small amounts to give fullness in places like the high part of the back, or the bulge of the stomach and cheeks. Each bit of clay is rubbed into the mass. The animal must be moist and of the same consistency as the pieces added.

Instead of punching parts in, a left-to-right movement with the flat padded side of the thumb or other finger is used to push the clay away. Instead of pinching or squeezing parts to make them smaller, clay is scraped away or pushed from some low part to a part which needs clay added. Projecting parts like tails and ears, if too thin, become brittle and break off; if they extend too far, they will crack or break with a slight knock. Fine forms are always compact. Guide children to see the beautiful curve of the tail placed along the back close to the back legs, or around to one side of the body thus leading our eye around to the head.

When a child is struggling with some part that collapses because the clay is soft or the part is too heavy or projects out too far, suggest placing a wad of paper, ball of clay, or block of wood under the part to support it until it dries. However, the part will no doubt break off later; thus, the child learns from experience.

Do not expect primary-grade children to model a finished piece which has subtle changes in contours. They may be able to see and feel them, but not to model them until the upper elementary level. Praise them for modeling strong, simple forms that do not break apart (see clay animals, pages 165, 261, 265, 267).

Modeling People
(Grade Two and Three)

CHILDREN OBSERVE THE SHAPES and sizes of forms found in people, such as the rounded shape of the head which is broadest at the top and smaller than the other main parts of the body; point out that a standing person would fit into a vertical cylinder.

Give each child a long lump of clay, which he places in a vertical position in front of him to make a standing person. By removing clay from each side of the top of the cylinder the child has a start with a smaller shape for the head. Encourage children to keep parts joined together, such as arms close to the body. They have learned ways to push the clay from a recessed part to a bulging part, and now should learn to add small amounts of clay to the mass to build out rounded forms. A wooden tool scraped along the side of the arm, for example, helps define the shape.

The first time a child models the figure, solidity, compactness, and stability should be stressed. In the child's language, parts must stay together, the figure must stand without tipping. Improvement will come in proportion to the child's ability to observe differences and his desire to do better. The teacher must help the child control his clay, keep it moist, join parts securely with slip, and to smooth out all cracks. Arms should be joined to the side of the figure. It is advisable for children to keep the two legs together, since the cylindrical forms of pants can be rounded with a tool, and a girl with a long skirt can also be easily modeled. Figures with short skirts need very sturdy legs for support.

While the clay is moist and plastic the

ANIMALS MODELED IN CLAY
Grade Three

Texture has been added for fur, feathers, and for the pattern on the turtle's back. The turtle would make a suitable paperweight.

figure may be slightly bent. Arms may hold something such as a baby or doll. Encourage children to carry out their own ideas in modeling.

Clay people and animals may be used in three-dimensional displays, such as sand tables and dioramas representing the farm, the zoo, animals in the woods, the community, things people do, or a nativity scene, for example. An animal or person may be used with a plant arrangement, with driftwood or woven straw, on the library table or somewhere else. Modeled pieces need a simple background to enhance their beauty.

BEFORE INTRODUCING pottery-making, have children feel examples of compact forms made of clay, that are solid and pleasing to hold, and tell them how primitive people make and fire their own dishes of clay. If you can, arrange a visit to a kiln, so the children can see how clay is stacked and fired; try to find a broken piece to see the hole on the inside which made an airpocket causing the piece to explode in the kiln, accentuating the importance of wedging clay and modeling well knit forms.

Procedure for making a coil bowl. (Clay that is to be fired should be well wedged before it is modeled.)

1. Each child makes a round clay base not less than four inches in diameter from a clay ball each child has patted out flat, to a thickness of one-half inch. The children should cover their bases with damp cloths while they roll the coils.

2. Each child rolls clay between his hands into a sausage shape about the thickness of his fist. He places the clay on a damp clayboard or on the underside of oil-cloth which covers his table.

3. The child places both hands with his fingers spread apart over the center of the lump of clay. As he rolls the clay slowly forward about 12″ he moves each hand *gradually* from the center outward (to lengthen the coil) using a very slight pressure all the time. The child leaves his hands on the coil and rolls it back, moving his hands gradually toward the center of the coil. The child continues the same movement until the coil is an even thickness, from ⅜″ to ½″, and long enough to go around the clay base, about 12″. If the coil is flat, the child has pressed the clay too hard. It is advisable to return flat rolls to the clay jar and for the child to start making a new roll with a fresh, moist piece of clay.

The child should make slight depressions with a stick around the circular base, and then add slip. The child places the coil directly above the edge of the base all the way around. The two ends should be cut on a slant at the point where they meet, scored with a stick, and joined together. The joint is smoothed by pushing the clay back and forth over the joining. If the part of the wall where the joining is made is thinner a small amount of clay should be worked into the wall at the weak points.

Precautions. The clay base and coils should be equally damp when they are joined together. The coils needed may be rolled and covered with a damp cloth, one after another, and added at the same time one above another on the clay base. This helps insure their being the same moisture. Level the bottom of the clay bowl by revolving the base around on a damp smooth surface, such as marble or formica.

Coils on the walls of the bowl that collapse are too moist. To prevent this, allow each coil to set a moment to stiffen before adding a new coil. Coils that crack when they are curved around the base, are too dry. Do not try to fill in cracks. Wrap the clay in a damp cloth, and roll the coils again later.

The coil method may easily be too difficult for some third graders; a hollowed-out ball method is much simpler and should be used by slower children.

Since clay becomes brittle when it is dry, try to avoid sharp, thin edges or small protruding parts that chip easily. These edges must be thick, rounded, and smooth. When the piece is entirely finished and

DEMONSTRATION OF THE COIL METHOD

partly dry it can be brushed with a damp sponge to remove *sharp* edges.

Decorating clay bowls. Allow clay pieces to set until they are firm so that line designs and textures will hold their shape.

Incised lines. Children may freely draw a line design directly on the clay bowl, with an orange stick or similar tool.

Textures can be pressed into the clay to make border designs or all-over patterns, with fingernail marks, nailhead marks, the padded end of a finger, the blunt end of a scissors, a wire potato masher or beater, a bent covered wire in loops or other shapes; a sawtooth edge of metal, a comb, or an irregular edge on heavy cardboard can be scraped around a bowl to make lines for texture. A plain area sets off a textured area. One kind of texture is usually best.

Seeds — pumpkin, watermelon, sunflower, or squash — may be pressed into the surface of clay which will not be fired.

Making a foot. A bowl that is to be fired must have a foot — a place to put the stilt, to raise the clay piece in the kiln when it is fired so air can circulate. To make a foot, turn the clay bowl upside down. Have the child make a circle on the bottom with a nail, a distance in from the edge equal to the width of the bowl's wall (*i.e.* if a wall is one-quarter inch thick, the circle should be one-quarter inch in from the edge all around the base). The inside of the circle is scraped away with the head of a nail to a depth of about one-eighth inch.

To dry clay bowls, place them one-half inch apart on two sticks one-half inch wide to allow air to circulate.

Firing. The best finish is to biscuit fire and glaze the clay in a kiln, which gives the piece a durable structure, a surface texture and color which is part of the material itself. The first firing called biscuit leaves the natural color of the clay and does not waterproof it. Glaze is added to biscuit and fired to add color and coating to the surface.

To insure the successful firing of modeled pieces, the following procedures must be followed:

1. Clay must be well wedged with all air bubbles removed before modeling.

2. Clay must be well built, in compact, solid forms of uniform thickness throughout.

3. No pieces with cracks should be fired. Some causes of cracks are: varying thicknesses (such as a thick animal body with thin legs, ears and tail) and degrees of dryness; poorly joined parts; too quickly drying (do not begin drying pieces near heat — a radiator, direct sunlight or a stove). Avoid pushing clay or overlapping clay, making crevices or air pockets.

4. Clay pieces must be *completely dry* when they are fired in the kiln.
It is very unlikely that pieces made by young children modeling for the first time would stand up under firing. Often there is an airpocket inside. Clay with some grog mixed in with the clay breaks less because it is more porous.

Substitutes for firing and glazing, for use where there is no access to a kiln, for pieces the child is keeping.

1. Polish when the clay is completely dry by rubbing with a glass rod or glass toothbrush container. (Clay object needs to have large plain areas.)

2. Tie a string around the clay and dip the clay piece into hot melted wax. (Wax crayons may be melted. Polish the clay piece when dry.

3. Paint wet or dry clay with powder paint, tempera, or poster colors. Thin paint will be absorbed into the clay. If a deep color is desired, paint must be the thickness of heavy cream. If borders are desired or an all-over pattern, the natural color of the clay is attractive used as one color. If background color is desired, paint it first. When it is thoroughly dry, paint on the all-over repeated design or border with opaque paint.

To waterproof an object, apply a coat of transparent shellac or brushing lacquer after the paint is dry.

4. Add design with waterproof oil paint (not advisable for children under 8). Children should not work with *oil*-soluble paint until they have developed fine coordination and are careful workers.

In painting clay objects, allow the color of the object itself as one color in the design. Instead of buying different color oil paints, use white or gray enamel, house paint, or rubber-base paint as a base color and fill several baby-food tins about half full of it. Add a different color of powder paint to each baby-food tin and mix thoroughly until the desired color is obtained. Be sure children use the one brush assigned to each different color. Place clean paper over the painting area for each new group of children.

Place the oil paint containers in the center of a work table, within easy reach of a group of children seated around the table. Have each child place his clay piece on top of a coffee can while he paints. A few children can paint at one time. It is advisable for the teacher to see how the work is progressing periodically. Show children how to revolve their coffee can with clay on top.

Dip a clean cloth in mineral spirits to wipe oil paint from fingers or the brush handle. Watch for brushes filled with oil that are placed on the working area — they can quickly stain clothing.

When each child finishes painting be sure he places the oil brush on a piece of oiled paper with the bristles facing the can of paint. If the brush is not going to be used immediately by another child, it should be cleaned while still soft. To clean oil brushes, place them immediately in mineral spirits until the paint is removed. Then wash them in warm soapy water.

Place the painted clay pieces out of the children's reach to dry for two days; a piece is finished when it is dry. These may be washed with water when they become soiled.

SKILLS ACQUIRED IN MODELING

By the third grade most children have learned:

How to change a lump of clay into a desired shape;

How to make a solid form that will stand and look well from all sides;

Ways to join clay together so it will not fall apart;

How to make bowls or dishes that will hold something without tipping;

Appropriate ways to decorate clay;

How to press the surface firmly to avoid cracks;

How to mend cracks;

How to keep walls uniform in thickness so they do not crack when drying;

How to avoid pinching clay;

The way to use a tool to take parts away;

To avoid pulling clay until it cracks;

To add clay to make parts larger;

To push clay from a too-large place to one not large enough;

To keep objects standing while modeling;

To have heavier parts at the bottom;

That a beautiful modeled piece is compact and feels good to hold.

After a child has learned all this, all his work should show this growth in understanding.

Clay — a kind of mud dug up out of the earth, consisting mainly of hydrated silicates of aluminum.

Biscuit — clay that has been fired once in the kiln.

Ceramics — a term used for any article made of clay and fired.

Glaze — the powdered mineral finish on fired clay that becomes glass when it is very hot.

Coil — a roll of clay.

Incised line — a line pressed into the clay with a tool: as a wire, a pencil, or a nail.

Kiln — an oven which reaches a tempera-ture much hotter than a stove, used for baking clay.

Pottery — a term used for dishes made of clay and fired in a kiln.

Sgraffito — a design scratched through a coating of slip, revealing the clay body underneath.

Slip — clay powder mixed with water until it is the consistency of cream.

Other materials modeled similar to clay are Asbestos Cement, see Appendix, page 275 and Salt and Flour mixture, see Appendix, page 283. Plasticine or modeline are substi-tutes for clay and do not harden.

W A L L   P L A Q U E

A First-Grader made this relief design by dig-ging away the top white layer of coated wall board around the white forms, making a dark background.

CHAPTER XXV

Art Fulfills a Basic Need

CHILDREN'S ART EXPRESSION is motivated by experiences which are significant to them. Each child gains ideas for his art through seeing, feeling, touching, and hearing. The experiences expressed in art may be ones in which the child tells his feeling, ones showing something that has happened to him, or something that he has made happen. The child needs to feel part of what he is expressing in visual form. Five- and six-year-old children picture anything they think of, remember, or imagine in symbolic form. Children free from adult formulas invent their own explanations of the symbols they have made.

Children must be given opportunities to see the beauties and wonders of the world around them, to touch things, to hear music, the sound of birds, the splash of water or the rumble of thunder, and to feel joy, love, and the rhythms of movement. Children must use imagination in a flexible way. Each child's desire to know more about the surrounding world leads him to discover how things move, how they grow, how they are alike or how they differ. The creative process results from the child's response to what he has seen or imagined.

At first he paints what his environment means to him, not what he sees. As he adds to his experience he grows in understanding and expression.

A child may need to concentrate on expressing a definite experience. By questioning or by directing observation, the teacher helps the child become personally involved and recall details. Dramatic play also may help him relive the experience he wishes to portray.

Children have a basic need to express themselves. Art materials must fit the developmental age of the child, and help him establish a relationship between the work and the idea. Experiences with many different materials help the child coordinate his motions and make him sensitive to the feel of things. Some children express their ideas through feeling and shaping a plastic material — such as clay — with their hands. Children in the primary grades often need the soothing feel of clay and the experience of changing the plastic material into new form, to release tension.

The child wants to use his hands — his natural tool for shaping, touching, and moving objects about — and to make new forms by re-arranging. The exploratory approach to the use of art materials helps the child discover the qualities of the material and what he can do with the material.

Child development comes when the re-creation of the child's experiences requires thinking, inventiveness, self-direction, imagination, individual self-expression, and offers the child opportunities to make new discoveries. Art is a natural form of expression for the child.

The child can honestly — and wants to — say of the work he has made in his own way, "This is Mine."

Appendix

INFORMATION CONCERNING ART MATERIALS

ADHESIVES

1. Carter cement is a strong adhering liquid for pasting cardboard.
2. Elmer's glue for wood, glass, rocks, seeds, cardboard.
3. Vegetable glue has a semi-opaque, pastel-like consistency for mounting pictures, dissolves with water and dries slowly.
4. Rye flour is better than wheat flour for making paste. Boil flour and water together until transparent.
5. Rubber cement, for mounting pictures, can be removed from paper without leaving mark. Spread evenly on the mount and the back of the picture, dry a few seconds, then press two surfaces together.
6. Duco cement adheres china or shells and dries quickly.
7. Soft solder or liquid solder for soldering metals, wood, and glass, is used to fasten loose bristles in brushes, and does not need heating.
8. Casco White Glue (flexible) is recommended for adhering felt and for joining wooden frames.
   Recipe
   1 cup Casco powder.
   1⅛ cups cold water.
   Pour water into mixing pot. Add Casco powder, stirring rapidly for one minute until the powder has absorbed the water. The glue thickens and becomes pastey. Let stand for thirty minutes, then stir one minute. It can be used then, and the next day.

ASBESTOS CEMENT
(Light-weight modeling material.)

Place water in container.

Stir wheat wallpaper paste into the water until it is the consistency of soft custard.

Add asbestos cement, stirring constantly. Continue to add cement and knead like bread dough until excess moisture is re-moved. If allowed to stand a short period of time, moisture will evaporate, and when ready to be used the mixture will not stick to the hands.

Mold and press the mixture into desired shape, and cover with a thin layer of paste;

smooth the surface. If you need to add more cement, cover area with thin layer of paste then add cement. This cement does not dry quickly.

You may use for modeling small objects like birds.

CLAY

TO MAKE CLAY FROM RAW MATERIALS

CLAY CONSISTS OF various igneous rocks that have been ground, crushed, and weathered until they become fine, plastic, workable material.

To separate clay from foreign matter.

1. Separate clay in small fragments and dry.

2. To pulverize, place the fragments in a strong cloth bag and pound with a mallet.

3. Sift powder through a ⅛″ wire mesh sieve or 16 or 20 mesh screen.

4. Fill a non-rust container half full of clear water.

5. Sprinkle or sift the clay powder into the water, distributing it evenly, until the powder extends above the water.

6. Allow to stand overnight; do not stir.

7. Pour off excess water.

8. Stir with the hand. The mixture should feel plastic.

9. If it does, pour it through a 40 mesh brass screen into a clay container; allow to stand overnight.

10. In the morning, siphon off clear water that has risen to the top.

If in step number 8, the mixture feels sandy, allow it to stand; the sand will settle to the bottom. Pour off the slip on top and proceed with step number 9. If the mixture feels sticky, some sand may be added.

TO PREPARE CLAY FLOUR OR POWDER

1. Use non-rust clay container with tight lid and handles: zinc-lined bin, galvanized iron, glazed earthenware, crock, or polyethylene can. Keep receptacle in cool place.

2. Place clay powder in gunny sack or flour sack about ¾ full.

3. Place sack of clay powder in non-rust container and cover with warm water, which helps clay to age. Allow to stand a minimum of 24 hours. Clay several weeks old is much more plastic than fresh clay; leave clay soaking in June for the following year. Mold on clay makes it more plastic.

4. Clay can be kneaded in the sack before it is removed.

MIXING LARGE AMOUNTS OF CLAY

A 20-gallon garbage can will hold 200 lbs. of clay.

Alternate four measures of clay powder with one measure of water until the container is nearly full. Keep airtight.

Clay stays in good condition more easily if a large quantity is prepared at once.

All clay must be wedged before it is modeled if the finished piece is to be fired. See Wedging, page 278.

Colored Slip, or Engobe

Underglaze colors which come in green, blue, yellow, turquoise, black, green, red brown, chocolate brown, and white can be used to make colored slip, as follows:

Mix one teaspoon of underglaze color with two tablespoons of white clay flour. A few drops of glycerine may be added to help the slip flow.

Add water gradually until the mixture is like thick cream.

The engobe, or colored slip, is painted on semi-moist clay with a soft brush. Avoid making one coat of colored slip too thick. The modeled piece must be made from the same clay as the engobe.

Clay pieces decorated with engobe are fired once for biscuit and a second time for a transparent glaze.

Clay Wedging Box

Materials.

Sturdy wooden box 2 ft. by 3 ft. by 6 in.

Tin strips to reinforce corners of box.

Wooden post 1 in. by 2 in. and 2 ft. long.

Pea gravel 3 in. deep in the bottom of the box.

Molding plaster of paris   100 lbs.

Hardware cloth or wire screen 23 in. by 35 in.

Piano wire or deep sea fishing wire   3 ft.

Turnbuckle, one.

Screw eyes, two.

Screws, three one inch.

Varnish to coat inside of box.

Directions for preparing box.

Place wedging box on a sturdy table in location it will remain.

Glue post to the center of inside of back of box, then insert three screws.

Cover inside of box with three coats of varnish.

Reinforce corners with tin bent and nailed to the outside of each corner of the box.

Directions for filling wedging box with plaster.

1. Cover the bottom of the box with pea gravel to a depth of 3 inches.
2. Pour in a layer of plaster of paris.
3. Place hardware cloth (½″) or wire screen over layer of plaster.
4. Fill box level with plaster.

Essentials for Mixing and Pouring Plaster

Use one batch of plaster to fill the entire box, because layers do not join well, and are likely to split or crack.

See Mixing plaster of paris, page 282.

Mix plaster in quantities of no more than one gallon at a time. Several eighth-grade boys or adults mix plaster in rotation about ten minutes apart to fill a large wedging box.

Hold the container of plaster close to the box. Pour the first batch into the box back and forth and up and down, smoothly and quickly. *Do not splash* when pouring, for splashing forms air bubbles. The tilt of the container and distance it is held from the wedging box govern the force with which it is poured. Pour one batch after another until the box is full.

If the surface is uneven, scrape it with *metal* scraper after plaster is thoroughly set and completely dry all the way through; this takes about ten days.

Place one screw eye on top of the verticle post and one into the center front of the box.

Fasten one end of the wire to the screw eye in the front of the box, extend the other end of the wire to one end of the turnbuckle. Cut the wire, fasten end to opposite end of the turnbuckle and extend to the screw eye on top of the post and fasten.

WEDGING CLAY

Purpose.

To free clay from all air bubbles.

To work into homogeneous mass, meaning to thoroughly mix hard and soft layers.

Process.

Screw turnbuckle until piano wire is taut.

Pick up a piece of clay in both hands and bring it down on the wire to cut into two pieces.

Lift the piece in the right hand and fling it down on the wedging table with the cut side up.

Lift the piece in the left hand and fling it down on the first piece with the uncut side meeting the cut side of the first piece. Roll and knead the two pieces together.

Lift up in hands and pat and work into a block form.

Repeat the above until the cut side is perfectly smooth, like the cut bread dough.

Form into oblong block and place in airtight container.

DYES

Green spirit stain to dye raffia (used for weaving).

	Mahogany	Dissolve
	Brown	in
Powder —	Rosewood	wood or
	Weathered oak	denatured
	Golden oak	alcohol

Color remover for cloth desired a different color.

1 tablespoon of ammonia

1 quart of water

Boil material in this solution to remove color.

Commercial dyes.

Read directions for kind of cloth, mordant and amount of time for cooking.

For Batik which requires a cold dye, use a dye called Batik dye.

Dye made from plants.

Gather plants young.

Collect roots in autumn, leaves when mature.

Collect ripe berries and seeds.

Tap root of dandelion ......dull magenta

Leaves of elderberry.................green

Purple elderberry ....blue-violet

Golden rod ....yellow

Pear leaves ....dull yellow
Shells and husks of walnuts......... brown
Powdered leaves of sumac
                                yellow-brown
Root of sumac...............................yellow
Berries of sumac ....purple
Sunflower seeds ....blue
Beets ....red-violet
Wild cherry roots.........................purple
Dahlia blossoms ....yellow-orange
Lily-of-the-valley leaves
                        light greenish-yellow
Marigold flowers.....................yellow-tan
Sassafras root bark...............rose-brown
Zinnia flowers .... light yellow or dark
                                greenish-yellow

To make dye from 1 pound of weeds, bark, or roots use 4 level teaspoons alum.

1. Soak plants 24 hours.
2. Boil 3 hours. Strain plant matter from dye. The plant may be chopped up and placed in a cheesecloth bag, covered with water and boiled.

Cloth.

1. The sizing must be removed from the cloth by washing before it is dyed.
2. *To treat the cloth before dying to make dye fast.*
   For wool, add ¼ oz. cream of tartar to alum bath, which consists of 1 oz. powdered alum and 1 gallon water. Boil cloth in the bath for 1 hour; rinse.
   For cotton, linen, rayon, add ¼ oz. washing soda to the water before boiling.
3. *To dye cloth,* cover it with water in a copper or enamel pan to which dye is added. Boil one hour. Stir with wooden paddle. Dry in shade. Or, to set the color, after cotton has boiled 5 minutes, stir in ½ cup of salt; after wool has boiled for 5 minutes add ½ cup vinegar.

FINGERPAINT

THREE RECIPES FOR MAKING YOUR OWN
(Cost is less.)

1. *Mix wallpaper paste* or wheat flour with water: gradually dust powder into water until it is the consistency of thick cream.
   Stir well.
2. *Laundry starch:* dissolve ½ cup of powdered starch in cold water until it is like thick cream; and gradually pour dissolved starch into 4 cups of boiling water.
   a) To make paint slippery, add to the above ¼ cup soap flakes.

   b) To keep paint from spoiling over a period of time, add ½ tablespoon of glycerine.
3. *Cornstarch.* Mix two heaping tablespoons of cornstarch with ¼ cup cold water until they are in solution.
   Add 1 pint of water, stir vigorously, and bring to a boil. Beat 1 tablespoon soap flakes into mixture. Cool.
4. Add powder-paint colors to liquid starch.

1. Shake 3½ cups of alcohol with ½ cup of transparent shellac and allow to settle.

Spray the clear solution which rises to the top, over chalk, or paint it over the back of the chalk painting.

2. Spray buttermilk over surface of chalk; or coat paper with buttermilk, and draw over wet paper with chalk.

3. Mix a small amount of glue with water. Dip chalk pictures in this mixture to set color.

4. Thin Evergrip Mucilage ½: spray, standing three feet from drawing, and repeat two or three times. This does not dull the colors.

LIQUID OPAQUE PAINTS

FORMULAS FOR MAKING PAINTS FROM POWDER PAINT AND TEMPERA

1. *Enamel.* Mix powder paint with clear shellac, lacquer, or spar varnish: pour liquid gradually into powder. The more varnish used, the more gloss there will be. The more powder paint used, the flatter the finish will be. Powder paint may be mixed with white enamel paint to obtain different colors.

2. *Oil paint.* Mix powder with linseed oil; by placing powder on glass; and adding a small amount of oil. Mix with palette knife. Solvent is turpentine.

3. *Silk-screen paint.* Mix tempera with ivory snow; whip up suds. Consistency like pudding. Solvent is water.

4. *Paint for glass.* Mix Bon-Ami with paint — powder in solution or tempera. Rub brush on soap, then dip into paint. Solvent is water.

5. *Wood stain.* Thin tempera with banana oil. Solvent is alcohol.

There are many fine, nonpoisonous, commercial paints on the market which have been thoroughly tested, and contain a preservative and binder. Lack of sufficient funds to purchase readymade paints is the main reason for making your own.

PAPER

STORE PAPER FLAT, and covered, to protect it from dust. Keep small amounts for daily use. Do not pull single sheets from large piles.

KINDS OF PAPER

Binder's Board. Heavy cardboard for notebook covers.

Bogus. Is rough and absorbent. For charcoal or chalk.

Butcher. Has pressed surface. For murals, book covers, fingerpaint, and scratched crayon.

Carbon. Comes in white and yellow, for stitchery.

Cardboard. Smooth and glazed or unglazed, pressed surface, white and colored. For posters, mats for pictures, gray on one side is cheaper than color on both sides. Shellac cardboard to make a clay-modeling surface.

Charcoal. Absorbent, white and colors. Tooth-edge for chalk and charcoal.

Craft. Slightly rough surface, absorbent, very pleasing texture, cream and colored. For printing.

Chipboard. Gray, or mottled gray, heavy with a rough surface, absorbent. For construction and portfolios.

Construction. Absorbent, slightly rough. White and in colors for greeting cards, program covers, paper construction. For silk screen and block prints, stencils, painting with tempera, crayon drawing.

Drawing. Absorbent, slightly rough. White. For watercolors, crayon, stencil.

Fibertint news. Absorbent, slightly hairy lines in paper, in colors (inexpensive). For powder paint, crayon, stencil, printing.

Fingerpaint. White, smooth, glazed surface. For fingerpainting, scratched crayon.

Japanese. Absorbent, very thin, fine texture in soft tints or in white for prints. (Kinds: Mino-silk, Woo Chang, Halsone).

Kraft. Smooth, hard-finish brown wrapping paper, used for crayon, powder paint, book covers, construction.

Ledger. Pressed surface, white. For lettering and pen drawing, watercolor, and paper sculpture.

Manila. Cream-color, absorbent. For watercolor, tempera, chalk, crayon, and prints.

Mimeo-news. Absorbent, white, heavier than unprinted news. For watercolor, crayon, chalk, prints.

Newsprint. Absorbent, light-weight, white. Used for painting in primary grades. Good for experimenting with brush and crayons.

Oatmeal. Absorbent texture, rough; similar to craft paper. For chalk and stencil.

Option bond. Pressed, semi-gloss on surface. (Cardboard with newsprint on one side.) Use colors for poster, lettering.

Option Bristol. Smooth surface; for lettering, book covers.

Paper towels. Rough, very absorbent; use wet for chalk drawing and as a final layer for papier mâché.

Parchment. Pressed, not absorbent, oil surface. For lettering, construction of lamp shades. To make a substitute for commercial parchment paper:

1. Use a spatula to spread oil paint in a very thin layer over a glass, marble, wax paper, or enamel. Use an earth color, such as burnt or raw umber or sienna.

2. Fold a piece of absorbent cloth to make a pad. Dip into turpentine if a transparent effect is desired. Dip into linseed oil if a more opaque surface is desired.

3. Pat the saturated cloth lightly on the oil paint.

4. Rub with a circular motion over the paper. Tag board or typing paper may be used. Start with a very small amount of color. Add more color if a deeper tone is desired.

The above method may be used over lettering done with India ink.

Photo paper. A light-sensitive paper used for photograms.

Poster. Colors, cut paper. Not as heavy as construction, transparent when placed in front of light. Use for stained-glass-window effect, also for cut-paper designs that require folds.

Sandpaper. Tan, rough, sandy surface. Used to smooth wood. For texture in a collage. For a sandpaper monotype print using a brayer and printer's ink: rub crayon in areas over surface, taking advantage of the rough texture. Grade 00 for sanding linoleum blocks. No. ½ for sanding soft wood. No. 1 for sanding rough wood.

Shelf paper. Pressed, smooth white surface. Used for fingerpaint, paper sculpture.

Screening. Cream-color, rough textured absorbent paper, inexpensive (tears easily). For chalk, powder paint, prints, murals.

Stencil. White, pressed, smooth oily surface. Cuts with a clean sharp edge. (Pen and India ink or pencil will "take" on surface.) For cutting stencil patterns.

Substitutes for stencil paper: heavy wax paper; frozen food boxes; wax-coated paper used on mimeograph machine (wax coating is needed to keep the moisture in the paint from soaking through the stencil pattern, thus smudging the paper or cloth); cover manila paper with linseed oil on one side and turpentine on the other.

Tag board. Pressed surface. 200 lb. cream, light-weight cardboard, lettering,

cut stencil, construction, charts and maps. Use ink, tempera paint.

Toilet tissue. White, absorbent. Use for small prints or stencils. As fine in appearance as Japanese papers.

Tracing. Pressed surface, white, thin transparent paper. Often used in making an all-over design by shifting the paper from one place to another to see various groupings for certain motifs. Will take ink, pencil.

Upson board. Heavy laminated cardboard $\frac{3}{16}''$ thick. Can be used to mount linoleum blocks for stamping.

Want-ad section of newspaper for children's first painting attempts.

Wax paper. Paraffin coated, white, transparent. For cutting stencils, under clay for modeling.

X-ray. Pressed surface, transparent, stencil, construction, mobiles. Cut into shapes.

Watercolor. Slightly rough surface, semi-absorbent, white; $15''$ by $22''$ or $22''$ by $30''$. For watercolor painting.

PLASTER OF PARIS

Amounts to use for mixing.

a. Approximate amount of *plaster* and *water* used for the following:

 For wedging box 2′ by 3′ by 6″ — 100 lbs. plaster added to 40 quarts of water.

 For a plaster bat 9″ by 9″ — 4 lbs. of

plaster added to 2¾ pts. of water.

 For a tile 6″ by 6″ — 1¾ lbs. of plaster added to 1 pt. water.

b. To estimate the amount of liquid plaster needed to fill a desired mold or container, fill the form with water. Use this quantity plus a small extra amount.

PROCESS OF MIXING PLASTER WITH WATER

1. Pour the cold water needed into a pail or bowl for mixing. The water should not fill the vessel more than halfway, because the plaster will swell the water.

2. Sift plaster powder through your fin-

gers or through a flour sifter carefully on to the surface of the water. Press out any lumps in the *dry* powder in your hand. The powder will be absorbed in the water, and will look milky. Continue to sift the plaster over the surface, evenly with an even speed. *Do not "dump" in a handful,* for this causes lumps and air bubbles, and do not sift it in too slowly.

Do not stir or shake plaster at any time while plaster is being added. When the plaster is no longer absorbed into the water and stands in an island above the surface about 1½ inches, *stop adding plaster.*

Allow it to stand about 1 minute.

Immerse a hand in liquid plaster. Move fingers around all through the mixture *easily. Do not stir vigorously,* or you will make air bubbles. If you feel any lumps, squeeze them out.

Lift your hand out periodically. When your fingers are coated with plaster like a glove, without plaster dripping from the fingers, the plaster should be poured *immediately.*

Pouring. Put the mold to be filled on a level surface. Hold vessel of plaster close to the form to be filled. Pour evenly and fairly fast, without splashing. If any air bubbles appear on the surface, touch them lightly; they must go into the plaster solution. Have a pan of water available. Wash the plaster *completely* from your hands *immediately.* (Plaster dries skin; use an oily lotion to lubricate your skin; dry plaster removed from your hands will pull hairs out with it.)

Poured plaster sets rapidly.

First it becomes warm. After it has cooled it is set and can be removed. While it is damp, remove rough edges with a knife or damp towel.

Set away to *dry thoroughly.* (This takes about a week for a large amount.)

Clean plaster containers immediately, while the plaster is still soft.

1. Wipe plaster from mixing vessel with crushed newspaper or paper towel.

2. Wash container with water. Pour this water, as well as the water in which you washed your hands, away outside, not down the drain or it will clog the plumbing.

To mix a small amount of plaster for small tiles or costume pins, use a coffee tin, which can be discarded later.

Coloring and finishing plaster (For poured pieces which are to remain in plaster as a finished product).

To color use powdered chalks with linseed oil, or mix water-soluble color with the water used for mixing the plaster.

To make a hard, washable surface, submerge objects completely in transparent shellac for about a month; the shellac penetrates the surface for about one-half inch, making it very hard.

SALT AND FLOUR MIXTURE FOR MODELING
(beads, birds, or small figures)

Recipe: Take equal parts of flour, salt, water; mix salt and flour together, and gradually add the water. Mix well and knead like dough.

To color, a. paint the modeled object with watercolor when it is finished; b. mix color with the dough as follows: powder paint with the flour and salt; measure liquid dye, vegetable coloring, tempera paint, or colored ink as part of the liquid. For example, to color a dough mixture of ½ cup salt, ½ cup flour, ½ cup water, add 4 tablespoons of tempera paint (½ cup water or 8 tablespoons of tempera equals 4 tablespoons of water). Mix the liquid coloring with the water.

The amount of coloring to use varies with the depth of color desired.

Keep this mixture in wax paper, and use it soon after it is made, for as soon as it is thoroughly dry, it becomes hard.

SHELLAC

Transparent shellac over a surface painted with water-soluble paint makes a hard, water-resistant surface.

Use shellac for wooden toys; over decorated papers used for book covers; wastepaper baskets or other objects handled a great deal. Mix shellac with alcohol to make fixative for chalk and charcoal drawings.

Shellac painted over wall board seals the surface for clay modeling.

Shellac used on drawing paper strengthens the edge for cut stencils. Watercolor paint does not soak through the cut stencil.

Shellac may be used over crayon.

A coat of shellac over papier-mâché objects protects them from dust.

Shellac may not dry if it is used on a damp day.

SOLVENTS

Solvents for thinning and cleaning.
(Consult labels on containers for correct solvent to use.)

For shellac use denatured alcohol.

For varnish use turpentine.

For oil paint use turpentine or mineral spirits.

For lacquer use lacquer thinner.

For enamel use turpentine.

For duco cement use acetone or lacquer thinner.

Thinner to make inks or oil paints on textiles more permanent.

Commercial thinners are sold with textile paints.

A substitute which is compounded by druggist consists of:

½ oz. oil of wintergreen.

½ oz. of 28% acetic acid.

4 oz. gum turpentine.

Use by the drop (in very small quantities).

Talcum dusted on a rubber brayer pre-

vents the roller from getting gummy.

Remove oil-base printer's ink from blocks and brayer with mineral spirits or turpentine: pour small amount of liquid on top layer of newspaper, roll brayer over liquid, and then on clean paper. Repeat until brayer is clean. Scrape surplus ink from glass. Wipe remaining ink from glass with rag soaked in mineral spirits. Wipe block clean.

Water-base printer's ink is removed with water.

Oily surface on linoleum is removed by rubbing oxydol over surface. Wash off with water.

Beeswax is dissolved in turpentine.

Thin damar varnish with turpentine.

Thin oil printer's ink with benzine or benzoil or carbona.

Remove glue from clothing with vinegar.

Protective hand cream.

Apply Protek cream to hands and under fingernails before working with oil inks, or wear rubber gloves.

Brush cleaners. Brush cleaners which come in powder form and require a soaking of the brush in the solution overnight are usually very strong caustic sodas and often ruin bristles. Only use them when the bristles are hard and stiff from standing too long without being cleaned. Gold Dust brush cleaner is recommended.

If oil brushes are washed in kerosene they must be thoroughly washed out before using for painting, for kerosene retards the drying of paint.

If you have no paint cleaner or turpentine for a brush that has been in enamel paint, rub the brustles of the brush in dry Dutch Cleanser and leave the cleanser on the brush until it is to be used again. Before using, simply rub powder out of the brush.

X-RAY FILM

X-ray film can be obtained from hospitals or medical clinics; it is a sheet of transparent plastic covered with a coating of chemically treated gelatin.

To remove x-ray picture:

Place film in enamel or glass container, and cover it with hot water.

Add ½ cup of washing bleach or powdered cleanser to one gallon of water, and stir until well mixed.

Allow the film to soak 15 to 30 minutes, or until gelatin slips off.

After gelatin is removed, run warm or cool water over the film until it is clear.

Use oil paint on the film if color is desired.

Flat material may be placed between two sheets of film for colored transparencies. The edges are bound together.

Cut shapes and use for mobiles or sculpture figures.

Sheets of plastic are expensive. X-ray paper is a useful discarded material.

Bibliography

by DOROTHY S. McILVAIN

"YOUR CHILD AND HIS ART"

By Viktor Lowenfeld

Published by The Macmillan Co., New York, 1957.

Questions by parents answered by Viktor Lowenfeld. Deals with average children and the contribution of creative activity to the child's happiness and his adjustment is emphasized.

"ART OF THE YOUNG CHILD"

By Jane Cooper Bland

Published by the Museum of Modern Art, New York, 1957.

For children three to five years.

"ART FOR THE FAMILY"

By Victor D'Amico

Published by Museum of Modern Art, 11 West 53rd St., New York.

Includes creative art processes for children, young people and adults.

"CHILDREN ARE ARTISTS"

By Daniel Mendelowitz

Publisher — Stanford University Press, Stanford, Cal., 1954.

Suggestions are made for the proper attitudes which parents and teachers should take toward children's art work in order to stimulate artistic expression.

"MEANING IN CRAFTS"

By Edward L. Mattil

Publisher, Prentice-Hall, Inc., 1959

Craft ideas intended to help develop good crafts programs which help with the creative, social, emotional, physical and aesthetic growth of children.

"USE OF NATIVE CRAFT MATERIALS"

By Margaret Eberhardt Shanklin

Publisher: The Manual Arts Press, 1947

Information concerning the gathering, preparing and use of native materials, as well as suggested adaptations.

"CREATING WITH PAPER"

By Pauline Johnson

Published — University of Washington Press, 1958.

Complete book of cutting, folding and constructing paper for all ages.

"OUR EXPANDING VISION,"
Books One, Two, Three

By Kelly Feareng, Clyde Martin, Evelyn Beard

Published by W. S. Benson & Co., Austin, Texas

A graded series designed to help children take ideas that they have perceived through all their senses and re-create them through art media.

"CHILDREN AND THEIR ART"

By Charles D. Gaitskell

Published — Harcourt, Brace and World Co.

Part one presents theoretical information for the teacher to develop his professional background. Part two suggests actual classroom activities in art.

"TEACHING ART IN THE ELEMENTARY SCHOOL"

By Margaret Hamilton Erdt, 1957

Published — Rinehart, Inc., New York

Experiences recorded attempt to show the role of the teacher in helping the child to realize his potential creative and aesthetic strengths.

"ART EDUCATION IN THE KINDERGARTEN"
BY CHARLES AND MARGARET GAITSKELL
PUBLISHED — CHAS. A. BENNETT CO., INC., PEORIA, ILL.

Topics included: what a young child produces in art; how he works; the supplies and equipment he requires; the guidance he needs and the progress he makes.

FILMS

ANIMULES 1951
PRODUCER, INTERNATIONAL FILM BUREAU
57 E. JACKSON BLVD., CHICAGO 4, ILL.   *11 min.*

BE GONE DULL CARE 1949
NATIONAL FILM BOARD OF CANADA
630 - 5TH AVE., NEW YORK, 20   *16 min.*

CARE OF ART MATERIALS 1948
YOUNG AMERICAN FILMS
18 E. 41ST ST., NEW YORK 17, N.Y.   *11 min.*

CHILDREN ARE CREATIVE 1952
CENTRAL WASHINGTON COLLEGE OF EDUCATION
BAILEY FILMS, INC.
6509 DE LONGPRE AVE., HOLLYWOOD 28, CAL.
11 min.

CREATIVE HAND SERIES

ART FROM SCRAP 1955
PRODUCER, CRAWLEY, INTERNATIONAL FILM
BUREAU   *5 min.*

BEGINNING OF PICTURE MAKING
PRODUCER, CRAWLEY, INTERNATIONAL FILM
BUREAU   *6 min.*

FIDDLE — de — dee 1947
NATIONAL FILM BOARD OF CANADA   *4 min.*

FINGER PAINTING 1949
INTERNATIONAL FILM BUREAU   *5 min.*

LOOM WEAVING 1951
INTERNATIONAL FILM BUREAU   *6 min.*

HOW TO MAKE A PUPPET 1953
PRODUCER, R. NISBAUER
BAILEY FILMS   *12 min.*

CHILD AS A POTTER 1953
LOBETT PRODUCTIONS
2002 TARAVAL ST., SAN FRANCISCO 16, CAL.
17 min.

MAKE A MOBILE 1948
DEPT. OF ART, U.C.L.A.
BAILEY FILMS   *10 min.*

MAKE A SPACE DESIGN
MUSEUM OF MODERN ART FILM LIBRARY
11 W. 53RD ST., NEW YORK 19   *30 min.*

MAKING A FEELING AND SEEING PICTURE 1952
MUSEUM OF MODERN ART
11 W. 53RD ST., NEW YORK 19   *30 min.*

TELL YOUR IDEAS WITH CLAY 1952
MUSEUM OF MODERN ART
11 W. 53RD ST., NEW YORK 19   *30 min.*

Index

Accordion-fold booklets, 142-144
Adhesive paper and sticker prints, 199, 200
Adhesives, kinds and use, 275
Adult standards, 11
Airplanes, 174
Animals
  baby, 161, 166
  booklet, 138
  caged, 137
  characterisitics, 135
  classroom, 177
  clay, 139, 141, 265-277
  farm, 164-167
  forms, 13, 212, 213
  from discarded materials, 221-223
  imaginary, 221-223
  live, 135-141, 166-171
  material, 45
  modeled in clay, 139, 141, 265-277
  pastured, 173
  penned, 170
  sheltered, 172
  underground, 164
  wild, 138
  woods, 164
Anxieties, 11
Appreciation, 29-33, 44, 45, 51-60, 94, 96,
  118, 119
Aprons, 84
Arms, 108
Arrangements for bulletin boards, 24
Arranging plant material, 29-33
Art, basis need, 273-274
Art development, 90
Art expression, 90, 273, 274
Art materials, 61-78, 275
  use of, 61-62
Arts, kindergarten, 61-68, 82-92, 147-158,
  178-192
Asebestos cement, 272, 275

Baby animals, 161, 166
Backgrounds

cloth, 25, 26
  felt, 133
  paper, 25, 133
Balls, clay, 260
Bamboo, 244
Beads, clay, 259
Bears, 162
Beauty appreciation, 57-60
Beauty in animals and plants, 15
Beginners with clay, 264, 265
Binder's board, 280
Birds, 104, 163, 164
Bird shape, 212
Birds, papier-mâché, 224
Birthday party, 105
Biscuit (clay), 272
Blueprint, materials and process, 199, 200
Blueprint project, 199
Boat (of wood), 40
Bogus (paper), 280
Booklets
  accordion-fold, 142-144
  construction, 142
  contents, 143
  covers, 143
  double-fold, 142
  materials, 142
  on animals, 138
  planning, 142-144
  single-section, 142
Box animals, 216-223
Boxes, cardboard, 133, 134
Box for movable pictures, 146
Box loom, 246
Brayer prints, 186
Brush, care of, 19, 21, 79, 85
Brush cleaners, 285
Brush painting (powder paint), 19, 21, 61,
  77, 79, 83-88, 284
Building blocks, 36, 37, 100
Buildings
  class discussion of, 122
  colors for, 132
  construction of, 121

observation of, 120-123
pictures of, 28
Bulletin boards, 23-28, 122
Bus driver, 125
Buttons, 45

Caged animals, 137
Camels (in zoo), 137
Candle holder, 260
Cardboard, 281
Cardboard construction, 133, 134
Cardboard loom, 244, 246
Care of brushes, 19, 21, 79, 83-88
Cars, 126, 129
Cats, 168, 169
Cement, 272, 275
Ceramics, 272
Chalk
  habits to encourage, 71, 72
  materials used with, 71
  methods, 189
  on wet paper, 72
  stencils, 189
  storing, 71
  uses of, 73
  variations, 191
  work space, 72
Chalk board, 81
Chalk to interpret music, 74
Characteristics of animals, 135
Charcoal paper, 281
Child
  characteristics, 1-7
  coordination, 61
  development, 43
  emotional stability, 15, 16
  learning qualities, 44
  spoiled, 15
Chipboard, 281
Clamps for easels, 79
Class discussion
  drawing and painting, 94
  buildings, 122
Classroom
  animals, 177
  comfort, 18
  design, 17-21
  discussion, 94, 122
  easels, 20
  floor plan, 18
  library, 19
  piano, 20

sand box, 20
science area, 20
sink areas, 18
space, 20
tables, 20
ventilation, 18
windows, 18
work bench, 18
Clay
  animals, 139, 141, 265-267
  beads, 259
  beginners, 264, 265
  biscuit, 272
  classroom preparation, 257
  cleaning up, 258, 259
  color combinations, 257
  finishing, 270, 271
  firing, 270
  flour, 276
  gifts, 261
  habits for children, 258
  materials, 165, 255-278
  mixing, 276
  modeling, 139, 141, 259, 264-267
  quality, 255
  stamping or stippling, 264
  stringing balls and disks, 259
  things to make, 259
  tools, 256
  vocabulary, 272
Cloth, 46
Cloth backgrounds, 25, 26
Clothes, removing paint from, 86
Coil method pottery, 268-269, 272
Collage — material, arrangement, etc., 52-56
Color, 45, 96-98, 150, 260
  choice of, 84, 97
  combinations, 96, 97, 179
  enjoyment of, 88
  in fruit, flowers, etc., 96
  matching, 97
  notations, 98
  selection, 97, 99
  teacher's knowledge of, 97
  variety, 99
Color plates 8 *pages following page* 98.
Comfort, 18
Committee, flower, 36
Community — stores, houses, construction,
  people, 118-133
Community mural, 194
Community projects, 124-128

Construction, in kindergarten, 33, 36-50, 201-203, 232-235, 246-259
Construction of booklets, 142-144
Construction of box animals, 216-233
Construction of buildings, 121, 122
Construction of doll house, 34
Construction paper, 281
Construction with cardboard, 133, 134
Containers, 62
Coordination of child, 61
Copying, 13
Cork board, 81
Covers for booklets, 143
Cows, 167
Craft paper, 281
Crayon, 67-71
Crayon and chalk, 21
Crayon on cloth, 70, 160
Creative abilities, 2
Creative expression — blocks and remedies, 10-14
Criticism, 10
Cut paper, 201, 209-215
Cut paper designs, 203-208
Cut paper forms, 206-210

Design, observation of, 88
Depicting fall season, 149-152
Development
    coordination, 61
    in art, 90
    in use of wood and tools, 43
    learning qualities, 44
    with building blocks, 37
Differences, individual, 14, 15
Diorama, 165, 170-172
Discarded materials, 221-223
"Discovery picture," 139, 140
Discussions
    buildings, 122
    group, 108
    painting and drawing, 94
Display
    pin-up boards, 27
    three-dimensional, 27
    two-dimensional, 25
Doll house
    construction, 34
    furniture, 34, 35
Double-fold booklets, 142
Drawing the human figure, 111-115
Drilling a hole, 40, 41

Ducks, 163
Dyes, 278-279

Easels (substitutes and use), 79-82
Eight-year-olds, 5-7
Elephants (in zoo), 135
Emotional characteristics
    eight-year-olds, 6
    five-and six-year-olds, 3
    seven-year-olds, 5
Emotional instability, 15, 16
Enamel, 280
Engobe, 277
Enjoyment of building blocks, 37
Enjoyment of color, 88
Experiences in rhythm, 59
Expression in art, 90, 273, 274

Fall season, appreciation of, 54-55
Fall season, color and depicting, 149-152
Farm
    animals, 164-171
    farmer, 173, 174
    mural, 174
    subjects for pictures, 173-176
    vegetation, 172
    visit to, 166
Farm, sandtable, 174, 177
Farm machines, 173
Fears, 3
Feel of things, 58
Felt background, 133
Felt or flannel for printing, 184
Fibertint news paper, 281
Fingerpaint, 62-66, 195, 279
Fingerpainting
    aprons, 62
    drying work, 65, 66
    hand and finger positions, 64
    instructions, 62-64
    materials, 62-66
    paper, 62
    preparation, 62, 63
    recipes for paint, 279
    to music, 64
    uses for, 66
    values of, 66, 67
Fireman, 125
Firing and glazing clay, 270
Five-year-olds, 1-4
Fixative
    for chalk and charcoal, 280

how to make, 280
Floor, painting on
  advantages, 82
  procedure, 82
Floor plan for classroom, 18
Flour for adhesive, 275
Flowers
  arrangement, 157
  display, 28, 260
  garden, 157, 172
  make-believe, 158
  panels, 173
  petal shapes, 157
  projects, 158, 159
  seed patterns, 150, 159
  springtime, 157
Footprints, 178
Frame for weaving rugs, 248
Frogs and tadpoles, 164
Fruits and vegetables (modeling), 259
"Funny man," 116
Furnishings for doll house, 21-23, 34, 35

Games, 103
Garbage collector, 125
Gardens, 172
Giraffes (in zoo), 137
Glazing clay, 270, 272
Glue, 275
Grade One
  arts, 62-68, 82-88, 95, 152-156, 178-185
  construction, 38-41, 47-51, 137-145,
    187-208, 260-263
  masks, 231-234
  materials, 45, 199-263
  mobiles, 50-51
  observation, 57, 101-104, 135-137,
    156-175
  puppets, 235-237
  six-year-olds, 1-4
  stabiles, 47-49
  wood construction, 39-41
Grade Two
  arts, 62-68, 72-93, 150, 183-193, 196
  collage, 52-53
  construction, 40-51, 142-145
  masks, 230-234
  observation, 156, 161-174
  puppets, 235-239
  seven-year-olds, 4-5
  stencils, 193
  things to make, 202-203

weaving, 242-250
Grade Three
  arts, 67-78, 108-114, 151-161, 178-186, 196,
    199, 251-272
  construction, 30, 50, 134, 142, 145,
    203-229
  doll house, 34-35
  eight-year-olds, 5-7
  masks, 230-234
  mobiles, 50
  observation, 33, 54, 115, 135-137, 153-156,
    161-165, 175
  puppets, 235-239
  puppet stage, 236
  stencils, 187-196
  stitches, 251-254
  weaving, 243-250
Ground, colors for, 132
Group discussion, 94, 108, 122
Growth in representation, 107
Growing things, appreciation of, 57-60

Hammer, use of, 39
Hibernating, 154
Holder for flowers, 260
Holding something, 116
Horses, 169, 170
Houses, 120
How things are planned, 119
How things grow, 118
How things work, 118
How to make modeling material, 275
Humor, 3

Ideas (for picture, games, toys, etc.),
  99-104
Illustrations List, 13-19
Imaginary animals, 221-223
Imagination, 3
  stimulation, 99, 116, 139
Incised line, 272
Instability, 15, 16
Instructions for fingerpainting, 62-66, 279
Interest span, 3, 5, 6, 12, 15
Interpreting music with fingerpaint, 64

Japanese paper, 281
Jars for paint, 86

Kangaroo, 135
Kiln, 272
Kindergarten

art, 61-68, 82-92, 147-158, 178-192
building blocks, 36, 37
child's world, 58
construction, 33, 36-50, 201-203, 232-235,
    246-259
daily surprises, 60
fingerpaint, 62-64
five-year-olds, 1-4
flower arrangement, 33
observation, 156-157, 161-164
playhouse, 22, 23
sharing table, 57
stabile, 47, 50
use of materials, 61, 147, 178-203, 255
wood construction, 38-40
Kings and Queens, 214, 215
Kites, 161
Kittens, 169
Knitting, 249, 250
Kraft paper, 281

Laminated paper, process and uses,
    227-229
Learning qualities, 44
Leaves, 150
Ledger paper, 281
Legs, 108
    position of, 112
Library, 18
Lions (in zoo), 135, 136
Live animals, 135
Looms
    cardboard, 244, 246
    Navajo, 245, 246
    simple, 242-247
    wooden box, 246, 247

Machinery, 4
Machines, 28, 103, 173
Make-believe flowers, 158
Making a "discovery" picture, 139, 140
Manila paper, 281
Masks
    materials, 232
    paper bag, 232, 233
    paper fold, 230
    primitive, 234
    shapes, 230
    types and use, 230-234
Materials, 10, 11, 14
    care of, 21
    for blueprints, 199

for booklets, 142
for bulletin boards, 23-26
for kindergarten arts, 62
for making animals, 45
for mobiles, 51
for printing, 178-200
using clay, 165, 255-278
Melted crayon transparencies, 71
Mental characteristics
    eight-year-olds, 6
    five- and six-year-olds, 2
Metal, 46
Milkman, 124
Mimeo-news, 281
Mixing clay, 276
Modeling clay animals and people, 139,
    141, 265-267
Modeling material (how to make), 275
Modeling mixture (salt and flour), 283, 284
Mobiles
    balancing objects, 51
    design, 49
    materials, 51
    new forms, 51
    uses for, 51
Monkeys, 135, 137
Monoprint process, 185-186
Movable tables, 81, 82
Movement (rhythmic), 59
Movement of things in space, 51
Moving men, 125
Moving picture making, 145
Moving picture (not movies) subjects, 144
Murals
    background, 148
    community, 194
    farm, 174
    mosaics, 148
    painting, 146
    second grade, 157
    size, 147
    stencil, 148
    subjects and making, 104-106, 126-129,
        145-152, 157-161, 174, 194
Music, interpretation in chalk, fingerpaint
    and watercolor, 64-78

Nails, how to use, 39, 40
Navajo loom, 245, 246
Neck, 110
Newsboy, 125
Newspaper, 62

Newsprint, 281
News subjects, 28

Oatmeal paper, 281
Observation
    buildings, 121
    of environment, 57
    of flowers, 157, 158
    in kindergarten, 156-157, 161-164
Observing and drawing people, 108-114
Oil paint, 280
Opaque paint, 75, 76, 280
Option bond, 281
Organization of bulletin board, 26
Ornaments, papier-mâché, 224, 225

Paint, 11, 21
    care of, 85
    combining and mixing, 75, 76
    formulas, 280
    for glass, 280
    liquid opaque, 280
    materials, 83, 84
Painting
    beginning, use and discussion, 83-94
    care of materials, 85, 86
    development in, 87, 88
    discovery of, 86, 87
    first experience, 83, 84, 87
    good habits, 84, 85
    jars, 86
Panels, flower, 173
Paper (kinds and use), 11, 28, 46, 227-229,
    280-282
Paper boxes and bowls, 228
Paper cutting, 201-215
Paper, laminated, 227-229
Paper plates, 230
Paper printing, 195
Paper project, 203
Paper shapes and design, 203
Paper things to make
    animals, 209
    bag mask, 233
    birds, 212
    chain, 202
    cylinder animals, 212-213
    people in a row, 205
    stencil, 195
Paper towels, 281
Paperweight, 262
Papier-mâché

animals, 225
    Christmas-tree ornaments, 224
    flowers, 224, 225
    modeling birds, 224
    painting, 227
    variations, 227
Parchment, 281
Parts of body, 110
Paste, flour, 275
Pasture animals, 173
Peep show, 25, 27
Pencil holder, 260
"People doing things," subject for painting,
    115
People (drawing them), 107-116
People who help families, 124, 125, 127
Perception, 2, 5, 89-91
Photo paper, 281
Physical characteristics
    five-and six-year-olds, 1
    seven-year-olds, 4
Piano, 20
Picnics, 104
Pictures of buildings, 28
Picture and game ideas, 99-104
Pictures of the seasons, 149
Picture subjects on farm, 173-176
Pigs, 167, 168
Pin-up boards, 27
Place cards, 211
Place mats, 188, 203, 204
Planning booklets, 142-144
Plant and flower arrangement, 29-36
    backgrounds, 33
    colors, 30
    containers, 31
    materials, 29, 30
Plaster, 277
Plaster of Paris, 282, 283
    coloring, 283
    mixing with water, 282
    pouring, 283
Play experience, 103, 126
Playhouse, 19
    group project, 22
    plan and furnishings, 21-23
Play rhythm, 59
Plywood easel, 81
Poster paper, 205, 281
Postman, 124
Pottery, 268-272
    bowl making, 268

coil method, 268
  decorating, 269
  precautions, 268
  textures, 269
Powder paint, 74-76, 280
  formula, 280
Praise, 9, 10, 13
Preparation of blueprints, 199, 200
Primitive masks, 234
Printed paper articles, 184
Process and uses of laminated paper,
    227-229
Projects, Grade Two, 40
Print making
  cleaning, 184
  colors, 179
  design, 181-182
  drying, 184
  felt block, 184
  flannel, 184
  making with vegetables, 182-184
  materials, 179
  potato print, 183
  process, 180-181
  shapes, 184
  stamping, 181
  suggestions, 182
Prints (materials and types), 178-200
Puppet dress patterns, 236
Puppets
  animal, 236
  cardboard, 235
  hand, 236
  paper or cloth bag, 237
  papier-mâché heads, 237, 238
  shadow, 239
  stage for, 239
  stick, 235
  stocking or cloth, 236, 241
  string, 235
Puppet stage, 239
Public service, 120
Punch and Judy shows, 236

Rabbits, baby, 161
Railway station, 126, 128
Recipes for fingerpaint, 279
Representation (growth and stages),
    89-94, 107
Rhythm experiences, 59, 60
  in play, 59
Rhythmic movement, 59

Roots, 164
Rubber cement, 275
Rugs, 246, 248

Sailboat making
  cabin, 41
  mast, 41
  sail, 41
Salt and flour mixture for modeling, 283,
    284
Sample lesson, 155, 170
Sample project — "Our Neighborhood," 133
Sample project, papier-mâché, 225, 226
Sandpaper, 281
Sandtable farm, 174-177
Saw, use of, 40
Saw, safety habits for, 40
Scissors, 61
  cutting, 201
  habits, 202
  learning to use, 201-202
Scrap paper, 202
Screening paper, 282
Screen prints, 194-200
  adhesive paper, 199
  cleaning, 196
  cut paper, 196
  stencil, 197
  stickers, 199
  wax crayon, 196-198
Seashore, 56
Seasons of the year, 28, 149-166
Seeds, 46, 269
Seed patterns, 150, 159
Seeing and feeling materials, 45
Seeing and touching picture, 54, 55
Self-achievement, 9
Self-confidence, 13
Self-expression, 8, 9, 10
Service station attendant, 124
Seven-year-olds, 4-5
Sewing, 251-252
Sgraffito, 264, 272
Shadow puppets, 239
Sharing table, 57
Shapes, similarity of, 100
Shelf paper, 202, 282
Shellac, use of, 284
Shells, 46
Sheltered animals, 170, 172
Shoulders, 109, 110
Silk screen paint, 280

Simple looms, 242-247
Single-section booklet, 142
Sink areas in classrooms, 18
Six-year-olds, 1-4
Sizes and shapes, 110
Slip (clay powder), 272
Snow, 155, 156
Social characteristics
  eight-year-olds, 7
  five-and six-year-olds, 4
Solder, 275
Solvents (for thinning and cleaning), 284
Space, 2
Spatter stencils, 192-193
Spoiled child, 15
Sponge stencils
  materials, 192
  methods, 192
Spool holder, 41, 42
Spool knitting, 249, 250
Sprayed stencils, 194
Spring season, 156-166
Squeegee, 194, 195
Squirrels, 162
Stabiles, 47-49
Stage for puppets, 239
Stages in representation, 107
"Stand-up" design, 49
Stencil paper, 282
Stencil prints, 187-196
Stencil process (for mural), 194
Stencils
  chalk, 189, 190
  cutting, 187, 188
  designs, 189
  group project, 194
  materials, 187
  methods, 187
  mural, 194
  paper, 187
  place mat, 188
  rubbing, 192
  screen print, 194-196
  spatter, 192, 193
  sponge, 192
  spray, 194
  use of design, 188
  variations, 194
Sticker prints and adhesive paper, 199, 200
Stimulation of ideas, 99-104, 116-139
Stitches (types and materials), 251-254
Stocking or cloth puppet, 236, 241

Stores
  clothing, 119
  food, 119
  hardware, 119
  subject for painting, 119
Street cleaners, 125
Stringing balls, beads and disks, 259
String puppets, 239, 240
Subjects for pictures, 101-104
Substitutes for easels, 80, 81
Sunflowers, 152
Surprises for the child, 60
Symbols, 107
Synthetics, 46

Tables (illustrative), 13-19
Tables (movable), 81, 82
Tadpoles and frogs, 164
Tag board, 282
Teacher qualities, 8
Teaching a technique, 12, 13
Tempera
  characteristics, 84
  formulas, 280
  mixing, 74, 75
  related colors, 75, 76
Tempera or powder paint, 74-76
Texture
  design, 54-56
  materials, 54
  sample projects, 54-56
Texture appreciation, 53
Thanksgiving Day, 152
Three-dimensional display, 25
Tile, clay
  designs, 263
  painting, 263
  underglaze, 263, 277
Tile making, 262-264
Time sense, 2
Toilet tissue, 282
Tools, 5, 10, 19, 103
Tools, cutting, 183
Tools and machines, 28
Tools for wood, 38
Toys, 103
Tracing paper, 282
Tractor, 173
Train (of wood), 42
Train and railroad station (observation
  and discussion), 126-130
Tree

mural making, 151
    sample lesson, 159
    sample project, 151
    third-grade project, 160
Trees, 100, 151-154, 159, 173
Trips (grades two and three)
    planning, 118
    suggestions, 118
Trips, sample, 120
Trip to zoo, 135-137
Trough, 79
Truck, 173
Turtles, 164
Two-dimensional display, 25

Underglaze, 263, 277
Underground life (roots, vegetable and
    animals), 164
Upson board, 282
Uses of chalk, 73

Vegetable life, 164, 173
Vegetables used for printing, 182, 183
Vegetation on farm, 172
Ventilation, 18
Visit to farm, 166
Vocabulary (clay), 272

Wallboard, 81, 82
Wall-hanging (crayon on cloth), 160
Walls, painting of, 123, 124
Want-ad paper, 282
Watercolor
    brush, 77
    characteristics, 77
    cleaning up, 78
    materials, 76-78
    paint, 77, 78
    paper, 282
    third-grade suggestions, 77
    used to interpret music, 78
    uses, 78
    with crayon, 69
    with stencil, 194
Watercolor paper, 282
Wax crayon, 66-71, 160, 196-197
    characteristics, 67
    on cloth, 70
    designs, 65
    with fingerpaint, 65

melted transparencies, 71
    rubbing process, 68
    screen print, 196, 197
    stain for wood, 69
    subjects, 69
    tools for scraping, 68
Wax paper, 282
Weaving, 242-250
    frame for rugs, 248
    looms, 243
    materials, 242, 244, 246, 248
    onion-skin bag, 248
    process, 244
    qualities, 249
    with rags, 246, 248
    weft and warp, 246, 248
Wedging box, 277
Wedging clay, 278
Wheelbarrow, 173
Wild animals, 138
Wings, 163
Winter
    animals, 153
    beauty of, 154
    clothing, 153
    fun, 156
    picture subjects, 152-156
    things to do, 153
Wire, 46
Wood, 38-48
Wood (appreciation), 44
Wood construction
    boat, 40
    boxes, 42
    materials, 39
    primary grades, 38
    tools, 38
    work bench, 38
Woodland animals, 164
Wood stain, 280
Work bench in classroom, 18
Working surface, 62
Workmen, 125
Wrapping-paper design, 157

X-ray film (to use), 285
X-ray paper, 282

Zoo animals, 135-137
Zoo trip, 135-137